Rock Doc

Neil Ratner, MD

Library of Congress Control Number:

2018906981

ISBN: 978-1-7323790-0-8 (Hardcover)

ISBN: 978-1-7323790-1-5 (Paperback)

ISBN: 978-1-7323790-2-2 (Ebook)

Printed by:
First printing: 2018

Publisher:
Rock Doc Entertainment LLC
46 Lower Byrdcliffe Road
Woodstock, NY 1249

THIS BOOK IS DEDICATED to all those that have been told by others, "You'll never." Whether it is an educational goal, your dream job, a place in the world you long to visit, or just peace of mind; it's not up to them. It's up to you. Only you are capable of changing your life and making your dreams a reality. Don't be defeated by others. Believe in yourself.

I also dedicate this book to Michael Jackson. MJ's presence was with me for much of the writing, and I hope readers will see and appreciate the fascinating, caring, and supportive Michael I knew.

Last and most importantly, I dedicate this book to Leann, my soulmate and partner for the last 42 years. Life is filled with ups and downs and the true test of a relationship is what happens when times get tough. Leann's love and support never wavered no matter how bad things got. Our bond has only strengthened, and I thank Leann for her infinite patience and tolerance in putting up with me for all these years.

Contents

1

Who Did You Say Was
Coming to the Office?

WHEN the phone rang in the middle of the day and the caller was Dr. Edgar Somers, I knew something was up.

"Neil, I am adding a patient to our schedule for tomorrow. He will call you in the next half hour."

I had been Director of Anesthesia for Dr. Somers in-office operating room on and off for the past eight years. I wondered what was so interesting about this patient that Somers had not only called me himself but had given out my number. (I usually got the patient's number and called the night before surgery.) Warily I asked, "Is there anything special I need to know?"

"Don't you want to know who it is?"

I could hear the excitement in Somers voice.

Edgar Somers, a well-known plastic surgeon, liked to impress me with the A-list celebrities he had as patients. That's the way it was in his business; the more famous the people you operated on were, the more of a star you became.

Usually I didn't care that much about the star power of our patients. I had been in the rock and roll business dealing with celebrities on a daily basis and, as a result, I didn't get impressed easily. This was helpful because in the specialty of anesthesia, it's essential to treat all patients alike. You develop a routine and it is necessary to stick to that routine. When a doctor starts making exceptions for celebrities, or anyone else for that matter, bad things happen.

"I don't know," I answered half-heartedly. "Should I care who the patient is?"

Dealing with the rich and famous could be a pain in the ass. Their desire for an extreme level of care and attention, their outrageous demands and their sense of entitlement, often made their cases far more difficult to handle than they had to be. Like the time a celebrated opera singer insisted that I use only one small vein on his thumb to insert the IV, or the time a Hollywood starlet claimed to be allergic to every drug known to man.

"Don't you want to guess?" Somers teased. He was enjoying this. If the smooth, fun-loving doctor hadn't become a surgeon, he surely would have been a comedian. However, I was quickly growing tired of the game.

"Hey, Edgar, let's stop the bullshit. Tell me who it is."

"Michael Jackson," he announced proudly.

Well, well, well. After all of these years.

I knew the King of Pop had been to Somers office before. When I had thought of starting an in-office anesthesia practice eight years earlier, I had approached Edgar Somers in part because I knew Michael had been a patient. It wasn't that I had any particular interest in Michael, but his presence indicated that Somers ran the kind of practice that would benefit from an office-based anesthesiologist.

I asked him about the up-coming procedure. "Nothing major," he said, "just some small facial work." It would take about an hour. We agreed I would use monitored sedation, and I asked about Michael's general state of health.

"Underweight and he has the skin condition vitiligo," Somers answered. "There are no other special issues."

What we didn't discuss was Michael's alleged drug problem. I was aware from what I had read in the press, that Michael had some kind of issue with painkillers and sleep meds. Years before I, too, had battled drug addiction. I was sensitive to patients with similar problems, and I had specific ways of dealing with their anesthesia: mainly, making sure they didn't feel high.

I hung up and gazed out my balcony window. My wife, Leann, and I lived in an apartment on the top floor of an Upper East Side building near Manhattan's East River. The views across the city and out over the water never failed to amaze me. Even better, the building was a convenient walking distance to the offices where I worked. I was finished with surgeries for the day and had planned to go to the gym. Now I paced around the living room as I waited for the call.

Half an hour later, the phone rang. I was nervous, and when I get anxious, my voice starts to quiver. I didn't want Michael to hear it. I waited a couple of rings, took a few deep breaths, and answered hello.

"Hello, Ratner."

I knew immediately from the high-pitched, almost childlike voice, it was Michael Jackson. I was a little surprised by the "Ratner," not "Dr. Ratner," or even "Neil."

I didn't know it then, but that was Michael. He used only last names or nicknames, although he didn't have one for himself. In our eight years together, he never called me "Neil" and I always called him "Michael."

We exchanged a few pleasantries. Then I got down to the business of talking about the anesthesia. Within a minute or two, he interrupted. "Ratner, are you going to use 'the milk?'"

I was taken aback by the question. By milk he meant propofol, a white milky substance very different from the alternative clear medications we also used. The introduction of propofol some years earlier had greatly improved the safety of in-office anesthesia. It also offered a much better experience for patients.

3

So much so they had begun asking for the drug, either by its chemical name, propofol, or its brand name, Diprivan.

I laughed to myself. Within the anesthesia community, propofol had a nickname, "Milk of amnesia." Michael knew our little inside joke. I assured him that propofol would be part of my anesthetic technique.

A unique aspect of what I did in the operating room was including the use of music through headphones. My experiences in the music business had taught me about the power of music. Great music comes from a deep emotional place and has the ability to generate similar emotions in listeners. Putting headphones on a patient had proven to be a valuable way to decrease anxiety and increase levels of relaxation.

I explained this to Michael. It was a topic of great interest to him. He had used headphones during anesthesia before and wondered how music affected altered states of consciousness. "Do you think it matters what type of music?" Michael mused.

"People often concentrate on lyrics, preventing them from relaxing," I replied. "So as long as it is non-worded and spiritually uplifting, it's up to you."

Next, I went through the usual checklist of health problems, allergies, and previous surgeries. He asked if I would call the anesthesiologist at Dr. Hoefflin's office. Michael was referred to Somers through his cosmetic surgeon in Beverly Hills, Dr. Steven Hoefflin. Somers and Hoefflin were buddies. When one of Hoefflin's patients was in New York and needed to be seen, he always sent them to Somers.

We spoke a few minutes more. I reminded him: nothing to eat or drink after midnight.

I called Hoefflin's office and spoke to the anesthesiologist. Michael had been there many times over the years. He had no previous problems with anesthesia, and, yes, they had been using propofol.

I would be lying if I said I wasn't pumped. My emotions were a mixture of fear and excitement. The fear was more or less the same reaction I had before every surgery. The Hippocratic Oath says: "Do No Harm." This was always my biggest concern. I felt that a little stage fright was a healthy response that kept me on my toes. The excitement came from being involved in a famous person's life. We all crave a little of that magic, and Michael Jackson was arguably the most famous entertainer in the world at that time. Of course, I had seen all kinds of stories about Michael, but I had learned long ago not to believe everything you see or read. It was much better to make your own determinations based, if possible, on personal experience.

I knew Somers would be watching me closely. As good as he was as a surgeon, if I screwed up he would get the blame. Patients quickly forget who the anesthesiologist was, but they always remember their surgeon!

The next day I got to the office early. The street entrance, in the middle of a block between Park and Madison avenues, opened to a plush waiting room with two couches, overstuffed comfortable chairs, and a table spread with the latest fashion magazines.

My domain was the back half of the office with its small, but adequate operating room and unusually large three-bed recovery room. Most offices barely had the space for a one-bed recovery area. With three beds, we could do three consecutive cases without worrying about finding a bed for the patient coming out of surgery.

Somers private line rang as a black SUV pulled up in front of the building. A tall, light-skinned Creole with an obvious attitude led Michael in. His name was Wayne Nagin, and he exuded a level of confidence I hadn't seen before in security people.

Seeing Michael Jackson close up for the first time was intense. Taller than I thought, he was wearing his signature outfit: black fedora, aviator sunglasses, red flannel shirt, black pants, white socks, and black loafers. We shook hands. His firm handshake surprised me. Michael followed me into the recovery room. I closed the curtain around the bed to give him some privacy while he changed into the gown. He left the fedora on the nightstand and handed me his glasses. I put them into the pocket of my scrubs.

Somers arrived and came into the recovery room to say hello. After their brief exchange, I wheeled Michael into the operating room.

I carefully searched the back of Michael's hand for a place to put the IV.

Shit, really bad veins.

I tried not to show my concern, but it was too late. Michael had been watching me the whole time, and I could hear him chuckling in his high-pitched way.

He he he....

"What's so funny?"

"They always have trouble," he remarked casually.

Assuming you don't knock out any teeth, damage a vocal cord, scratch a cornea, or do something else calamitous, the worst thing you can do as an anesthesiologist is not get the IV in quickly and efficiently. No matter how good the anesthesia experience, sending a patient home with a big black-and-blue hand has consequences. When they see the marks from the multiple IV stabs, they remember the pain and anxiety that went with it.

While I prepared to insert the IV, the nurse attached Michael to an EKG monitor, a blood pressure machine, and a pulse oximeter. Somers and his surgical assistant scrubbed their hands at the sink just outside the OR. I found a vein.

It wasn't very big, but it was adequate.

One stab and it was in.

"You're good," Michael said.

I could see by his face he meant it. Now, I was the one smiling.

I told Michael, "Think good thoughts." I placed the headphones over his ears and cranked up the classical piece he brought, and I put him to sleep.

The procedure was fast and uncomplicated and took little more than half an hour. Michael woke up quickly and didn't say much. He rested in the recovery room for about an hour. After changing back into his clothes, he put on the fedora, and I handed him back his sunglasses. Michael gave me a hug and a smile. Wayne Nagin led the way out of the office into the waiting SUV.

Finally, I let out a big sigh of relief. I think I had been holding my breath the whole time.

Every few months, I got a call about another small procedure. All were facial surgeries, usually nothing more than a simple revision of something that had been done before.

Within a few months, Michael and I became friends which was funny because Somers had insisted, "You'll never be friends with Michael Jackson."

"You'll never," was something I had heard many times before in regard to every goal I told others I was going to achieve.

His new name for me was "Rat." I didn't love the nickname; it had too many negative connotations. But Michael got a big charge out of using it so the name stuck!

2

So You Want To Be A Rock Star

I was born with rhythms in my head and from a very young age, I tapped them out on any available surface. My mother constantly told me, "Neil, please stop banging on the table!"

Eventually my parents decided to give me drum lessons. I played on a practice pad for many months until they realized I was serious. Only then did they buy me my first drum set. Once I had it, I could be in a band. By the time I was twelve, I was playing together with a group of friends.

In high school, I formed a band called the Knights of Soul. Ralph Raiola, the lead singer, and our big attraction, was the definition of "blue-eyed soul." When he went down on his knees and sang in falsetto, he made the girls cry. I truly believed we would be offered a record deal, and I was disappointed when it never happened. But it was just as well because there was no way my parents would have accepted the fact that I was ditching college, especially to try to make a living as a rock-and-roll musician.

As a kid I dreamed of two different career paths. Either I would become a successful rock and roll drummer, or I would study hard and become a physician. I was fascinated by the human body and it was easy for me to see myself as a doctor in some faraway place saving lives. I had applied to a few different universities and I was accepted at the University of Vermont, as a pre-med student with a major in biology. This meant plenty of intensive classes, but as much as I could, I kept my nights and weekends free to play in a folk-rock band called Talbots Bus. I was committed to becoming a doctor, but I was also ready to consider becoming a professional musician.

It was 1968, and although college campuses were hotbeds- of dissent, the protests in and around our university tended to be small. This was to change one Sunday in October. An anti-war group organized a large concert on campus with nationally known speakers and a couple of name bands out of Boston and New York City. Talbots Bus was one of the few local groups asked to play.

I strongly objected to America's involvement in Vietnam, and the idea that we would be a part of the concert excited me. The day of the show, I proudly wore an American flag T-shirt as a symbol of protest. As far as I was concerned, the war was a matter of making profits and a way to destroy the flower power culture of the sixties.

There were four of us in the band: Tony: electrified acoustic guitar; his girlfriend Betty: vocals; Billy Parker: bass, and me on drums. We were all against the war, especially Tony, the leader of the group. As a huge Dylan fan, he knew the right choice to close our set: "Masters of War," a song about how pointless and corrupt warfare is.

More than five thousand people gathered on the green. Standing on the side of the stage looking out over the audience of students, professors, young families, and other locals felt overwhelming. We went on late in the afternoon. "Masters of War" was our fourth and last song. Tony began singing quietly while playing an acoustic guitar.

It didn't take long for the crowd to see where we were going. By the next to last verse, Betty was singing harmony, and Billy and I were providing a driving, steady rhythm. Everyone was on their feet yelling and cheering. The audience hit a fever pitch, and all of us except Tony stopped playing.

For the final verse, Tony played and sang softly, the way he had at the beginning of the song:

...And I'll stand over your grave
'til I'm sure that you're dead!

After a moment of silence, the crowd erupted and didn't stop cheering, stomping, and applauding for many minutes. I had never played for more than a couple of hundred people. This was completely different. The experience of being on stage, performing in front of such a large audience, and watching them cheer our music was intoxicating. Now I knew what it felt like to be a rock star and I wanted more!

Still, I wasn't quite ready to give up my dream of becoming a doctor. I finished my sophomore year and was accepted into a summer training program at Flower Fifth Avenue Hospital in New York City to become a licensed operating room technician. It was very difficult to get into medical school, and I hoped that completing this summer program would help get me a spot.

I sublet an apartment on the outskirts of the East Village. By day, the streets were fairly ordinary except for the ever-present flower children milling about, but at night, the scene came alive. Crowds flocked to productions like *Oh! Calcutta!*––an avant-garde show performed mostly in the nude; they crowded the Fillmore East––rock and roll's premiere venue (and my second home for the summer) and the Electric Circus––a club that radiated psychedelia and glamour, with its walls askew, loud music, intense lighting, and multimedia performances by Andy Warhol and his entourage.

My apartment was on the ground floor. After repeatedly hearing loud music coming from above, I went to investigate. The upstairs neighbors were members of the rock group, The McCoys, which years before had produced the hit song "Hang On Sloopy." Rick Derringer, the lead singer and guitarist, lived with his wife, Liz, in one apartment, while Randy Hobbs and Rick's brother lived next door. Rick and Randy had started to play with Johnny Winter, a Texas-born, albino guitar phenomenon recently signed by Columbia Records' new president, Clive Davis.

Puddie, my on-again, off-again girlfriend, moved in with me for the summer. Rick and I hit it off, as did Puddie and Liz, and the four of us became buddies. The Derringers knew all kinds of interesting people in the New York underground scene, many of whom would visit unannounced. On any given day, anyone from a member of Andy Warhol's Factory to Patti Smith or Todd Rundgren could be found sitting in their living room.

I formed a band for the summer with some friends from high school, and we played a few gigs at a small club in Long Island. I invited Rick to come along to one show. Hanging out with him and his friends had ignited the idea of quitting school to become a rock musician. My fantasy was that sometime in the future he would be asked if he knew a good drummer and he would think of me. He enjoyed our set and, on the way home, told me he was surprised by how well I played.

I reluctantly returned to UVM that fall and began to muddle my way through the year's curriculum, but I focused more on bringing some of the energy of New York's music scene to Burlington. Partnering with two friends, I got the owner of the beautiful old Flynn Theater to agree to let us to start booking concerts there.

Our first question was who to book. I wondered if I could persuade Rick to do our first gig. He was playing in Johnny Winter's band, which was still doing theater-size shows.

Rick was comfortable with the idea, but he thought the band's manager would argue that playing at an unknown venue in a market no one cared much about would be a lost opportunity. I tried to sweeten the deal, assuring Rick that they would get most of the money, and we would party hearty and supply whatever the band needed.

The band had a gig not far from the University of Vermont a few weeks later. He invited me there and said we could talk more. The show was my first time seeing Rick and Johnny on stage together. It was a great pairing. They traded guitar licks in a unique and incredibly dynamic way. After the show, we partied until the wee hours and had such a good time that as I was leaving, I jokingly said they should come back to Burlington with me.

Moments later in the hotel lobby, Teddy Slatus, their road manager, confronted me. He looked upset, but I couldn't imagine what I had done wrong.

"Neil, we have a problem! Rick and Johnny want to go with you." He must be joking.

The look on his face told me otherwise.

"I have to get back to the city," he continued, "and I am not going to leave them on their own."

Rick wandered into the lobby and came over to see what was going on. He insisted I would be the perfect person to look after them. Teddy was still unhappy and called Johnny on the house phone. When Johnny enthusiastically endorsed the idea, he had no choice but to agree. I became the "babysitter" for the weekend.

I booked rooms at the Holiday Inn close to UVM, and the next day gave them a tour of the university and the area. That night Johnny and Rick wanted to go out, and I suggested a club where some friends were playing. When we walked in, the room got silent. The crowd was dumbstruck.

By the end of the night, Johnny and Rick were jamming with the band. Word spread quickly, and the club filled to capacity, while a large crowd spilled onto the street. It was light outside by the time we left. I dropped the guys back at the hotel, and they flew back to the city on Sunday.

Rick and Johnny said it was one of the best weekends they had spent in years. Teddy and their flamboyant manager, Steve Paul, were pleased, and it had been a great experience for me. I realized I was good at taking care of people. It was different from hanging out with friends and having a good time. Really taking care of someone meant not always giving them what they wanted. I had to be the "designated driver" so to speak, and I took those responsibilities seriously. In essence, it was my earliest experience as a road manager, and I am sure the way I handled myself that weekend had a lot to do with Rick offering me my first job in the music business.

Right before summer vacation, Puddie phoned me unexpectedly and said I had to call Rick; he had exciting news for me about Edgar Winter and his new band.

I can't believe it, I thought. *My chance at becoming a rock star is moments away.*

I dialed quickly. Rick answered.

"Hey, Rick, Puddie told me to call."

"Neil, I am glad it's you. You know Johnny Winter's brother, Edgar? Well, he just formed a band, and I know you would be perfect as the road manager."

Road manager? That's not what you're supposed to say.

Rick must have read my thoughts.

"I know you want to be the drummer, but the band is made up of old friends from Texas and Louisiana, and they have been waiting to play together for years. You'll make contacts, meet people. Who knows what will happen in the future."

He was pushing me to take the job.

I didn't want to be in school anymore, and my career as a drummer wasn't going anywhere. This was an opportunity to get into the music business. The problem was I had no idea what a job as a road manager meant. Rick assured me that Steve Paul, who was both Edgar and Johnny Winters' manager, and Teddy Slatus, Johnny's road manager, would train me, and that I had more than enough smarts. With a bit of reluctance and a lot of excitement, I walked out of college and took the gig as road manager for Edgar Winter's band.

3

Another Brick In The Wall

EDGAR was a full albino just like his older brother. He was tall and lanky with shoulder-length blond hair, red eyes, and very light white skin. If I hadn't already met Johnny, meeting Edgar would have been a shock. Most of the rest of the band were good old boys. Being their road manager was a real education. New words and expressions like "sha," "gumbo," and "crawfish" became part of my vocabulary.

Singer Jerry LaCroix was a star in his own right. He had a distinctive, gravelly voice, perfect for white Southern R&B. He and Edgar went way back, and the band was the realization of their childhood dreams, so they co-headlined, officially naming themselves Edgar Winter's White Trash featuring Jerry LaCroix.

Still, Edgar was the draw. He was a master musician, and it didn't hurt that he looked outrageous. It was his band, and everyone knew it. This caused tension between Jerry and Edgar. One of my primary jobs was to defuse the almost constant bickering that existed between them, often made worse by their wives.

We didn't go on the road until a few months after I'd become their road manager, while Edgar and the band were working in the CBS studios in New York City on their debut album. I was with them in the studio as well, and my initial excitement lasted about two weeks. Then the reality set in: take after take of the same thing. I was happy to be the go-to guy: go to the coffee shop, go to the music store, go to the pharmacy. As the hours in the studio dragged on, I looked forward to someone sending me anywhere just so I could leave for a while.

Meanwhile, Steve Paul and I were getting on well. I was a quick learner and in addition, I think he saw my business potential. He took me along to important business meetings, including one renegotiating Johnny's record deal with Columbia's Clive Davis.

This was my first time in a meeting with a record company president. Even though I was an observer, I felt like I had taken an important step forward. Steve walked in like he owned the place. He introduced me as Edgar's new road manager. Clive was gracious. He told me he thought Edgar was fantastic and that he was on his way to becoming a big star. During the negotiations, Steve and Clive threw numbers back and forth, each justifying why they were right. Clive wasn't going to let Johnny Winter walk away, and I am sure he knew the meeting was going to cost him more money; it was just a matter of how much. I realized that most of what was going on was posturing and attitude. The meeting was like a poker game, and it was a good lesson for me on negotiating and doing business.

Once the band did go on the road, I learned another important aspect of being a road manager. It happened during my first gig.

"Neil, WHAT THE FUCK happened to the sound!?!?!"

Barbara, Edgar Winter's wife, who had delivered these words, was not happy. We had just finished playing at a medium-sized club in Buffalo, her hometown. During the show, she had been sitting in the back with a sizeable group of family and friends.

The weather coming up from the city had been atrocious. More than half a foot of freshly dropped snow had covered most of New York State. The ride was painfully slow, and the band hadn't had time for a sound check. I was nervous. In addition, we didn't travel with a sound system. It was my responsibility to make sure the venue supplied one, and I had. But I had never thought about exactly who would be behind the mixing board.

By the time I settled the band into the hotel and got back to the club, the place was filling up. I looked around for the sound guy to give him our set list. The promoter was on stage talking to one of my roadies.

"Where's the sound guy?" I asked.

"It's the band's responsibility," he shouted back.

"What do you mean? It's *your* sound system! Who runs the board?"

I was starting to feel massively apprehensive.

"We rent the sound system and mixing board whenever we need it, and it doesn't come with anybody. I told you, it's the band's responsibility."

I didn't know what to do. I couldn't tell Edgar. I certainly never intended to be the soundman, nor did I feel qualified. But I was pushed into a corner and believed I had no choice. The channels on the board were labeled with the names of the microphones they controlled. All I needed to do was create a good balance between the vocals and instruments.

I went to the hotel and got the band. On the way back, Edgar asked, "How's the club, Neil? I am worried that we didn't have a sound check."

He's worried! I thought. *He should only know.*

"Don't worry, Edgar. It's a good club with a very adequate sound system."

We didn't play to a full house, but the crowd loved the show and the band felt it. During the set, Edgar signaled to me a couple times to turn up his mike. That was it! I thought, under the circumstances, things had gone well.

But then Barbara walked up to me. I knew by her expression that something was wrong. She went into a tirade and compared the sound to listening to a bunch of toy instruments. I didn't know what to say. To sit there and make excuses would have been ridiculous.

I took her back to the dressing room. She started to tell Edgar how bad it sounded out front. He didn't say anything.

"What did you think, Edgar?" I asked.

"It sounded all right to me, Neil, but all I heard were the stage monitors. Barbara was out front."

I could tell he was upset.

"Sorry, Edgar. It won't happen again."

In the end, he was cool about what happened, but I wasn't.

What a stupid mistake. How foolish I was to think I could mix the band!

I should have thought about a sound technician when I picked my road crew!

I faced a steep learning curve, but over many weeks, my work became easier. About eight months after I had started, Rick's words, "Who knows what will happen in the future?" took on new meaning.

Edgar's powerful drummer, Bobby Ramirez, had a problem. Years of playing hard and fast had left his hands looking like raw meat. The news from a hand specialist was not good: Bobby needed a small operation and wouldn't be able to pick up his sticks for at least a month.

I didn't want to be the drummer in Edgar's band. Bobby was great and one of my best friends, but I definitely wanted to fill in for him during the one important gig he would miss at the Capitol Theater in Port Chester, New York. I was sure that if I did a decent job, word would get out and possibly catapult me into a job as a drummer. Not that being a road manager was bad. I was learning a lot, but it wasn't the same as performing, and I began an unrelenting campaign.

Bobby was my biggest supporter. He had heard me play, knew I could cut it, and even offered to coach me. But the reaction of the rest of the band was lukewarm at best. Their main concern was not my ability as a drummer, but the loss of a road manager.

"Come on!" I pleaded, adding that Paul Hoffman, one of our road crew, would work out just fine taking over for me that night.

I couldn't budge Edgar Winter or Jerry LaCroix, the leaders of the band. I even offered to pay for an extra roadie. No dice. I was bummed out big time, and I made sure they knew it.

Bobby had the operation. During rehearsals for the Capitol Theater show, Edgar filled in as the drummer. A replacement still had not been chosen. One night, rehearsal went very late. I left, went to my room and took a Quaalude. The 'lude had taken its effect, and I was sedated and drifting off when Edgar burst into my room.

"OK, Neil, here is your chance."

"What?"

"Now or never, Neil. Come try out for the band."

"You have got to be fucking kidding me. Not now, Edgar."

Edgar had asked me if I was going to return when I left to go to my room. Of course it was a setup. He didn't know I would take a Quaalude, but he guessed I might smoke a joint or two and go to sleep.

I knew the songs. I had secretly practiced them when the band was not around. Although my style was different from Bobby's, I was sure my playing would be more than sufficient. Not that night. I played everything at half speed. My arms and legs just wouldn't move the way I wanted them to. It was a joke, and I was crushed.

I sulked for days. Bobby Columbe, from the band Blood, Sweat and Tears, got us an OK fill-in. Like I said, he was OK. After the gig, most of the guys admitted I would have done a better job.

"No kidding!" I answered sarcastically.

Over time, I accepted the fact that I wasn't going to make my living as a rock drummer. I began to understand the business side of music and realized there were great opportunities in touring, management, and production.

Toward the end of the six years I was in the music business, I finally got the opportunity to play professionally. Greg Lake, of the band Emerson, Lake, & Palmer, and I co-produced a record for an artist named Michael Baldwin, who came to our notice through a business connection of my father's.

I am not sure how much actual producing I did, although I gave suggestions. But I did get to play drums for the album. Greg was demanding and getting the parts down exactly the way he wanted was hard. It didn't help that I was intimidated playing alongside him and the other world-class musicians brought in for the sessions. But when I got it right, what a rush!

...

I stayed with Edgar about a year. Learning how to be a good road manager was much more difficult than I had expected. It took a lot of attention to detail. We weren't a very important band, especially at the beginning, and we played clubs, theaters, and even high schools. Many of the crowds were small, but we slowly built a loyal following. By the time I left, the band had national prominence. We parted ways amicably and I began looking for a new job.

A lawyer I knew got me an interview with Dee Anthony, a well-known manager who was in need of an assistant. Dee could have been a character in one of the Godfather movies. Born in the Bronx as Anthony D'Addario, he was Italian through and through, short and heavyset with salt-and-pepper hair and a full beard. Dee managed Humble Pie, Peter Frampton, the J Geils band, and Emerson, Lake & Palmer. He was extremely knowledgeable, well respected, and rumored to be connected. Whether or not he was didn't matter; he was like Don Corleone to his groups, and they seemed to enjoy treating him that way.

Dee and I hit it off immediately, and he asked about my family background. I told him that my father and uncle owned a trucking and warehousing company, and that as a kid, I often went to work with my father. He got a big kick out of the fact that I considered the shop stewards "Dutch uncles." He hired me that day as his special assistant and began teaching me the business right away.

"Neil, this is the most important lesson I can teach you...

Number one: Get the money.

Number two: Remember to get the money.

Number three: Don't forget to always remember to get the

money!"

His groups were doing very well. Humble Pie's album *Rockin' the Fillmore* was rising up the charts. A few months later, the boys in the band gave him a Silver Cloud Rolls Royce as a thank-you.

"See, stick with me," Dee said, looking at me, "and you will have a few of these by the time you get to be my age."

Our relationship was close. That bode well for me, but there was one problem: his younger brother and partner, Bill. The only thing I will say about Bill is he always had the best-looking dry-cleaned jeans and a year-round golden-brown tan. Bill and I got along, but in the back of my mind, I knew that I could only go so far.

Dee sent me on some East Coast tour dates with Humble Pie, and in March 1972, on the Emerson, Lake & Palmer U.S. tour. ELP had released *Tarkus,* their second album, about a year before. They were preparing their next album, *Trilogy*. ELP was big time and very important to Dee.

My primary job was to do box office—collect the money—something I had done as road manager for Edgar Winter. Groups were paid a guaranteed amount upfront, with a percentage of the gate to be paid in cash at the concert. In the days before computers, no one used bank transfers and trust between parties was limited. Someone representing the group would physically go to the box office during the show and count ticket stubs.

ELP had their own tour manager, but he had his hands full with a large crew and the group's elaborate staging. When Dee suggested that I go on the tour with them, even though it was an additional expense, the band was more than agreeable. Of course, Dee had a hidden agenda. He didn't want to go on the whole tour, and I could be his eyes and ears when he wasn't there. I hadn't been on a major tour with an A-list group, and I was psyched. It was time to take the next step in my music business education.

4

It's Only Rock And Roll

DECEMBER 10, 2017 would have been Greg Lake's 70th birthday, a fitting day for the celebration of his life planned for that afternoon. He had died almost a year earlier from pancreatic cancer.

I was very taken back and honored when Greg's wife, Regina, asked me to come to London and be one of the speakers at the event, each of us representing a different chapter in Greg's life.

Among the other speakers was Carl Palmer, the only surviving member of the band. I hadn't seen Carl in over 40 years and it felt good to reconnect and catch up. There were many other familiar faces from the old days and it was hard for me to stay in the moment.

As I sat in the beautiful old church in London waiting for the tribute to begin, the memories of my time with Greg and the band came rushing back to me like a stream overflowing in a storm.

Emerson Lake & Palmer was a super-group, and each of the trio was a master musician in his own right.

Keith Emerson was one of the world's best and most dynamic keyboard players. He appeared on stage like something from outer space, wearing tight silver-gray pants and a short silver jacket accented by extremely exaggerated shoulders. Knee-high black leather boots with heavy silver buckles completed the outfit.

The centerpiece of his rig was a Moog synthesizer, a massive piece of electronics with many crossed wires and flashing colored lights, which stood above his Hammond B3 organ. Keith's love and knowledge of classical music and his groundbreaking use of electronics set the tone for the band.

Greg Lake, lead vocalist and guitar and bass player, would take the stage wearing a beautiful custom-made white leather suit. He provided forceful and smooth vocals, beautiful guitar parts, and a constant driving bass. Behind Greg were racks of guitars and stacks of amplifiers.

Carl Palmer, a remarkable drummer and percussionist, completed the rhythm section. Much of the time he also complimented Keith's keyboards with intricate melodies played on a variety of percussion instruments. He was the most underdressed, but this didn't matter because by the middle of a set, he was usually drenched in sweat and shirtless. Carl had the biggest drum kit I had ever seen. It was engraved and made of stainless steel and flanked by two huge Chinese gongs.

The three were complicated people with distinct personalities. Keith Emerson was a real rock star and a dominant presence on stage. Offstage, he was shy, soft-spoken, and withdrawn. Greg Lake was the opposite. He was a charmer: personable, and gregarious with a big heart. Carl Palmer, the youngest of the three, was good-natured, fun-loving, and a disciplined martial artist.

It didn't take long for me, as Dee's stand-in, to make myself an indispensable part of the entourage. I was not only doing box office, but the band began to rely on me for much more. Although the band had a tour manager he was preoccupied with equipment and production problems, and I filled in as the band's personal assistant and spokesperson. After a few gigs, I got in the habit of leading ELP from the dressing room to the stage. The excitement was palpable as the crowd noise grew louder and louder. We often stood for a few minutes backstage soaking it all in.

"Ladies and Gentleman, please welcome ...

"Emerson.......... Lake............. and.......... Palmer!"

I would send them onto the stage with a smile, a nod, and the words, "Have a great show!!"

When Keith began the first few notes of their opening song, "Hoedown," the crowd would go crazy, and my heart would pump as if I were the one on stage.

Late in March, when we played the convention center in Miami, Greg told me someone was flying in from London whom he wanted me to meet. What I didn't know was that ELP had been looking for a new manager to replace my boss, Dee.

We arrived at the sound check, and Greg walked me over to a well-dressed gentleman sitting alone in the front row. He had medium-length dark hair and looked to be a little older than I was. His arms and legs were crossed, and he wore a stern expression. Greg introduced me to Stewart Young, the group's new manager, a chartered accountant and graduate of the London School of Economics. When ELP had started looking for a new manager, Stewart's father (their accountant) suggested it could be a good job for him. Stewart was unsure at first, because he knew little about the business. The band assured him he would be fine and sent him to New York to get some advice.

Stewart's first stop was at the office of Frank Barcelona, the head of Premier Talent, which was the band's booking agent. Frank impressed upon him the need for an experienced tour manager. Greg had filled Stewart in about my role, so he knew the tour was running smoothly and the band was happy. That was enough for him, and he offered me the job as full-time tour manager for Emerson, Lake & Palmer. The group based themselves in London, so I would have to move to the UK. It was a big decision. Things were going well with Dee, and I didn't think I was ready to leave him yet.

At first I couldn't understand why the band had hired Stewart, since he had no experience in the music business. Many of the people involved in management had a background as either lawyers or accountants and that was where Stewart certainly had the right pedigree. And as I got to know him, I realized that he was a very shrewd businessman with a gift for numbers. I liked Stewart. He was a bit arrogant but that could serve him well as a negotiator. And he loved music. That was what we had most in common and, after a short while, I understood why the band had chosen him.

He stayed with the tour a few days while I gave the decision to leave Dee a lot of thought. In the end, I felt the opportunity to live in Europe and work for one of the biggest bands in the world was too good to pass up, and I accepted the offer. But first, we had to finish the tour: April 15, Philadelphia; April 17, Detroit; April 18, Dayton; April 19, Chicago; April 20, Kent State University; April 21, Louisville; April 22, Fort Worth. On and on it went, and we were only half way through.

Managing large numbers of people with so much equipment was not an easy task, especially with the lack of simple tools like cellphones and computers. Remember, this was 1972.

A big part of being a tour manager was managing logistics, and I was good at it. During summer vacations, I had worked for my father in one of his warehouses. Trucks came loaded with goods that needed to be sorted and moved out to multiple destinations.

It had been a lesson in logistics. I also loved the challenge of getting the group on stage every night. Edgar Winter and Jerry LaCroix had often been at odds before shows, to the point where a few times, Jerry refused to go on. I had learned how to be a good mediator so that both sides felt they gained something and peace prevailed.

The situation was different with Emerson, Lake & Palmer. There were three of them, and each thought he was the star attraction. Keith Emerson, with his outrageous equipment and stage antics, stole much of the attention, but that didn't stop Greg and Carl from demanding equal treatment. When the three were at odds, it was usually about business matters such as where and when to tour or the type and cost of production. Getting one of them to compromise required finesse and was a delicate balancing act.

Soon after the tour ended, I moved to London and almost immediately began to prepare for a European tour. The second show would be in Berlin at the Deutschland Halle, a building built primarily for Hitler's 1938 summer Olympics. Berlin was a divided and tense city in 1972.

The concert sold out but didn't go well. Something went wrong with the onstage monitors, and ELP came offstage unhappy and angry. However, the crowd absolutely loved the show and was going wild. The foot stomping began. The audience wanted an encore.

I noticed fire hoses lined up in the back of the hall on my way into the dressing room, where the band members were sitting by themselves sulking. I told them they needed to get back on stage.

"No encore," Greg said, taking the lead.

I went out to tell the promoter, who was waving his hands wildly and shouting, "Where are they? Where are they?"

"No encore," I told him.

He went nuts.

"They have to do an encore. The people won't leave. You have seen the hoses. The riot police are on the way!"

As crazy as it sounded, he was telling me that the hoses would be turned on the crowd, and we were at an indoor venue.

Rushing back to the dressing room, I saw, to my horror, what looked like a small army of helmeted German storm troopers moving in.

Out of breath and as calmly as I could, I explained the situation. Greg said he understood, but there would be NO encore. I ratcheted up my insistence and pointed out the press consequences of not going on. That got their attention, and I went on to explain that any damage done to the venue or our equipment, for that matter, would be an additional huge expense. I could see they were considering going back on stage. My final plea was on behalf of the fans. In the end, the band didn't want to see anyone get hurt, and to the delight of the audience and the relief of the promoter, they played the encore.

Later during the tour, before our show in Paris, Johnny Hallyday, the French Elvis, came to our hotel to say hello. I was intrigued to hear about the way he toured. Much like a circus, Johnny, his musicians, and crew traveled with their own venue along with everything else they needed to put on a show. Their tent went up just outside of whatever town they were booked in, making the tour completely self-contained and ending the need for outside companies.

I liked the idea of having everything in-house. Most groups had their sound, lighting, trucking, and staging all done by different vendors. This could and did get confusing and expensive.

As ELP's tours grew more and more complicated, I couldn't get the idea of an all-in-one company out of my mind. A phone call from Puddie, my old girlfriend, helped to make this a reality. She was now living in London and married to Peter Watts, soundman and road manager for Pink Floyd. Peter had been married before and had two kids who lived with their mother, Miv. Naomi Watts, the older of the two, went on to become a famous actress but unfortunately Peter died of a drug overdose in 1976 years before she became well-known.

Peter's good friend, Jim Morris, was a co-partner of a hot sound and lighting company. I met him and listened carefully as he described his production ideas for the future, which were not so different from mine. I went to Peter for some advice. As he listened to my idea, he started smiling. It turned out that Jim's partner, a technical genius named Bill Kelsey, wanted to strike out on his own. This meant Jim would be left with all of the sound and lighting equipment, and he was looking for a new partner. Jim and I joined forces and became Circus Talents Ltd.

There was one more piece of the puzzle: transportation. My father had been watching my career from the sidelines. At first he disapproved. When I left college to join Edgar Winter, he took away the car and money and didn't speak to me for a few years. It was different now. He understood that what I was doing was real. He had seen me go from road manager to tour manager.

Now I was creating a serious business and he wanted in. Not only did he agree to participate in Circus Talents, but he also wanted to come on tour. Emerson, Lake & Palmer became our first big clients. and I went to talk to Greg Lake about my father coming on the road. Much to my surprise, he was all for it. Greg was very much of a family man, and he was interested in my on again, off again father-son relationship.

My father met us in London a few days before the tour began. Greg was on top of every detail, getting him a room at the Dorchester, the fanciest Hotel in London, and insisting on inviting him to his Mews house for a proper English dinner.

The night couldn't have gone any better and by the end of the evening, it was as if Greg and my father had known each other forever. In later years, whenever my father told the story of going on the road, he always began the tale with the fabulous dinner at Greg's.

Greg was also very much involved in the design of the production and together we created a portable proscenium arch enclosing a 96,000-watt lighting system bright enough for film and video. The lights were placed on four towers sitting on the corners of the stage. In addition, we custom designed a twenty-four-channel sound mixing board. My father provided special air ride trailers to minimize the potential damage to Keith's multiple keyboards and synthesizers, which needed special care, along with Carl Palmer's drum set, worth about $15,000 (a lot of money in those days).

The idea of the proscenium arch with full curtaining (60-foot wide by 30-foot deep) was to create a theatrical atmosphere. We wanted to provide a multimedia environment that could be reproduced night after night. Both Greg and I knew from experience that the more comfortable the group was on stage, the better the show. What better way to ensure this than to travel with your own theater? Once set up, it was massive. The only place big enough for us to rehearse in was the famous Shepperton film studios outside of London.

The name of the tour was Get Me a Ladder, and it was scheduled to last the better part of four months. ELP insisted I go on the entire tour, and I did. We had seventy-seven roadies, three tractor-trailers, twenty tons of equipment, and a film crew. (This was 1973.) Logistics were a nightmare. It took close to five hours to set up the stage and four hours to break it down. The crew almost never left before 2 a.m., then drove through the night to the next city. That meant little to no sleep night after night.

We were losing road crew at a rate of one a week. In the middle of the tour, I hired a doctor to come give everybody B-12 shots. (B-12 keeps nerves and blood cells healthy and is known as the energy vitamin.)

As much as my father tried to prep himself for the road, nothing could have prepared him. He had seen the conceptual drawings for the production but had never seen it fully assembled. I could see he was impressed. The music was a bit much for him though. As a child, he'd had an operation to remove an eardrum, and loud noise bothered him. He got a special pair of earplugs for the tour.

Both the band and crew liked him and called him "Coach." It was weird having him on the road though. I knew he would be cool about the women who were part of the scene. Drugs were something else. I am sure he knew what was going on, but I tried to be careful around him.

After a week of spending almost every night in a different country, I could see that my father was ready to go home. It had been an incredible bonding experience and an opportunity to understand each other better. He isn't a man of many words, but I could tell he was proud of what I had accomplished. Every son is looking for approval from his father and in many ways, a father son relationship is incomplete without it. I had waited a long time for my father to see that I too was a good businessman and I reveled in the knowledge that he finally got it.

Pink Floyd went into the Abbey Road Studios in January 1973 to finish up the Dark Side of The Moon album which led to a phone call from Peter.

He invited me to come to the studio the following night. The band was finally mixing the album, and Roger Waters was planning to record anyone in the studio who was willing to answer a series of questions he had created. Roger wanted a more human feeling to the record and thought people's spontaneous answers would give him just that. He initially planned to use the answers as a segue between songs but as he mixed them into the recording, he realized what an integral part of the album they were.

I was very excited and couldn't wait to go. As fate would have it, instead of Abbey Road Studios, I ended up in the emergency room of a London hospital, writhing in pain with my first attack of what turned out to be kidney stones.

Peter told me about the evening a few days later. Roger asked anyone, and everyone present in the studio, including roadies, studio staff and invited guests, to answer his questions. Paul and Linda McCartney showed up but apparently their answers ended up on the cutting room floor. Although their new guitar player, Henry McCullough, made it into the record with the memorable line, "I don't know. I was really drunk at the time."

Roadie, Chris Adamson, opens the album with his line, "I've been mad for fucking years – absolutely years." And my friends, Peter and Puddie, are very well represented. Peter contributed the repeated laughter during "Brain Damage" and "Speak to Me"

Puddie can be heard saying, "the geezer is cruising for a bruising," used in the segue between "Money" and "Us and Them," and her words, "I never said I was frightened of dying," are heard halfway through, "The Great Gig in the Sky."

Maybe the best lines came from Abbey Road's big Irish doorman, Gerry O'Driscol. Among them were, "I am not frightened of dying. Any time will do. I don't mind. Why should I be frightened of dying? There's no reason for it – you've got to go sometime."

And of course, his words at the very end of the album: "There is no dark side in the moon, really. As a matter of fact, it's all dark."

Before the ELP tour had started, I was sitting in Peter and Puddie's London apartment one day, listening to Peter talk about the upcoming leg of Pink Floyd's Dark Side of the Moon tour. The band had been out on tour using their own sound, lighting, and production equipment. But Peter knew it could be much better. "The production on this leg of the tour," he told me, "is going to be the most intense ever. I am going to be the first to do quadraphonic sound live, and I want Circus Talents to be a part of this tour. I have spoken to Steve and he agrees." Steve was Steve O'Rourke, Pink Floyd's manager.

My team joined Pink Floyd's Dark Side of the Moon tour during a short U.S. segment in March of 1973, the same month that the album was released. I was in Europe with ELP, but Jim, my partner, was in the States and went out with them. After the tour finished, they came back to London. Peter and Arthur Max, Pink Floyd's lighting designer, had some new ideas they needed to work on before starting out again.

While in London, the band was doing two gigs at Earl's Court. Peter invited me to a rehearsal. He was excited for me to see one of their new tricks. I couldn't believe my eyes. They had the balls to fly a relatively big model airplane on a guide wire from the back of the venue to the back of the stage, simulating the plane's destruction right above Nick Mason. It was great!

The Dark Side of the Moon tour caused a real buzz in London, and everyone wanted a ticket, even other rock stars. Carl Palmer called and asked if I was going. I invited him to come with me. Peter, by then, had perfected his version of surround sound, and the band sounded better than any other band I ever heard. Aside from the airplane, there were cool pyrotechnics, four black backup singers, and a sax player. Carl and I left shaking our heads.

The next part of the tour was in the States again, but this time the venues were much bigger, mostly outdoor stadiums. A couple of guys in the crew knew a great sign painter. Why not paint the *Dark Side of the Moon* album cover on the side of two of my trailers? Whenever possible, my drivers would drop the trailers on either side of the stage for effect.

I went to about thirteen shows, all on the East Coast, with the first at a stadium in Jersey City. The trailers parked by the sides of the stage looked amazing, and the production was state of the art. It wasn't until years later, though, that I came to fully appreciate the music. Don't get me wrong; it was great, but it wasn't the same as smoking a joint or two and listening with headphones. Besides I was working.

I didn't hang with the band much. I spent most of the time with Peter, the crew, and the backup singers. The tour went well. Peter and Steve, the band's manager, were satisfied. So much so, that after the tour, Peter approached me about doing more work together. The concept I had thought of a few years earlier was succeeding, and I was hitting my stride.

5

Life In The Fast Lane

IN THE early '70s, Steve Paul, Edgar Winter's manager, held court almost every night in the back room of Max's Kansas City, a downtown restaurant and club in Manhattan. Steve wasn't alone. Andy Warhol, Robert Rauschenberg, Lou Reed, David Bowie, and a host of other artists and rock stars also made Max's their late-night home.

As Edgar's road manager, I split my time between the band's house in upstate New York and the city. When I stayed overnight in Manhattan, I also ended my days hanging out with Steve at Max's.

Steve was an unusual character. He was very smart, very gay and wore only blue velvet. *Newsweek* once described him as, "a combination of sincerity, egotism, and coffeehouse literacy," and a "pseudo-poetic, stream of consciousness speech." The author went on to include a typical Steve Paulism: "I'm searching, always searching for a self-actualization through personal reality within a larger world reality."

Steve had owned an iconic New York Club called The Scene, which was famous as the place where Hendrix played his first major show in New York. It also showcased many acts that went on to become huge, including Jeff Beck, Pink Floyd, The Doors, Traffic, and Fleetwood Mac.

Drag queens, music moguls, rock stars, and movie stars hopped between the tables at Max's. It didn't matter if they stayed a minute or all night; they knew it was *the* place to be seen. The Velvet Underground was the house band and it was at Max's that they played their final performance with Lou Reed.

Patti Smith was Steve's secretary. With her dirty jeans, ripped T-shirt, ratty hair, and incredible mind, she was punk before the word existed. She didn't try to be that way; that was who she was. Robert Mapplethorpe, the photographer, was her boyfriend, and they were part of the nightly backroom crowd. I knew Patti a little from the office, and we talked at Max's, but it was at the Chelsea Hotel where I got to know her best. That's where she and Mapplethorpe lived.

The Chelsea Hotel was a landmark notable for the numerous writers, artists and musicians who stayed there over the years. Leonard Cohen, a longtime resident, immortalized the hotel in his song "Chelsea #2." It begins:

I remember you well in the Chelsea Hotel
You were talking so brave and so sweet

When I was in the city, Steve often booked me a room at the Chelsea, and Patti and I would talk late into the night. She wrote beautiful poetry and had started to experiment with performance (putting spoken word to music). I was impressed by her drive and determination; she had something to say and was not going to be denied.

Being on the road with Edgar in the early days was difficult. There weren't any Lear jets or limousines. If the distances weren't too far, we drove in rented cars. We usually stayed at Holiday Inns and sometimes shared rooms. In many cities, the audience barely knew who we were, and we played in all types of places, including high school auditoriums.

As my career progressed, the lifestyle improved. Emerson, Lake & Palmer toured in a rented private jet and were ferried around in large stretch limos, usually one for each of the guys. Everywhere we went we were treated like royalty and had suites in the best hotels and meals in Michelin-starred restaurants. The drugs were plentiful and of high quality, and then there were the groupies, an important and ever-present part of touring. Besides the obvious, they provided support and companionship and often traveled with the band. Emerson, Lake & Palmer seemed to attract a particularly sophisticated group of young ladies.

Nice hotel rooms, good food, and female companionship all helped to make touring more pleasant but being a tour manager was tough. Most mornings I got the band up and out to the airport for either a commercial or a private flight to the next city. After I checked the group into the hotel, I went to the venue. Once things were set up and the road crew was ready for the sound check, I went back to the hotel to get the group. One hour before the show, I gave a pep talk in the dressing room and made sure there were no bad vibes. I was also responsible for getting the group onstage as close to schedule as possible—always a challenge. During the concert, I listened to the show from different places around the venue to make sure the sound and lights were good. I also stopped at the box office to count ticket stubs and "get the money." Then I headed backstage to give the band towels when they came off the stage and see that they went back out for an encore.

After the show, I still had to get the band to the hotel and make sure the crew loaded out quickly and efficiently. I tried to go to sleep by 2 a.m. or 3 a.m. at the latest since I knew it would start all over again early the next day.

Some gigs, like Mar Y Sol, a three-day rock festival in Puerto Rico, were much harder than others. Emerson, Lake & Palmer toured with tons of specialized equipment, so the promoter arranged for a cargo plane to meet us in Jacksonville, Florida, our last stop before Puerto Rico. Alice Cooper, the Allman Brothers, Faces with Rod Stewart, and Black Sabbath were all scheduled to perform there, and most had their own equipment. ELP was afraid the scene at San Juan airport would be chaotic and elected me to go on the plane with the gear to keep track of it all.

I have a history of motion sickness, and although I am usually OK with flying, this time I was worried, especially when I realized there was no navigator on the flight, and I would have to sit in his jump seat. We left Jacksonville at about 3 a.m. under light rain. As the plane climbed higher, the first thing I noticed was the drop in temperature. There was limited heat and it was cold. I had never traveled in the cockpit before, and I was amazed by the small size of the windshield, especially considering that the aircraft was a very large old military cargo plane. The rain started coming down in sheets, and it didn't seem as if the pilot could see anything. Then the turbulence started, and I thought the flight would never end. We finally made it to San Juan in the early morning. Somehow, I didn't throw up, but I felt like shit.

I got the equipment loaded onto trucks to be driven to the festival grounds on the other side of the island. Then I took a waiting two-seater for the short flight to meet the trucks. It was Sunday morning, and the festival had started the day before, but when I arrived, things were quiet. The acts didn't start until 3 p.m. After our equipment was away in a safe location, I took a helicopter to the Cerromar Hotel. The helicopters were being used to get the artists to and from the venue.

I hadn't slept and needed a nap, but ELP had just arrived. The atmosphere at the hotel was cool. Rock stars could be seen milling about at the many restaurants, bars, and pools within the complex. Then nighttime came, and we heard from some of the groups that there were major problems with the sound system. A rumor had also spread that two people had drowned. I was worried.

Things got confusing. The promoter's representatives were telling multiple groups to get ready, but there weren't enough helicopters. I remember them frantically trying to get John McLaughlin of the Mahavishnu Orchestra on a helicopter to the gig. He was to have been on an earlier one, but someone gave his seat away. When ELP got the call, I made sure there were enough helicopter seats, but we arrived only to find technical problems of our own. Keith's organ kept shorting out, and the road crew couldn't find the cause. It was after 1 a.m. when the band finally got on stage, and almost 4 a.m. by the time we got back to the hotel. I went right to my room, collapsed on the bed, and fell asleep with my clothes on.

Working for Emerson, Lake & Palmer and living in London took some getting used to. London was like New York City, but on Valium, slower and more civilized. I drank tea, not coffee, ate fish and chips instead of burgers, and most difficult of all, drove on the wrong side of the road.

Greg offered me a room in his townhouse. He lived there with his girlfriend, Anita, and their two Irish setters, Oliver and Cromwell. The house was beautiful, and they made me feel right at home.

A few months after I arrived, I fell very ill. It turned out I had to be hospitalized, and I needed a minor operation. Greg was amazing. It was as if he was the brother I never had. Although I had a sister, Robin, who I was close with when we were children, in recent years we had gone in opposite directions and we now had very little contact. Greg got me the best doctors and a bed in the prestigious Harley Street Clinic. After the procedure, I didn't want to put him out, but Greg would have no part of it. He insisted I return to his home to recuperate.

Fortunately, I recovered fully. got my own place and was able to quickly get back to work. Our office was at 16 Curzon Street right off Hyde Park. I spent my days planning our next European tour. There were hotels to book, promoters to call, and meetings with Stewart and the band. At night, I would often go to The Speakeasy, London's version of Max's.

There was a real contrast between my time on the road and in the office, but as hard as touring was, after a few weeks at home, I couldn't wait to get back out there. The touring lifestyle was unique and something, for better or worse, that I tried to share with my friends.

When I was just starting out, and Steve Paul told me I needed a road crew for Edgar Winter's White Trash, the only people I really considered were my friends from college, Paul Hoffman and Ashley Lewis. I probably should have looked for more experienced people, but, fortunately, Paul and Ashley worked out pretty well. The next two friends I tapped, not so much.

Paul Shweitzer and I had been close through grade school, high school, and college. Paul was a guitar player, and we had played in many bands together throughout those years. Although he never asked me, I knew Paul wanted to come out on the road.

Greg Lake needed a guitar roadie, someone to string and tune his many guitars every night. I thought the gig would be perfect for Paul. He was excited when he arrived, but that didn't last long.

After only a week, I could see that he was struggling. I'll never forget what he looked like before the show in Jacksonville. He was sitting on the floor of the stage surrounded by five or six guitars, all in a state of being half stung with guitar strings, new and used, everywhere. He looked like he hadn't slept since the tour started.

I put my hand on his shoulder and said, "Hey, Paul have you had enough?"

He looked at me with a blank stare and nodded his head. I sent him home later that night. He had a big smile on his face and a sack filled with ten pounds of beautiful Florida oranges. Although the job didn't work out, I felt good that I had given him the opportunity. At least he had a story for his grandkids.

Kenny Marshall, another friend from the University of Vermont, was pissed off that I had not chosen him to be in Edgar Winter's road crew. Kenny was about 5'7", slightly built and not athletic in any way. Being a roadie was very demanding, and I knew he would never be able to hack it. Kenny was aware of my concerns but let me know that at some point he expected a job.

He came to visit me at Edgar's house in Clinton Corners, a small town a short distance from NYC, in early August 1971. We had a gig not too far away at Gaelic Park in the Bronx. I didn't think it would be a big deal to let him drive Edgar and a couple guys in the band. I gave him detailed driving directions (no cell phones or GPS), and I told him to make sure to leave himself plenty of time.

I left early to check out the venue, a medium-sized open-air gig with a good stage and sound system. We were sandwiched between Looking Glass, the opening act, and Ten Years After, the headliner.

The concert was about to begin and no Kenny. Looking Glass had about a twenty-minute set. Howard Stein, the promoter, was not happy.

"If Edgar isn't here by the time Looking Glass goes off stage, forget about it."

What could I say? Their set ended, and Howard told my guys to break down Edgar's stuff. I begged for a little more time.

"Ten minutes!" Howard barked back.

I was trying to remain calm but found myself pacing back and forth behind the stage. The ten minutes sped by, and Howard gave the signal for my roadies to move our equipment off stage. At that moment, Kenny's car pulled up and came to a screeching halt, and, although he had a curfew, Howard let us do a much-shortened set of three songs.

I was livid. Kenny did his best to apologize, but I did not want to hear it. Edgar wouldn't drive back to Rhinebeck with him. I asked Paul to take them back. Kenny loaded out with Ashley and some crew from Gaelic Park. Then, unbeknownst to me, Ashley took off with a girl and told Kenny to drive the twenty-foot rented U-Haul truck with all of the band's equipment back to the hotel at LaGuardia Airport, where the crew was staying. Kenny had never driven any type of truck before, but for some reason, decided to do it anyway.

I went back to the house. My anger had subsided. I wasn't quite ready to forgive him, but I had to have some pity on him, especially when he told me what happened in the car. After having gotten lost once, nobody trusted him, arguments ensued, and they kept going around in circles until Kenny took control again and got them to the gig.

About four hours later, he called. I could hear from his voice that something was wrong. After what he described as an unbelievably harrowing drive, he arrived at the Holiday Inn, where the front entrance included a low concrete overhang. The truck was higher than the concrete, and as Kenny drove, he proceeded to peel back the top of the truck as if it were the lid of a sardine can. He was able to back out, but the truck and the concrete awning were badly damaged.

Nobody was injured, and the equipment was intact. I told Kenny to go home and never to call me again. Luckily, insurance covered the damage. It was a few years before we spoke, but we reminisce and laugh about it today.

That's when I learned that including friends in everything you do certainly has limits. But helping each other is an important part of any friendship and an important part of my life. I have been through some extremely difficult times and without the support of friends, I am not sure how I would have made it.

Years later, this philosophy would play a role when Michael Jackson and I became friends, and he reached out to me. It wasn't in my nature to turn a friend away, especially when I was in a uniquely qualified position to help.

By 1974, the rock and roll lifestyle had started to take its toll. I was in London when I was stricken with the worst pain I had ever experienced. A friend drove me to the Harley Street Clinic, a prestigious British hospital. The diagnosis: kidney stones. The doctor admitted me for a few days.

It was late one night when an American film called *Not as a Stranger* came on the TV. The story followed a group of medical students on their journey to becoming successful physicians. As I watched, it seemed as if Dr. Aarons, the head surgeon, was talking directly to me when he was lecturing the interns: "I can see the picture you have of yourself already... a country road and an old Ford. It's a white house and you are Saint George complete in spotless armor. You get to a farmhouse. There's this man bleeding to death. Now alone, without instruments, without assistance, you perform an impossible operation, and because your heart is pure, you save him."

The desire to become a doctor was suddenly reignited in me. It had been buried somewhere deep inside but had never gone away. I don't know if it was the kidney stones, the pain meds, the movie, or what, but I began to cry, and I continued for a long time. The music business was hard, and I constantly had to play the tough guy when really, I was a softie inside. I was proud of what I had accomplished, but I was looking for something different both emotionally and intellectually, and I wanted to make more of a personal difference in other people's lives.

I decided then and there to go back to school to become a physician, and once I got out of the hospital, I put my plan into action. Jim was eager to buy me out of Circus Talents and take the equipment, so getting out of the business was easy.

About a year later I found out why Jim was so anxious to buy me out. I got a phone call from Stewart Young, who was still managing ELP, and who had an interesting story to tell me. Stewart had been visited by agents from Scotland Yard questioning him about his relationship to Jim Morris. Unbeknownst to me, Jim had been using our speaker cabinets to smuggle large quantities of hashish from Europe into the US.

Jim had been dealing with a man named Howard Marks (Mr. Nice), who at the time, was one of the largest hashish smugglers in the world. Every time Circus Talents did a tour for ELP or Pink Floyd or whomever, the speaker cabinets were packed with the hidden hash. Since the equipment was only temporarily in the US, assuming there were no problems with the paperwork, inspection of the equipment was minimal. After the tours were finished Jim made sure the speaker cabinets were packed with bricks so that the weight of the cabinets when they left the US would be the same as when they had arrived.

Marks was eventually caught, convicted and served seven years. In his autobiography, titled Mr. Nice, he tells the story of the first shipment using this scheme. It was in 1973, at a time when none of our groups were going on tour in the US. Jim was so sure of the plan that he got four out-of-work musicians to form a fictitious group called Laughing Grass. The group acted as if they had a tour booked in California beginning in LA. Jim took our speaker cabinets out to a location in the remote French countryside where they were packed with a few hundred kilos of hash. They were then shipped from Paris through New York to LA without incident.

Fortunately, neither Stewart nor I were implicated and as far as I know, my ex-partner, Jim, disappeared and was never prosecuted.

6

The Long And Winding Road

LIKE I said, leaving was easy. Reaching my goal of becoming a doctor, a hell of a lot tougher. Almost everyone I spoke to about going back to school said I would never be successful, but I was determined, and the negativity I heard just strengthened my resolve. After all, I had heard it all before in relation to the music business.

With few college credits to my name, I felt lucky to be accepted into a pre-med program at Hofstra University in Long Island. I lived in a basement apartment close to school and worked my ass off, graduating less than two years later with a B+ average.

I'd grown up in Long Island and at Hofstra, I reconnected with a few old friends from high school. My friend Paul Shweitzer's sister had married into the family that owned the Nevele, one of the premier hotels in the Catskill mountains, a couple hours north of NYC.

About a year after I began classes, Paul invited me and a group of friends to go to the Nevele for Labor Day weekend. Our activities included seeing Ike and Tina Turner at Monticello Raceway, not far from the hotel. The show was terrific and afterwards we all went to a strip club across from the Raceway for a couple of drinks.

I didn't pay much attention to the first few dancers and then Leann took the stage. I don't know if it was her big blue eyes or her long sexy legs, but I became mesmerized and decided I would try to speak to her. When she came out of the backstage door, I was there waiting. At first she didn't want to know about me at all. I was just another stage door Johnny. But I kept talking and when I invited her to lunch at the Nevele the next day, her tone changed. The afternoon went well, and we started dating.

Leann lived in New Jersey about an hour from my apartment and over the next year things began to get serious. As I got to know her better I learned that Leann was a trained dancer and had worked in Vegas and off Broadway and studied with some of the best teachers in NYC. Being a professional dancer was a very tough competitive business and stripping was a good way to make extra money.

We got along well. She was easy to talk to, fun to be with and we connected spiritually. Leann had been a chanting Nichiren Shoshu Buddhist for many years and I was very attracted to her Buddhist way of thinking.

Graduation from Hofstra was fast approaching, and I began applying to Medical schools.

American medical schools had a glut of applicants in those years. Admissions committees didn't value my music business experience, and I was rejected across the board. But there was still hope: a few foreign medical schools were accepting the overflow of Americans determined enough to take that difficult route toward becoming a physician.

By this time, Leann and I wanted to get married, but I worried about taking her with me on what I knew would be a long and difficult road, not only for me but for her as well. We spoke about the hardships we both would have to endure, and Leann assured me that she was willing and ready for whatever was ahead of us. My parents tried hard to dissuade me from getting married. They were overjoyed that I had gone back to school and deathly afraid that a new marriage would derail my efforts at becoming a physician. I appreciated their concern but the feelings I had for Leann were too strong and we got engaged.

After careful consideration, I chose to attend the Universidad Autonoma in Guadalajara, Mexico, a school sensitive to the small number of spots available in American medical schools. In fact, by its sheer number of U.S. students, Autonoma was the largest American medical school in the world. The only problem was that its courses were in Spanish. To be accepted, I first had to pass a language exam. Four months of intensive Spanish classes helped me jump that hurdle.

Leann and I got married on July 25, 1976, a month and a half before the semester started at the Autonoma, and we spent our honeymoon driving the 2600 miles from New York to Guadalajara Mexico.

Once in school in Mexico, I quickly realized that although my Spanish was good enough to get by in everyday life, it was woefully inadequate for following the complex lectures and lab discussions I needed to learn medicine. The only upside was that I was not alone. Most Americans faced the same predicament. What's more, we confronted a Catch-22. To stay in school, we had to pass exams in Spanish, but eventually, to practice in the United States, we would have to pass extensive English-language licensing exams.

A group of fellow Cuban-American students came up with a solution. They needed help with English, and we needed help with Spanish, so we held joint study groups three or four nights a week. They taught us enough additional Spanish to get by on our exams at school, and we helped them to understand the American textbooks, so they, too, could pass the U.S. licensing exams.

After four years, I became proficient in Spanish, a skill I value highly. Not only did it enable me to get by in Mexico, but it also became invaluable for living in a world with such a large Latino population.

As hard as the language was for me, it was twice as hard for Leann. She didn't know a word of Spanish when we arrived. I tried to teach her a few words and expressions, but she basically picked it up as she went along. Leann is a real go getter and before too long she got a job as a dance instructor at a local Mexican Dance Academy. The owners, and many of the students, were bilingual and over time her ear became very accustomed to Spanish and although she couldn't speak the language that well, her understanding of Spanish increased by leaps and bounds.

Unlike most of the American students at the medical school who lived clustered together and only hung out with other Americans, we lived in a Mexican neighborhood and embraced the culture. And for both Leann and me, it was the start of a love affair with the third world. We traveled throughout the country and found exotic places and interesting people, and the whole Mexican experience brought us closer together.

Once each semester, the medical students were required to go into the countryside for a few weeks to treat the poor and disadvantaged. Most of the people we saw were "campesinos" (peasant farmers) and their families. They lived simply in homes with no appliances, few pieces of furniture, and, often, no bathroom. They also had little access to either clean drinking water or electricity and almost no access to medical care unless they traveled many miles over rutted dirt roads. What I saw opened my eyes to the poverty that many in the world live in, and, importantly, taught me how to help people in remote clinics with little available medical technology. This experience, along with time spent working as a surgical resident in the emergency room of Queens General Hospital, combined to help me years later when I did a series of charity projects in Africa.

After finishing four years of medical school, as a foreign medical graduate, I was required to complete an extra year of clinical training in a U.S. hospital. Although I had briefly gone through the different specialties during my last two years of medical school, I was still unsure of the type of physician I wanted to be.

I spent the first four months of the year assigned to the surgical service, and this time around, the specialty intrigued me. I was especially taken with the idea of being able to diagnosis a problem in the human body and fix it mechanically, using my hands and a few specialized instruments.

When I was ten, I'd seen an exhibit called The Invisible Man at the American Museum of Natural History in New York City. It featured a life-sized glass figure with all of its internal organs and physiology visible from the outside. The image never left me. Now I was in the operating room seeing those organs for real, and it fascinated me. I finished the year and passed the U.S. licensing exams. Once licensed in the U.S., I was eligible to apply to American residency programs and I was accepted into a surgical residency program at Long Island Jewish Hospital in New York.

I never served in the military, but I imagine it must be similar to being in a residency. Both are rigorous, highly structured environments where you start at the bottom and learn through experience. In surgery, the familiar expression, "see one, do one, teach one," epitomizes this approach. Unfortunately, "see one" spans the first few years, which are spent mainly holding retractors and carefully watching a surgeon's every move.

The residency was extremely competitive, with two residents being asked to not return at the end of each year. We started at 6 a.m. and never finished before 7 p.m. and spent every other night on call.

As much as I liked surgery, what I was seeing at the other end of the table intrigued me. This was the domain of the anesthesiologist. What intrigued me was the idea that it is possible to put patients quickly and efficiently into a completely unconscious state, and just as easily, wake them up. As I watched, I realized anesthesiologists not only had to be good academically, but also skillful at procedures, calm in stressful situations, and able to think fast on their feet. The shorter cases, performed with just sedation, particularly interested me because they required a keen sense of timing and attention to detail, skills I had picked up as a drummer and tour manager.

I was accepted into a three-year anesthesia program at Beth Israel Hospital in New York City. Credit for time spent in surgery reduced that to two years. My new specialty suited me well, but I didn't love working in hospital operating rooms. They were impersonal, antiseptic, and generally unfriendly. What's more, they were cold, literally bone-chilling. (Surgeons work under hot lights and sweating is taboo. Anesthesiologists, meanwhile, are far from the lights.) I found it impossible to wear enough gowns layered over my scrubs to keep warm. Inevitably, I went home with frozen extremities.

In the last year of residency, we were required to create a research study. Most of my fellow students devised highly technical studies that involved a lot of time in the animal lab. My project was about the effects of music on patients under anesthesia. When I told the program director, he laughed and said it wasn't a serious enough topic, but I persisted. Eventually he allowed me to do a very limited version of what I had planned, and my results were valuable in demonstrating the power of music in relaxing patients although the program director still poo-pooed the study.

By now, it was May 1985. My residency finished at the end of June, and I needed a plan. The residents graduating with me were split between pursuing specialty anesthesia residencies and going right into private practice in a hospital-based anesthesia group. I wasn't particularly interested in either option.

I did have an idea, though. There were a couple of anesthesia residents moonlighting part-time in the offices of a few plastic surgeons. I wondered if full-time, office-based work was a viable career option. As far as I knew, no one was doing that in New York City.

My colleagues weren't keen on making a living outside the hospital. It mostly involved giving a combination of IV drugs to relax the patients and block the pain of surgery, which was called conscious sedation. This type of anesthesia was lo-tech science and lots of intuition, and it was just what I liked about the specialty: the sixth sense of knowing how much of what drug to give at exactly the right time.

For surgeons and patients alike, office operations offered distinct advantages. Patients generally didn't like going to the hospital, especially for cosmetic surgery. The fewer staff they saw and the more privacy they had, the better. For surgeons, the multiple advantages of office-based surgery included the ability to build a strong, trusting relationship with the anesthesiologist. This happened less often in the hospital, where each day the surgeon was assigned someone different. In an office setting, surgeons would also be able to use their own nursing staff, a distinct advantage over the alternative. And finally, they could schedule patients at their convenience. Hospitals often had cosmetic surgeons working in the afternoon, an inconvenient time for both the surgeon and the patient.

I weighed potential problems. The monitors available at the time, tended to be bulky and geared toward hospital use, and many of the anesthetic drugs were long-acting depressants with multiple side effects; okay for general anesthesia, but not really effective for short office cases. Another problem was the lack of backup. Hospital ORs were filled with doctors and nurses of all types. When something went wrong, within seconds professionals were on the scene. Not so in offices.

This was less of a problem in my case, because as a second-year surgical resident, I had worked in the emergency room of Queens General Hospital (a level-three trauma center) to gain experience. I was the first doctor a potential surgical patient saw. If the problem was simple, like needing sutures, I handled the case. My main job, however, was to evaluate and help stabilize patients needing surgery.

I worked mostly on weekends when the ER was like an intense knife-and-gun-wound repair shop. At times I thought the borough of Queens was at war. Tough as that was, the most difficult cases were the auto accident victims, who often arrived with multiple life-threatening injuries. I learned to stay cool and make quick, intelligent decisions in the face of real emergencies.

I decided to approach a cosmetic surgeon about my idea of full-time work in an office OR, but who? A small paragraph in the *New York Post* jumped out at me:

"Michael Jackson was seen yesterday leaving the office of his favorite New York plastic surgeon, Dr. Edgar Somers. It is believed Michael was receiving treatment for the scalp burns he suffered during the filming of a Pepsi commercial a few years ago."

What caught my eye was both Michael Jackson's name, and the mention of Dr. Edgar Somers. I knew him, sort of. I had never been assigned to one of his cases, but I had seen him in the doctor's lounge. Like most of the other cosmetic surgeons, Somers was well groomed, well dressed, and projected an attitude of confidence. Word among the residents was that he was a good guy, pleasant to work with.

His day at the hospital was Tuesday. It seemed best to approach him after he came out of surgery, and I felt positive that I would be successful with my proposal.

I didn't want Somers to know I was a resident, so I put on a long white coat with the nondescript title "Anesthesiology Department" written over the breast pocket. He walked out of the OR alone. I came up the hall from behind and tapped him on the shoulder.

"Hello, Dr. Somers, my name is Dr. Neil Ratner."

"Hello Dr. Ratner, nice to meet you," he said. "What can I do for you?"

"Dr. Somers, I have heard a lot about you. I know you have a busy office practice with important patients. I would like to ask you a question."

"Sure, go ahead."

"Who gives anesthesia in your office?"

"Well, what do you mean? I give some sedation."

"Yes, I am sure you do, but don't you have an anesthesiologist come in for bigger cases?"

I could see the wheels turning in his mind. I had his attention. It was time to move in for the finish.

"Dr. Somers, if you had an anesthesiologist come to your office, you could do many of your hospital cases right there. I would work with you to make sure your OR had the right equipment. Don't you think many of your patients would prefer to have surgery in the office?"

From the look of intense interest on his face, I knew what he would say next, and I wasn't disappointed.

"When can you start?" I was pretty sure he wouldn't question my credentials because he just assumed I was an anesthesiologist on staff at the hospital. Whether he asked around about who I was, I don't really know. A week after my residency finished, I was on board in his office, and my technique both pleased and intrigued him.

During my training I had concentrated on the smaller cases and especially on the goal of keeping a patient comfortable and immobile without using general anesthesia.

When cases were done in the hospital under local anesthesia with sedation (conscious sedation), commonly, patients moved around because most anesthesiologists were uncomfortable keeping patients in anything but a very light state. Surgeons hated to work on a moving target, but it was the accepted norm. I had a clear enough understanding of the medications and their combinations that I was comfortable keeping patients in a deeper state. My patients almost never moved during surgery, and the surgeons couldn't believe it.

Office anesthesia was especially challenging and took great attention to detail. When a patient is under general anesthesia, it's a matter of watching the monitors. With a patient under conscious sedation, while the monitors are still very important, it's also crucial to watch the patient. They will tell you in advance, with small movements and muscle twitches, when it's time for more or less medication.

Somers had never seen an anesthesiologist do what I did. He couldn't believe it was possible to keep a patient so deep, yet have that person wake up so fast and without nausea. (Every plastic surgeon's nightmare is a beautifully done facelift ruined by the trauma of post-op retching and vomiting.) It took real skill to mix the right medications and give them in a way so that the patient woke up smoothly.

Doctors, and especially cosmetic surgeons, love to brag, and Somers was no different. By the beginning of August, I was overwhelmed with requests to give anesthesia in other offices.

Scheduling was the problem. Even with juggling, I could only cover three or four offices. Eventually, other anesthesiologists realized the wisdom of what I had started. Some worked for me on their days off; others went into the field on their own.

In those days, minimal regulations governed office surgery, and most office environments were inadequately outfitted. It was my job to create a safe operating environment for all concerned, especially the patient.

I traveled from office to office and brought whatever I needed. Every patient had to be properly monitored with a minimum of EKG, blood pressure cuff, and a way to gauge respiration.

I also kept oxygen and a crash cart on hand (a case filled with emergency drugs and supplies). Somewhat later, the invention of a small, portable non-invasive machine, called a pulse oximeter, proved revolutionary. It measured the blood oxygen saturation level from heartbeat to heartbeat. Not having to estimate this through the combination of a stethoscope on the chest and a visual inspection of the blood in the surgical field cut my stress level in half. More importantly, it made surgery in general, and anesthesia in particular, safer whether done in an office or a hospital.

By 1995, I was settled in my career with a busy, successful practice in office anesthesia. My marriage was good, and Leann and I were enjoying all the benefits of my being a successful doctor in NYC and then a phone call changed everything.

7

One Night Only

THE table was set, the turkey carved, and Leann and I were about to serve dinner to my parents when the phone rang.

"Rat, what are you doing?"

Michael Jackson sounded shaky. He was living in Manhattan, at the Four Seasons Hotel, while rehearsing for an upcoming HBO special. I had given him anesthesia for a small procedure at Somers office earlier in the week, and I hadn't expected to hear from him until after the holiday weekend.

"It's Thanksgiving Day, Michael. I am having dinner with my family."

He began to cry. It was disturbing, especially because I knew he was probably alone. Michael had been brought up as a Jehovah's Witness and didn't celebrate holidays. It had been more than a year since we had first met in Somers office. Although I saw him occasionally when he was in New York, we had become friendly, mostly through late night telephone calls—something Michael was known for.

It was a difficult time for him, and the stress was taking its toll. The Jordy Chandler child molestation charges had finally been dropped, but the experience had devastated him personally, and the *History* album, which had been released in June, was not selling well.

In fact, Somers and I had spoken about how pale and tired Michael looked. He had lost weight and never seemed to drink enough water.

"Rat they're killing me... too many rehearsals. They are working me too much."

I wasn't exactly sure if he was talking about his management, HBO, or the concert promoter. What did concern me was that Michael seemed to be at his breaking point.

He continued through the sobs. "They don't know how hard I work.... They don't understand.... They are killing me.... You gotta help. You gotta help me, Rat!"

I heard what he was saying, and I felt bad for him, but I was not sure how I could help him. "What would you like me to do?"

There was a pause.

"Rat, I need you to be my doctor. I need you to work with me."

We had spoken about touring with doctors. Michael knew I was not interested in the job of tour doctor, taking care of all the performers, road crew, and staff that travelled with any major musician. We had also talked about the possibility of my being his personal physician on the road, but there were no plans for an immediate tour. This had to be something else.

Michael was shy, and it wasn't easy to become friends. My ponytail and earring helped, but what really connected us was music. Michael loved hearing about my early days of rock and roll. We laughed about stories of broken-down tour buses, small town gigs, and the blunders of inexperienced road crews, like the time my crew for Edgar Winter's White Trash had chained a truck fully loaded with the band's equipment to a parking meter on Fifth Avenue and 13th Street the night before our tour started. The lock, chain, and parking meter were all exactly in the same place when they returned in the morning, but, of course, the truck was MIA.

I was jarred back into the present by the startling sound of Michael screaming.

"Call Mensch! Call Mensch!!"

"OK, OK, calm down and tell me who Mensch is."

Bernie Mensch had been Michael's personal physician in California for many years. Michael had told him how he was feeling, and because he knew Michael's medical history, Mensch was concerned. Michael wanted me to work with Mensch to help him through the rehearsals and upcoming shows.

I still wasn't sure how I could help, but I took Mensch's number and told Michael I would call him. By now he had stopped crying, so we said our good-byes and agreed to speak the next day.

I didn't know what to think, and when I explained the phone call to my parents and Leann, they just looked at me. None of us knew what to say. I figured it would make more sense after I spoke with Mensch and I phoned him first thing in the morning. He was expecting my call.

"Dr. Ratner, so glad you called. Michael has told me a lot about you."

"Good things, I hope," I replied with a laugh.

"Only good things, but I am afraid our 'little buddy' isn't doing very well."

He explained that Michael had a pattern of poor nutrition, dehydration, and sleeplessness, especially when he was on tour or before important events like the upcoming HBO taping. We spoke about Michael's mental state and the fact that the sleep meds he had been prescribed weren't helping and could, potentially, become an addiction. I asked if Michael had gotten any kind of psychological therapy. Mensch's answer was vague but left me with the impression that it had been tried without success. Neither he nor I had a good solution, and the show was only a few weeks away. I told him I would think about what I could do to help on my end.

The easiest problem to fix was the dehydration. An IV with a saline solution for an hour or so either before or after rehearsal could take care of that problem, and it was a common practice used by doctors to treat both professional athletes and performers. Michael's nutritional deficits could be aided by adding supplements to the infusion. The biggest problem was Michael's lack of sleep.

As an anesthesiologist, I considered myself a sleep technologist. Many people would argue that the state of unconsciousness an anesthesiologist produces—whether light or deep—is not sleep at all, and I would agree. However, certain medications create a sleeplike state not unlike that produced by most sleeping pills. I wondered if there was a non-addictive medication I could use on a temporary basis to replace the sleeping pills.

Propofol had become available in late 1986, and I had begun using it in my office anesthesia practice that year. The first time was in Tillman's office. As I injected the propofol into the IV, he took one look at the medication and just about had a heart attack.

"What's that? Stop! It's not clear! It must be contaminated."

I had to calm him down.

"Edgar, chill! It's a new medication, and it's meant to be milky white."

I explained propofol's dynamics and after the surgery gave him a few articles about the drug. It was a good lesson for me. I avoided the same reaction from the other surgeons I worked with by educating them about the drug before I used it in the OR.

Propofol is classified as a "sedative hypnotic" and is dose dependent, producing a range of effects from sedation to general anesthesia. One of the major advantages of using propofol is its ability to keep a patient in a light sleeplike state from which they could be woken up quickly with few to no side effects.

Until the introduction of propofol, Sodium Pentothal was the best drug we had for putting a patient to sleep at the start of surgery. Pentothal depressed respiration and lowered blood pressure (as did most anesthetics), but it was difficult to control, long acting, and highly nauseating. Propofol also depressed respiration and blood pressure, but to a much lesser extent. It was much easier to control and, more importantly, it wore off within minutes with little to no nausea. By late 1995, I had used propofol, conservatively, in more than five thousand cases.

I considered whether using propofol might help as a temporary solution to Michael's sleep problem. The more I explored the possibility, the more sense it made. The studies I read about burn patients who were given repeated propofol infusions over a series of weeks to months indicated no residual effects, and I couldn't find a single article on addiction to propofol.

I called Mensch and explained my thoughts about temporarily correcting Michael's problems. We agreed the solution was not ideal, but it seemed to be the best course of action under the circumstances. Lee gave me permission to use the recovery room in his office for the treatments, as long as it was late in the day when most of his patients were gone.

When Michael and I spoke next, I explained the treatment plan and stressed that its main purpose would be to give him fluids and supplements with the added benefit of a few hours of "sleep." He understood that this was not a substitute for a genuine good night's sleep, but only a temporary solution. We would explore other ways to address his problems once the shows were finished. I also told Michael that this was serious business and that he would need to be fully monitored, just as if he were having surgery. He said he understood. There was one more thing I needed him to agree to before I was willing to move forward, and that was to let me severely limit his use of tranquilizers and sleeping pills for the few weeks that we would be working together. (My hope was this would wean him off them forever.)

I set up a schedule of four treatments spaced out over the two weeks left before the show. Each would be no more than three hours, and each treatment would be separated by three or four days. Michael would come to Somers office in the late afternoon following rehearsal. This way I could gauge his maximum level of dehydration and fatigue. We also timed the treatments for the late afternoon because it meant Michael would leave the office in the early evening. My experience with other patients had taught me that Michael would be tired for at least a few more hours, and I hoped it would be the start of a better night's sleep.

The first two treatments went exactly according to plan. Michael looked a little better and said he had more energy. I felt a sense of relief that the measures were working. I knew what I was doing was an off-label use but seeing him improve gave me confidence that I had come up with a helpful solution.

I was waiting for him at Somers office for the third infusion, and he was late as usual. I didn't like bothering Wayne, Michael's head of security, but more than two hours had passed, and I was getting tired of sitting tight. I reached for the phone.

As I started dialing, Conchita, Dr. Somers office manager, came running into the recovery room, shouting to me.

"Pick up the phone for Wayne. It's an emergency!"

My heart was racing as I took the call.

"Ratner, he's on the ground! What should we do?"

"Wayne, what are you talking about?"

"He collapsed during rehearsal, and he is on the floor of the stage at the Beacon. EMS is here. What should we do? They want to take him to the hospital."

"Wayne, is he breathing? Is he conscious?"

"Yes, he is breathing and conscious. They are getting ready to take him out of here. What do you want us to do?"

Wayne needed an answer fast.

I was freaked and had no idea what could be wrong. A heart attack? A stroke? Something else entirely? It certainly had nothing to do with the treatments. I had seen Michael the week before and had monitored him on two separate occasions for three hours each time with no sign of any impending problems.

Michael needed to get to a hospital where there would be doctors who knew him. I had no hospital affiliations, but Dr. Somers was on staff at Doctors Hospital nearby, and I was sure that he could put together a team.

Conchita was standing in the doorway of the recovery room wearing an expression of horror.

I took a firm grip of her arm, "Conchita, get hold of Dr. Somers and tell him what's going on."

She hurried to her desk to make the call. I got back on the phone with Wayne.

"Do you know where they are taking him?"

"I don't know, Ratner."

Conchita shouted from the front.

"Neil, pick up the other line for Dr. Somers."

I told Wayne to hold on, and I spoke to Somers. He said he would arrange everything and insisted that MJ go to Doctors Hospital. I hung up with Somers and got back to Wayne.

"Let me talk to the EMS guy."

I told him who I was and asked about Michael's condition. He said he was conscious and talking, with low blood pressure and a rapid, but stable, pulse.

They were taking him to Roosevelt Hospital. I told them that they had to take him to Doctors Hospital. We argued. Protocol said Roosevelt because it was the closest. I was getting angry.

"Are you kidding? Do you have any idea what it will be like at Roosevelt? It's already on every wire service. He needs to go where we can best take care of him. This is Michael Jackson. Don't be foolish!"

He told me to hold on. I overheard him discussing it with his partner. Finally...

"OK, we will meet you at Doctors Hospital."

I took a cab and got out in front of the emergency room entrance. There were already two or three satellite trucks, five police cars, and a rapidly growing crowd of photographers, spectators, and fans.

Dr. Somers arrived at the same time, and we walked into the ER together. Michael had been wheeled in a few minutes before. Wayne was standing at the door doing his best to control the flow of people and information. The scene was becoming chaotic.

Inside the trauma room, Michael was on a stretcher surrounded by an array of medical personnel. The nurses were cutting off his clothes and hooking him up to monitors. At the same time, doctors were poking, prodding, asking questions and yelling orders.

I went straight to the head of the stretcher to comfort Michael. He had an oxygen mask over his face. His eyes were wet, and he was sobbing.

I felt very badly for my friend, and I did everything I could to look calm and confident.

I squeezed his hand.

"Hey, Michael, don't worry. You'll be OK. You're in good hands."

He turned his head. I could see the fear in his eyes as he gave me a half smile and nodded in agreement.

ROCK DOC

8

Doctors Killed My Father

MICHAEL'S condition was serious, but stable. The medical team in the ER had made a preliminary diagnosis of dehydration with a possible arrhythmia, and they were transferring Michael to the intensive care unit where he could be carefully monitored and evaluated further.

I was relieved the ER doctors had found nothing more serious. I was also a little surprised that Michael's dehydration was so severe. I thought we had been making progress on that front, but I hadn't seen him in four days. Michael obviously wasn't paying attention to drinking enough fluids, although it was a point I was continually stressing.

Each of the ICU's ten individual glass cubicles faced a central nurses' station. The hospital placed Michael in the cubicle farthest from the entrance to the unit to give him extra privacy.

He and I spoke for a few minutes. Michael had been mildly sedated in the ER and was calm now. I told him not to worry and to try to get some sleep. I would see him first thing in the morning. He asked if Mensch knew what was going on, and I said I had already spoken to Mensch; he was taking a red eye from Los Angeles.

I left Michael and introduced myself to Dr. Bill Alleyne, the head of the Critical Care Department. He was a large black man with a soft, trustworthy manner and an easy smile. Turned out he was also a fan. I knew Michael would like him.

He was primarily concerned that MJ might have an underlying problem with his heart rhythm, possibly caused by a combination of dehydration and poor nutrition. Michael was a poor eater, especially when he was on the road. He often skipped meals or barely picked at his plate, and when he did eat, it was basically take-out or fast food. I had tried hard to impress upon him the need to eat nutritious foods on a regular basis. His excuse was always the same, "It's hard to eat good on the road, Rat, but I eat very well at Neverland."

As part of his treatment plan, Michael would receive a special form of intravenous feeding called hyperalimentation, designed to correct nutritional deficiencies.

It was almost 11 p.m. I had been in the emergency room for five hours after a full day in the operating room. I felt exhausted and I needed some rest. Wayne saw me getting ready to leave and grabbed my arm.

"Ratner, where are you going?"

"I'm tired, Wayne. I am going home."

"You can't leave yet."

I was a little taken aback.

"Why not? What's the problem?"

"Ratner, you're his doctor now. Nobody has talked to his family. You've got to do it. His brothers Jermaine and Randy have been calling every fifteen minutes. I said you would call back. After that, you have to go out to the waiting room and talk to his sisters, Janet and Rebe."

I hadn't thought about Michael's family. It had never occurred to me that I would be the one to have to talk to them. I thought they would talk to Dr. Somers or Dr. Alleyne, but both had left. Wayne had decided it was up to me.

He gave me a phone number for Michael's brothers who were waiting for the call together. Both got on the telephone. Their first question was why nobody had talked to them sooner. I formally introduced myself, apologized, and explained that the situation had been chaotic. I told them about Michael's condition and that he was in the ICU as a precaution. They asked how long he would be there. I told them I wasn't sure and added that Mensch, whom they knew, was on his way from LA and would get back to them the next day with more details. They seemed satisfied and thanked me.

I went to the waiting room where Michael's sisters, Janet and Rebe, were sitting quietly. Their main concern was that Michael was going to be OK. I assured them he was not in any danger and explained that he was in the ICU so he could be watched closely.

I checked on Michael one last time, said goodnight to Wayne, and split. The scene outside the hospital was like something out of a movie. The cops had blocked off the street and barricades were everywhere–– with a sea of photographers to my left and a throng of fans behind barricades to my right. The fans had set up for an all-night vigil and were holding candles and chanting, "Michael! Michael!" Behind them stretched a huge array of get-well signs, flowers, and stuffed animals.

I walked the short distance to my apartment. Leann was eager to hear about the day's events. She hadn't met Michael yet, but I knew it was only a matter of time. I also knew that when they did meet they would get along well, in part because Leann, like Michael, was a dancer. She and I spent a little time talking, and I went to bed.

At 2 a.m. the phone rang. The resident in charge of the ICU was on the other end of the line. Michael couldn't sleep and had asked him to call me. The resident said the sleeping medication they had given him was totally ineffective. I explained that I had tried low-dose propofol. I told him it seemed effective for short periods, but I hadn't used it for longer than three hours. He seemed interested and said he would try it.

I had an early case the next day, and it was late morning before I arrived at the ICU. Wayne was talking to someone I assumed to be Dr. Bernie Mensch. I waved and went right into Michael's cubicle. His energy level seemed much better, and we talked about the great care he was getting. When a nurse came in to draw blood, I walked over to Mensch. He greeted me warmly, and we briefly discussed Michael's condition. From that point on, Mensch ran the show, and I slipped into the background. Michael's team called a news conference to dispel rumors of drugs, AIDS, or a hoax. I was invited, but I had a case and didn't go.

The next afternoon, I arrived to find Lisa Marie Presley Jackson in the cubicle with Michael. Wayne had told me she would be coming, which wasn't surprising, of course, since they were married. I hadn't met Lisa, and I didn't want to bother them, but Michael saw me at the nurse's station and waved me over.

"Hey, Rat, meet Lisa."

The first thing that struck me about Elvis Presley's only daughter was her piercing blue eyes, very much like her father's. She had dark hair, was shorter than I expected, and was dressed conservatively in a black pants suit. I felt a little odd since Michael didn't indicate who I was, so I shook her hand and explained that I was a doctor involved in his care. She just looked at me with a curious, hard-to-read expression.

Michael was in a playful mood and starting to feel like himself again. I stayed for a few minutes and then excused myself. As I walked out of the cubicle, I heard, "The Rat has left the building."

At the end of Elvis Presley concerts, announcers would say, "Elvis has left the building." It was a way of signaling "No encore. Time to leave." The phrase became so famous producers recorded it on many of Elvis's live records. In fact, the expression had become a catch phrase and punch line for anyone exiting for any reason.

I could hear MJ laughing as I walked to the nurses' station, and I was incredibly embarrassed. For Michael to say that line in front of Elvis's daughter was too much!

Lisa Marie didn't stay long. As she came out of Michael's room, she walked over to me and asked if we could speak privately. I hadn't heard her voice before, and its similarity to Elvis's freaked me out. I couldn't imagine what she wanted to talk about, but she came right to the point.

"I don't know who you are, but I don't like so many doctors around Michael."

Her words were dark and foreboding.

Before I could respond, she got right in my face and looked me in the eyes.

"I don't like doctors," she stated. "Doctors killed my father, and I won't let them kill my husband!"

Without another word, Lisa Marie turned and walked out of the ICU. It was a chilling experience and left me flabbergasted.

Michael responded well to the IV feedings. The arrhythmia never developed, the blood tests were back to normal, and his hospital stay was coming to an end.

Before Mensch headed back to LA, we spoke a little about an idea I had to try some form of Eastern medicine with Michael. Mensch liked the idea. I said I would keep him posted.

I had no personal experience or contacts to go by, so I asked around for recommendations. The name Jerry Go came up repeatedly. He seemed highly regarded, especially when dealing with lifestyle and nutritional issues. A friend who had worked with him set up a phone call. I explained the situation, and Jerry was definitely interested in helping. He thought he could assist Michael in a variety of ways using acupuncture, herbal medicine, and specialized techniques of moving energy around that he had developed. I told him I would get back to him after Michael was out of the hospital.

Before leaving, Michael asked if he could visit the other patients in the ICU. Dr. Alleyne gave the OK and took him into a few of the other cubicles. Alleyne told me later about one patient who was moved by the experience.

"I can die now," she said to the doctor. "I have prayed with Michael Jackson!"

On the morning of Michael's discharge, the scene outside the hospital was madness. There were more photographers, fans, and satellite trucks than I had seen the entire time he was in the hospital. Mensch had asked me to accompany Michael back to the hotel. His hair and makeup artist had been at the hospital earlier to make sure everything was perfect. Michael slipped on a long black coat, wrapped a black chenille scarf around his neck, and donned his signature black fedora. He left off his sunglasses and the usual tape on his nose.

As he walked out of the hospital, he gave a big smile and waved to the crowd enthusiastically. Michael wanted everyone to know he was healthy and strong.

We made it through the crush of fans and paparazzi and into a waiting van. As the vehicle pulled away, a group of fans carrying huge get-well cards ran with us. The driver began to speed up, but Michael stopped him.

"Slow down," he yelled. "Wayne, get the cards."

The driver stopped the van, and Wayne retrieved the offerings. As we drove away, the fans shouted in unison, "We love you, Michael!"

Michael opened the window, stuck his head out and shouted back, "I love you more!"

Wayne knew that both the front and back entrances to the Four Seasons Hotel would be thick with paparazzi, so the van pulled to a stop in front of a side door leading into the kitchen. Michael, Wayne, and I burst through the doorway. The shocked looks on the faces of the kitchen staff was priceless.

"Oh, my God, it's Michael Jackson! It's Michael Jackson!"

"Hi, Michael!"

"Get well, Michael!"

Michael stopped to shake a few hands as we moved quickly to the service elevators. Wayne was a master at his job, and we made it up to Michael's suite without so much as the click of a single camera.

We were on the fifty-second floor in an expansive suite with huge windows and spectacular views of Manhattan. Michael went into a bedroom to change and told me to have something to eat. I took a sandwich from one of the many platters in the living room overflowing with food.

Michael emerged in a plain white V-neck T-shirt and black cotton pants with a stripe down the side. I asked if he was hungry. He grabbed a cookie and relaxed on the couch.

"Michael, I have an idea I want to run by you," I said. "How would you feel about seeing a practitioner of Chinese medicine?"

"I've seen people like that before, Rat," he answered.

"And did they help you?" I asked hopefully.

"Sometimes."

His answer seemed tentative.

"I have been in contact with a practitioner named Jerry Go here in New York who, I think, may be able to help you."

"Help how?"

"Teach you about nutrition and work with you on sleeping better. He uses herbs, acupuncture, and massage. He has some great techniques."

"Did you talk to Mensch? What does he think?"

"Mensch is into it."

The phone rang.

"Answer it, Rat."

I picked it up. It was Lisa Marie.

His expression instantly changed from contentment to anger. I expected him to take the call in the other room, but he motioned for me to stay.

I could hear only his side of the conversation and couldn't tell exactly what they were talking about, but Michael became increasingly agitated and paced as he spoke. After five minutes, he hung up.

"Rat, I'm not sure I can stay married to her."

I didn't want to have this conversation, especially in light of what Lisa Marie had said to me a few days before. I made a comment and quickly changed the subject. It was time to go.

As I was saying goodbye, I noticed a cool-looking video camera on a table near the door. Michael saw me looking at it.

"Hey, Rat, don't leave yet."

He ran into another room and came back with a brand new Sony video camera.

"Michael, you don't have to do that."

I was embarrassed.

"Take it, Rat. You deserve it."

"For what?"

Michael didn't answer. The gratitude in his eyes was unmistakable. I smiled.

"Michael, I am going to arrange for you to see Jerry Go."

"OK, Rat."

Within a day, Jerry came to the Four Seasons and consulted with Michael. I spoke with Michael that evening.

Hey, Rat, thanks for sending Go. I really like him."

"Great. I thought you would."

I didn't want to ask too many details. I was beginning to understand Michael better, and I knew how hard it was for him to accept new people. And the fact that Michael was willing to give Jerry Go a chance, spoke volumes about the trust that was developing in our relationship.

Go worked with Michael a few times in New York, and at the end of the two weeks, Michael looked and felt good. He had gained a few pounds and seemed to have more energy. Most importantly, he had a new positive attitude about himself and his health. He was even going to fly Go out to California for additional treatments. I was happy to see the changes, and I hoped they would continue.

Four months passed, and Wayne called.

"Ratner, who the fuck is Jerry Go?"

"What's the matter, Wayne?"

"I said, who the fuck is Jerry Go!"

"He is a Chinese healer I arranged for Michael to see."

"Yeah, well, I just got a bill from him for one million dollars!"

I nearly fell off my chair in shock. *The balls!* I couldn't believe it.

"Michael liked him and flew him out to Neverland," Wayne continued. "Go brought his wife and two kids, and they stayed for over a month. We couldn't get rid of the motherfucker. And he had the nerve to send this bill!"

The whole thing was so outrageous I couldn't control myself and burst out laughing.

"Ratner, what's so funny?" Wayne said. He started to laugh as well.

Luckily, the absurdity ended without any major fuss. Go was paid a greatly reduced and far more reasonable amount. Even so, his stab at ripping off Michael bothered me. I had never liked people who inflated their prices when it came to celebrities, and as I came to see, this approach seemed particularly commonplace when it came to Michael Jackson.

9

On The Road Again

A few weeks after I'd spoken to Wayne, I got an unexpected call from Christine, Michael's personal secretary.

"Is your passport up to date?" she asked.

"No, as a matter of fact, I have to renew it."

"Send it to me. Michael wants you to go on the HIStory tour."

Wow!!!!!

The tour was scheduled to begin in October and would last more than a year. Christine didn't have all the details and promised to send me the itinerary when she did.

I hadn't seen Michael in months. We had spoken about touring in the past, and he knew the only way I would come along would be as his personal physician. Is that what Christine was saying?

I didn't want to ask her, but as soon as I hung up I called Mensch. He knew Christine was going to call me and had planned to speak to me later that day. Michael had expressed concerns about going on the road again. He was worried that the grueling schedule would put his health in jeopardy, and they had discussed the possibility of employing a personal physician for the tour. Of course, Mensch was Michael's first choice, but Bernie didn't have a partner and couldn't be away from his practice for long periods. I was Michael's second choice, and Bernie wholeheartedly agreed.

We spoke about the potential health issues Michael might have on tour. Poor nutrition, dehydration, and sleeplessness dominated our conversation. It was a pattern that Michael fell into easily, and we discussed various ways of combating it.

I was worried about being away from my practice for so long and leaving Leann was a big concern. She was OK with the idea, as long as she could come on tour to meet me every month or so. Mensch told me not to worry. He would speak to Michael about that, and he would join the tour to relieve me for a few days every six weeks or so. I asked him about compensation. We talked rough numbers. He said management would work it out.

I got my passport back in June, but that was it. I never got any other information. No phone calls. No details. I waited a while longer. At the end of August, I called Mensch.

"Hey, Bernie, it's Neil. How are you?"

"Great, Neil. Nice to hear from you."

"Bernie, I thought by now I would have heard from someone about the tour."

"Oh, yeah. I have been meaning to call you. Sorry."

I could hear it in Mensch's voice. I wasn't going.

"Management doesn't want to pay for a full-time personal physician," he continued. "They think it's too expensive. They want you to be available if needed."

"That's a drag."

"Sorry, Neil. It's out of my control."

I was bummed out, but also a little relieved. It was a long tour, and I wasn't sure how long I wanted to be away. Later I saw a news clip of Michael arriving in Prague for the first show. There he was in a gold lamé outfit stepping out of his private jet to the cheers of several hundred fans. It looked intense, and I have to admit, I was a little envious.

Time went by and nobody contacted me. Finally, more than a year later, I got the call, but by then my life had changed significantly.

...

Beginning in the early '90s, in vitro fertilization had become the rage, especially among older women who were dealing with infertility and who felt their biological clocks ticking. Most fertility specialists were getting ready to set up office ORs, and I knew it was simply a matter of time before they would be looking for anesthesiologists. I joined the New York Fertility Society as a way to talk to gynecologists about providing them with office anesthesia. The response was overwhelming and before too long I was working with multiple gynecologists, helping them to set up their in-office surgical suites. Niels Lauerson, a prominent, all-purpose ob-gyn who also was a fertility specialist, was particularly interested and one of the first to approach me.

Lauerson was well known from his books and daytime talk show appearances and had a huge practice. The famous and the not-so-famous, from high society and rock stars to Orthodox Jews and gypsies, crowded into his office on Park Avenue and 74th Street in Manhattan. They all sat for hours in a small room with too few chairs, an old TV, and a dimly lit fish tank waiting for their turn with the doctor.

Niels was tall with curly blond hair and a thick Danish accent. He was good looking, flamboyant, and arrogant, and the hundred or so patients he saw a day treated him as if he were a member of their family, often bringing him gifts and inviting him to their special occasions.

Lauerson's office consisted of two floors with his private office, waiting room and multiple treatment rooms located on the ground floor. I created an operating theater and a recovery area in the two large rooms next to the fertility lab on the second floor. Lauerson loved the idea of operating in his office instead of at the hospital, and we not only did fertility cases, but also many other types of gynecological surgeries such as D&Cs (dilation and curettage) and laparoscopies.

Lauerson felt that every woman, rich or poor, celebrity or homemaker, deserved the right to have a baby. He also thought insurance companies should be responsible for paying for at least one round of fertility treatments, especially because many of the causes of infertility, like endometriosis, were gynecological.

For me, this created a moral and ethical dilemma. Lauerson intended to bill the fertility procedures as if they were gynecological issues. Morally, I felt he was right, but ethically, I knew better. Still, somehow, I convinced myself that going along with his scheme to defraud insurance companies would be OK because I didn't charge any more than the going rate for anesthesia in New York, and I delivered good service. In addition, and most importantly, I believed these were Lauerson's patients and his operative reports containing his diagnosis; I was just an outside provider.

I knew what I was doing was a risk, but I also knew that slightly altering a diagnosis a little to fit with what insurance companies were willing to pay was a common practice among doctors. I had seen it often with regard to nasal surgery. A diagnosis would be listed as deviated nasal septum when, in fact, the purpose of the operation was cosmetic.

I also foolishly thought that if we got caught, it would be Lauerson's problem, not mine. But fraud is fraud, and I played an important role in propagating this one. Now the consequences of our actions were about to hit home.

The Friday before Labor Day weekend 1997 was a slow workday. It was late in the afternoon, and I was at my apartment speaking to a friend on the phone about plans for the holiday when I heard the intercom ring from the lobby.

"Dr. Ratner, Linda is down here to see you."

"I am not expecting anyone," I replied. "Please find out what she wants."

"She says she is a good friend and needs to talk to you."

This annoyed me. It sounded like someone was trying to sell me something.

"Tell her I don't know who she is, and if she won't tell me what this is about, she can leave."

There was a pause.

"Dr. Ratner, she just showed me her identification. She is an FBI agent, and she wants you to come down right now."

My stomach sank, and as I rode down the elevator, the sick feeling grew. Lauerson had told me that a few weeks earlier the FBI had interviewed a patient about the fertility procedures she'd had in his office.

Linda was tall and pretty with long blond hair. She was dressed in a well-fitted black pants suit with a white button-down shirt. After showing me her identification, she handed me a piece of paper. It was a subpoena for my anesthesia records at two fertility offices. She acted friendly, however, and said I was not a target of the investigation and that I had nothing to fear in talking to her.

Feeling nervous, I started to talk without thinking. As the conversation got into the billing practices at the offices, I realized my mistake. I needed to shut up and talk to a lawyer. I ended our meeting then and there, telling her I had to get to work.

"You're not planning to go to Dr. Lauerson's office, are you?" Linda asked.

"Yes, I have a case there."

"I don't think so," she replied.

I went to the telephone in the lobby and called the office. Lauerson got on the phone. He stuttered when he was angry.

"Ggggggget over here right now! Right now!! Of course, we are doing the case. We have to do the case. Fuck them! Fuck them! Who do they think they are? Get over here now!!"

I had never heard him so angry. I told Linda, yes, I had a case. She gave me an incredulous look and said she would see me at his office.

The scene at Park and 74th was out of control and crawling with feds. They were at every door and in every room except the operating room.

Niels's eyes shot fire. He looked like an angry bull ready to charge. An FBI agent put on scrubs to come into the OR. That was it.

"You can't fucking go in there!" Niels screamed at the agent and shoved him out of the way.

He was inches from the man's face, and from Niels' expression, I thought he would deck the agent. Another agent jumped in, and cooler heads prevailed. They stayed out of the OR, and we did the fertility procedure under great duress.

I felt bad for the patient. She was obviously aware of what was going on, and I had to calm her down before putting her to sleep. Afterward, when she was ready to leave, I did my best to shield her from the chaos happening all around us. I walked her out of the recovery room and down the stairs to a waiting car.

Agents were going through the office taking out every computer and filing cabinet they could find. I realized this was extremely serious, and I was scared. I needed to get home and call a lawyer.

...

Two weeks later, Michael showed up unexpectedly at Somers office. I was in surgery elsewhere and unavailable, so they called one of my associates. It didn't go well; Michael had an allergic reaction to one of the meds. I received a message to come over as soon as I could.

By the time I got there, Michael was doing much better. He was sleeping, and I didn't wake him. Wayne looked angry and asked me to take a walk.

"Ratner, you are coming with us to Africa," he said.

I didn't know what he was talking about. I had my own problems, and I had lost track of their schedule.

"You should have been on the whole HIStory tour. No more bullshit. You're coming with us on this last leg."

"Why now, Wayne? What happened?"

He responded vaguely.

I didn't want to go. I was dealing with lawyers, and I was highly concerned about potential legal problems.

"I can't go, Wayne."

"Ratner, you're coming. I don't want to hear it. We'll make you an offer you can't refuse."

I tried to explain that it wasn't about money, but he wouldn't listen.

"Ratner, it's only three weeks in South Africa, and you will be well taken care of."

I didn't want to argue any longer. It was, after all, a once-in-a-lifetime opportunity.

After the incident in Lauerson's office, I had started to work with a lawyer. First, I cleared the trip with him and arranged to have my practice covered. Next, I called Mensch. I needed to know what was going on with Michael. He was not encouraging. Michael's bad habits hadn't changed much. He was eating poorly, not drinking enough fluids, and was chronically tired from a lack of sleep. Bernie mentioned something about German doctors who were brought in for part of the tour, but whatever they were doing, and Mensch didn't elaborate, wasn't working.

I had given Michael's problems a lot of thought. I felt the treatment regime I had started in New York could be successful, if controlled and used sparingly. Of course, he would be fully monitored, and I would be right there at all times. In addition, I would make sure I had oxygen, a defibrillator, and a crash cart.

This leg of the tour was only three weeks, and the concerts were not on consecutive days. That would give me the ability to separate the treatments and make them available only either the night before or the night after a show, depending on Michael's medical condition.

Off-label use of medications for unapproved indications is common and perfectly legal. Doctors treat patients with off-label medications all of the time. Still, I was well aware that using propofol for this purpose was unorthodox and would be controversial. I was not advocating propofol as a sleep medication for anyone else but Michael and, even then, only as part of a treatment regime while he was touring. This was a one-of-a-kind treatment for a very difficult patient in a unique situation, and I believed it was the best possible solution under the circumstances.

I was going to South Africa.

10

Off To See The Wizard

MY first trip to the African continent had been with Leann two years earlier. We flew in to Amboseli National Park in Kenya with Mount Kilimanjaro in the background, and while descending, caught sight of a herd of zebra crossing the savannah. It literally took my breath away. Then we stepped off the small plane and were greeted by Maasai warriors, tall, proud-looking young men adorned with beautiful beaded jewelry and wearing tartan cloths wrapped around their muscular bodies. They carried the luggage to the great room of our lodge, where we just sat and marveled at the fact that we were in Africa.

Leann had suggested the photographic safari. As a kid, she had watched Tarzan movies and the animals, especially the lions, had mesmerized her. That first trip, she had an opportunity to observe a pride up close. Seeing the large predators sent a rush of adrenaline flooding through our bodies, and as thrilled as I was, for Leann it was the realization of a dream. The look of gratification on her face was one I'll never forget.

Africa is special. It's the only place left on Earth where you can see large numbers of predators and prey living as they have for thousands of years. We spent hours watching lions stalking herds of zebra, and families of cheetahs hunting groups of gazelles.

As much as we were intrigued by the animals, it was the people of Africa that we came to love. During that trip, we visited a Samburu village in a remote part of Northern Kenya. The Samburu, who live simply in mud and dung huts, are one of many ethnic groups in Kenya. Cattle are their most prized possessions and provide them with a livelihood and their primary source of food. The villagers spoke a unique dialect of Swahili, which forced us to communicate with hand gestures, smiles, and some translation help from our guide. Seeing a sick Samburu child there moved me, and I made a commitment to help them in any way that I could.

By September 1997, when I agreed to go to South Africa with Michael, Leann and I had returned to Kenya a few times and had started to work on a project creating a clinic for the Samburu village. Our love of the bush had also taken us to South Africa. I was not only glad to be going back, but also happy Leann would be joining us. As part of the deal, Wayne had agreed to arrange for her to meet us in Sun City for the last week of the tour.

Wayne was still in New York, and I went to see him to pick up my ticket for the flight two weeks away. As he handed it to me, I glanced down and did a double take: Fort Lauderdale.

"What's this, Wayne?"

"You're not going straight to South Africa," he answered.

"Florida? Of all places?"

"Don't be a wise-guy, Ratner. Michael has business in the Bahamas first. He and I are going there to meet Jerry Inzerillo. The three of us will meet you in Florida, and we will all go to South Africa together on a private jet.

"Who is Jerry Inzerillo?"

"You know Sun City in South Africa?"

I knew it was a famous resort with multiple hotels, casinos, and golf courses. I also knew a little about its creator, a Jewish South African entrepreneur named Sol Kerzner.

"Ratner, the place is going to blow your mind. Michael loves it. We will be based there most of the time."

"OK, but what does Jerry Inzerillo have to do with Sun City?"

"Ratner, you ask too many questions, but since Jerry is coming with us, I will tell you. Jerry ran Sol's company for years and introduced Michael to him. Jerry will be our contact in South Africa. He's good people; you'll like him."

Wayne was right. I got to know Jerry well during those three weeks. He was cool and more important, a good friend to Michael.

Packing wasn't easy. I wanted to be prepared to treat all kinds of problems. I was not Michael's sleep doctor. I was his personal physician, and this was serious business.

It might have seemed strange that Michael chose me, an anesthesiologist, as a personal physician, but it wasn't really. Patients came to the operating room with a wide range of problems, and each of these medical conditions affected how the patient would react to anesthesia. So it was my job to know and understand a myriad of different types of medical issues and chronic diseases.

I had already begun to broaden my knowledge of general medicine as a result of the project in Kenya, setting up the clinic, and I felt comfortable that I would be able to handle any medical problems that came up.

I arrived in Florida in the afternoon and learned the group would be returning from the Bahamas late that evening. I was to meet them in the lobby the next morning.

At 8:30 a.m., I went downstairs to get a cup of coffee. Jerry Inzerillo was there having breakfast. He introduced himself, and we made small talk as we waited for the others. Then the elevator door opened, and Wayne came out followed by Michael, and next to him, a young boy. I was stunned. After the Jordy Chandler child molestation charges, I didn't think Michael would have a kid join him on tour again. Wayne and I had discussed Jordy Chandler, and Wayne was adamant that the allegations were all about getting money out of Michael. I tended to agree.

Michael and I had talked openly about countless subjects, including children. He felt his association with them was misunderstood. To Michael, in many ways, the world was a dark and foreboding place, and the innocence of children was its one bright spot. Having been locked in the basement rehearsing with his brothers for most of his early years, Michael was forever trying to recapture what he felt he had lost. As for sexually deviant behavior, I hadn't seen anything that would trigger an alert, but with a little boy on tour, I vowed to be extra observant. If there were even the slightest indication of anything untoward, I would be forced not only to quit, but also to take action to stop it.

Michael came over and gave me a hug.

"Hey, Rat, this is Doo Doo," he said pointing to his companion.

Doo Doo looked like a miniature Michael. They were dressed alike in military-style jackets, white T-shirts, and black pants. Their outfits were finished off with black shoes, white socks, aviator sunglasses, and, of course, black fedoras.

I guessed Doo Doo's age was between ten and thirteen. He was short with dark eyes and long black hair pulled back into a ponytail. As soon as I could, I took Wayne aside and asked him what was up. He explained the boy's real name was Omar and that he was the son of Riz, another member of Michael's security team, whom I had met in New York. Riz and the rest of the security detail were traveling with the road crew and would meet us in South Africa, while Omar's mother was at home in Sweden. They were both cool about Omar coming along and hanging with Michael.

Then Wayne surprised me with another change to our itinerary. We would be spending that night in Paris to pick up Michael's manager, Tarek Ben Amir, the following day. Michael's business partner, Prince Al-Waleed, a Saudi royal, had chosen Tarek for the job.

We flew to Paris on a luxurious G3 private jet. Wayne, Jerry, and I spent the flight drinking wine, eating, and talking. Michael and Doo Doo watched movies.

After we arrived at our hotel on a small street next to the Champs-Elysées, Michael and Doo Doo went to their respective rooms. I didn't see either until the next morning.

I had a suite with a stunning view of the Eiffel Tower. I looked out at the beautiful September evening in the City of Lights, and then hungry, headed to Café Figaro, a famous Parisian bistro right around the corner. I sat outside, ordered a drink and dinner, and watched the flow of people walking down the Champs-Elysées. I felt as if I were in a movie.

When I left the music business more than twenty years before, I never expected to be on tour again, let alone with someone who was possibly the most famous entertainer in the world. I was looking forward to experiencing Michael's shows, and I wanted to see how far concert production had come since my days on the road.

Still, my thoughts lingered on the seriousness of the responsibility I had undertaken. One of the first rules of medicine is "do no harm," and I took that rule to heart. I needed to pay close attention to Michael's eating and drinking habits, treat him only when necessary, and keep him away from the Valium and Demerol that other MDs had seen fit to prescribe.

Later that evening, Jerry and I had a few drinks in my suite, with the Eiffel Tower as our backdrop. Jerry had been in the hotel business since he was thirteen, having followed in the footsteps of his father, who coincidentally had introduced him to Michael. Jerry was president of Sol Kerzner's company when Sun City was built. In addition to being COO of Sun City, Jerry had been involved in every aspect of the design of the part of Sun City called the Lost city and its centerpiece, the Palace Hotel. He no longer ran Sun City but was extremely proud of his accomplishments. The Palace would be our base of operations once we finished our six nights in Cape Town.

This trip was auspicious to Jerry for a number of reasons. He and Michael had been friends for years, and he had turned Michael on to Sun City. Jerry beamed when he spoke of how much Michael loved the place. Jerry was also proud of having introduced Michael to Nelson Mandela and a deep friendship between the two was beginning to flourish. On top of this, Jerry was getting married while we were in Cape Town, and his buddy Michael Jackson was going to be his best man.

The next day we met the manager, Tarek Ben Amir, at the airport. Although he was to have come alone, Tarek had brought his wife and two kids along for the twelve-hour overnight flight, and despite knowing that Michael needed to be rested for his South Africa appearances, he demanded the only bedroom on the plane. Wayne confronted him while Michael kept quiet.

After a tense discussion, Tarek and his family retreated to the front of the cabin where there were a few comfortable couches. Jerry, Wayne, and I found reclining lounge chairs in the middle of the plane, and Michael retired to the bedroom. Doo Doo fell asleep on one of the chairs near us.

Tarek was pissed and never came back to talk to Michael or anyone else. Wayne vented about his attitude, and I was just glad I didn't have to get involved.

We had a long flight with little sleep. Our plane neared Cape Town as the sun was rising, and I watched Michael transform himself. (His dresser, makeup artist, and hair stylist were not with us.) He changed into a military-style jacket, white T-shirt, and black pants, and began carefully applying makeup to his face, eyes, and lips. I wasn't quite sure why Michael was preparing as if he were going on stage. It was 7 a.m., and I thought we were headed straight to the hotel.

As we made our approach, I looked out of the window and couldn't believe what I saw. Thousands of people had lined the roads and thousands more were at the airport. They must have been waiting for hours. Now I understood: Our arrival was a major public event.

We landed and taxied to a spot away from the terminal. Wayne was the first off the plane. The crowds thronged behind a fence about one hundred yards away and massed along an access road leading out of the airport. The press, packed tightly together, stood behind a separate part of the fence. There seemed to be almost as many reporters, video camera crews, and photographers as there were fans.

Wayne gave a signal and Michael stepped from the plane. I watched from a window as the fans went berserk, waving signs, screaming, dancing, singing, and yelling as loud as they could. Michael stopped a few times to wave as he descended the steps and got into a waiting van.

The trip had left me tired and bleary-eyed. Wayne directed me to a black SUV half-filled with South African security personnel. Security occupied at least two other cars. There was also a vehicle for Tarek and his family and the one in which Michael, Wayne, and Jerry rode. A full police motorcycle escort with sirens screaming accompanied us into Cape Town.

Our destination was the Table Bay Hotel in the harbor complex. I had a room directly across from Michael's suite with beautiful views of the waterfront. Michael was scheduled for two rehearsals and two shows in Cape Town before we left for Sun City, and this was an ideal spot to spend our down time.

I showered and lay down for a nap. Fifteen minutes later, Wayne started banging on my door.

"Ratner, get up. We're going shopping."

I could hear him laughing.

"What's the matter? You tired or something? Open up."

I wasn't amused. I stumbled out of bed and opened the door.

"A little. What's up?"

"Michael is going shopping in fifteen minutes, and he wants you to come."

"I'll pass, Wayne."

"He wants you to go," Wayne insisted. "Come on, Ratner, we are just going to walk around the complex. We won't be out for more than an hour."

Our entourage included Michael, Doo Doo, me, Wayne, and three other security guards. Wayne warned me that we would be moving fast, and I would need to pay attention and keep up. He led the way with the rest of the security team forming a circle around Michael and Doo Doo. I positioned myself on the outside of the circle. That was a big mistake.

We swept into a large modern indoor shopping center connected to the hotel. Within minutes, shoppers recognized Michael and all hell broke loose. People began running towards us from every direction. Wayne was moving so fast that I couldn't keep up. The next thing I knew, my group was in a record store, and I wasn't. I was being pushed and shoved in the middle of a frenetic crowd. Luckily, Wayne saw me, made his way through the throng, and brought me into the store. He was laughing again.

"Ratner, I told you to keep up."

"OK, Wayne, I got it this time."

Michael had watched the episode unfold and came over to advise me. He, too, was laughing, although I didn't see what was so funny.

"Hey, Rat, it's like a hurricane."

"What?"

"When I go out in public and the fans are all around me, it's like a hurricane."

He paused for a moment to let me think about what he had said and asked rhetorically, "What's in the middle of the hurricane, Rat?"

"The eye?"

"That's right. The middle of the hurricane is the calmest place."

I got it. Stay close to him and I would be OK. We tried to go to a few more stores. It was impossible. The crowds were too large and unmanageable. Our shopping trip was over. I had traveled with famous musicians before, but most could go out in public without being mobbed. This was another level of celebrity. Michael handled the frenzy like a pro, but he had years of experience. His problem was he didn't know how to stop it. As a result, he couldn't go out among the public anywhere in the world without being recognized.

I never did take my nap. I ate an early dinner, called Leann, and tried to get a good night's sleep. I tossed and turned all night and couldn't stop thinking about what it would be like to be Michael Jackson and never have the ability to be anonymous again.

11

I'm Dancing As Fast As I Can

ALTHOUGH I had been to Johannesburg before, I'd never visited Cape Town. The waterfront was bustling with restaurants, shops, dockside boats, sidewalk vendors, and street performers. I ordered breakfast at an outdoor café and took my first good look at Table Mountain, the imposing, flat-topped elevation that dominates the landscape a short distance beyond the city.

After a while, Wayne called, and I met the group in front of the hotel. We were going to a toy store and a hospital. As we drove from the harbor, we passed upscale neighborhoods that reminded me of communities in Miami or San Francisco, but with a major difference: high protective walls, topped with crushed glass or barbed wire, surrounded virtually every home, large or small. The security measures were stark reminders of where we were.

Michael had a weakness for toy stores, and we had the Toys 'R' Us to ourselves as it had been closed to the public.

"Hey, Neil, grab a toy doctor's bag, and let me take a picture of you with Michael," Jerry called from an aisle.

Michael came running over with a little red plastic doctor's bag.

"Here, Rat, take it!" Michael said smiling. "Jerry, come and shoot the picture."

We mugged for the camera as Jerry snapped a photo and we joked about it as we left the store. The next stop was an HIV children's hospital on the outskirts of the city. I knew Michael made a habit of going to children's hospitals while on tour, and I was glad he wanted me to accompany him.

On the way there, Michael and Jerry discussed Nelson Mandela. Jerry knew the president of South Africa well from his years working for Sol Kerzner, and he told Michael that Mandela was planning to come to one of the concerts. Michael's eyes lit up, and he raved about what an unbelievable person Mandela was.

We exited our white van to an intense crush of reporters and cameras. It still wasn't easy for me to anticipate the mob scene. One photographer pressed against me with a hot bulb and seared a hole right through my leather jacket. I jumped away just in time to avoid getting burned. Michael didn't see it happen, and I didn't tell him.

Inside, Wayne took control. Only a few of the photographers were permitted to join us to see the patients. The children stayed in large communal wards with twenty or so beds lined against each wall. It was heartwarming to watch Michael with the kids, and I was impressed that he never seemed to be put off by how sick any of the children were. Some spoke English, some didn't. Some knew who he was, others didn't, but they all related to him. It was something about his manner, the little *he he he,* and the natural way he interacted with them. It struck me that he never left a bedside until he got a smile, and these were not photo-ops. Michael focused his attention on each child without regard to the photographers.

Walking to the next ward, I turned to say I was moved by his bedside manner. Michael put his hand on my shoulder and looked at me.

"They're children," he said. "They're innocent."

There was nothing else to say. I saw a deeper side of Michael that afternoon, a sensitive, caring adult who appreciated the suffering of those children.

Back at the hotel, Michael and I chatted about his own health.

"I'm not sleeping at all," he admitted.

To be honest, he looked it!

He went on to say he hadn't slept on the plane ride or during the previous night in Cape Town. The first show was the following night, and he was highly concerned about his ability to function at peak form. I wasn't surprised because I knew Africa inspired Michael, and he wanted his performances to be perfect. The extra stress was showing. Even though he had a lot of nervous energy, he looked tired and drawn. I had expected this conversation and had scheduled a treatment for that evening.

I needed to plan the treatments because they would take place at night, and I would stay awake to monitor Michael for the duration. That meant adjusting my schedule by sleeping during the day. I had already told Wayne I would not be available the next day until late afternoon.

The years I had spent as a resident had taught me how to operate on almost no sleep. Being on call had meant catching naps in small uncomfortable rooms in some far-off corner of the hospital and having to wake up at a moment's notice to deal with potentially life-threatening situations.

Before I left Michael's suite, there was one more thing I needed to bring up. Mensch had told me that he had given Michael a prescription for Ativan for anxiety. I wasn't sure whether Michael was an addict, although I had suspicions that he was dependent on Ativan and other Valium-type drugs. It was time to share a part of my life with him. I was a recovering drug addict. Rehab and recovery are all about sharing your stories, and a user learns best from someone like himself. I was hopeful that we could relate on this level.

I started the conversation by talking about the events of the day. We laughed about the trip to Toys "R" Us. Things got more serious when we turned to the children with HIV.

"You know, Michael, most people would have been afraid to get as close to the kids as you did."

"You have to touch them, Rat, otherwise they don't feel wanted. People pretend to care. Kids know."

"I think ignorance and disinformation have a lot to do with people's fears, especially here," I noted.

Michael nodded and asked about my experiences treating people with the virus. This gave me the opening I was looking for.

"As an anesthesiologist, I am always careful. I wear gloves and wash my hands a lot. The greatest danger for us is getting stuck with a dirty needle."

"In my practice, it's the patients I don't know about who worry me," I added.

"What do you mean?"

"If we know a patient is HIV positive, we take all necessary precautions. But when a patient hasn't been tested and looks perfectly normal, you can tend to get cavalier and not be as careful."

He listened with interest.

"Actually, Michael, there is another disease that is a bigger problem for anesthesiologists."

"Really, what's that?"

"Drug addiction."

Michael got quiet.

"We have the keys to the candy cabinet," I continued.

He laughed.

"Every so often you'll hear a story about an anesthesiologist found dead in a hospital bathroom with a needle in his arm. Anesthesiologists live in a world with moments of terror and hours of boredom. It's not for everyone."

Michael was smart. He could see where I was going.

"You, Rat?"

"Yeah me, Michael. Not quite that bad. Obviously, I didn't die. I got addicted to narcotics and ended up in a rehab. It was eight years ago, and I am one of the lucky ones. I worked hard. I went through a program and years of therapy, and I watch myself carefully. I understand why I became addicted, and I never want to go back there."

He didn't say anything. I didn't want to get preachy or go into excessive detail, but I wasn't finished.

"You know, I thought I was clever. I really didn't get it. Even at the beginning of rehab, I was still totally in my head, explaining away any feelings that came up in my heart. The counselor asked me, 'So, Neil, where did your best thinking get you?'

"My best thinking had taken me to the depths of addiction, all the while deluding myself into believing I could handle it. After all, I had a very good practice, went to work every day, and nobody knew. Or so it seemed to me.

"Actually, I looked like death warmed over. I was barely holding it together, and everyone knew something was wrong. As they say, *denial* is the hallmark of the disease. It took time, but eventually I got the message."

I had said enough. I hoped we could start a conversation about drugs and addiction in the future. All I wanted to do right then was to convince him to give me the pills.

"Michael, I want you to give me the Ativan. I promise I will give you one if you need it, but I have to make sure you don't inadvertently take one before the treatment tonight."

He didn't say anything. I could see he was thinking about it. He got up and went into the bathroom. He came back with two vials of pills.

"OK, here."

There was no way to be sure that he had given me all the bottles. I would have to watch him carefully. The important thing was that he knew I was aware of his problem. He also knew that as a recovering addict, I would know from personal experience if he were high.

I showed back up at Michael's suite at 10:45 p.m. He came to the door wearing a white T-shirt, pajama bottoms patterned with African animals, and a doo-rag covering his head.

There are multiple explanations for how doo rags came into use: from a way to identify light skinned slaves from whites, to a time in the 19th Century when poor laborers and slaves needed something to tie their hair back with. But by the '90s, the head coverings had become more of an urban fashion statement. To me, it looked like Michael was wearing a pair of pantyhose on his head. Later, when I saw the scars from the burns he'd received while doing a Pepsi commercial years before, I realized why

Michael felt the need to cover his head. The scars were much more extensive and severe than I had expected.

We went into the bedroom and I set up the room, making it a safe place to work, just as I had done when I started giving anesthesia in doctors' offices. Back then, I often had to convert small side rooms equipped with little more than a reclining chair into work areas where I felt comfortable giving anesthesia. Then, and now, I ensured that I had everything I needed with me, including monitors, portable oxygen, and equipment for emergencies and resuscitation.

"Don't you love Africa?" Michael continued talking as he made himself comfortable on the bed. "You know Mandela is coming to tomorrow's show. I really admire him."

"So do I. As a matter of fact, he is someone I respect greatly. Do you think there is a chance I could get to meet him or, at least, shake his hand?"

"Don't worry, Rat. You'll meet him."

Michael had his headphones out, and we had the music chosen. He had meditated before I got there and was in a good mental state. We talked a while longer, mostly about the show the next day. I started the IV and put him to sleep.

The worst part about the time I spent in the suite that night was the loud, constant chanting of the fans on the street below. Other than that, everything went smoothly. Michael opened his eyes around 8 a.m. I waited and when he was ready, walked him to the bathroom. We didn't speak much. He was still tired and went back to bed for a while.

At 9 a.m., we exchanged a few words. He thanked me and said he would see me later. I was satisfied that he was OK and walked across the hall to my room. Wayne was outside the door of the suite setting up a large "Men in Black" display with life-size cutouts of Will Smith and Tommy Lee Jones.

"Good morning, Wayne. What's this?"

"Hey Rat, Michael saw this in front of the movie theater yesterday. You know him. I had to go early this morning and work out a deal to get it here."

I was tired and didn't think much about it.

"That's nice. Goodnight. See you later."

As I got into bed, I heard what sounded like a heated discussion outside my room.

"Where you going tough guy?" "Where you going tough guy?"

The words repeated themselves over and over again. I opened the door and saw Wayne walking back and forth past the cutouts. Each time he walked past either Tommy Lee Jones or Will Smith, his footfall triggered a recording.

"Wayne, this won't do. I can't sleep with this shit going off every time someone goes in or out of his room."

Wayne started laughing. He thought it was funny.

"Ratner, this is what Michael wants. If you don't like it talk to him."

Michael was a fan of oversized cutouts and thought it would be cool to have them at the entrance to his suite. I didn't want to deal with Michael right then. I figured I could handle it. After all, how many people would be going in and out of his room during the day?

It was a nightmare. By the afternoon, I hated both Will Smith and Tommy Lee Jones.

12

The Princess And The King

JUST four short weeks before our first Cape Town show, Princess Diana had died tragically from injuries she received during a car crash while being chased by paparazzi in a tunnel in Paris.

Michael was in Belgium when Wayne told him what happened. He watched as Michael crumpled to his knees and began to cry. Michael and Diana had met only once, before a concert in London in 1988, but the pair had forged a bond strengthened through hours of secret late-night phone calls. Michael was heartbroken and cancelled the next day's concert. He dedicated his following show to Diana and had started every show since then with a tribute to the fallen princess.

Diana, known as the people's princess, was beloved around the world. During her marriage to Prince Charles, she traveled extensively, raising money for causes including HIV-AIDS and ridding war-torn countries of landmines. Diana, the mother of Prince William and Prince Harry, was also a passionate advocate for children.

On the short ride to Greenpoint Stadium in Cape Town, Michael told me to be at the front of the stage when the concert began so I would have a clear view of the Jumbotron screen.

The stadium was set up so that the area immediately in front of the approximately six-foot-high stage could be used by photographers and security personnel. Fans stood behind barricades placed at the back of this security zone, approximately 10 feet from the front of the stage. I positioned myself near a few photographers and waited. "Smile," written by Charlie Chaplin and a favorite of Michael's, began to play.

Smile though your heart is aching,
Smile though your heart is breaking...

A video montage of Diana's life flashed across the screen as the music changed from "Smile" to Michael's song "Gone Too Soon." Originally recorded in memory of Ryan White, a young teenager who fought AIDS valiantly, it was also a great song to describe Diana.

Born to amuse, to inspire, to delight
Here one day, gone one night

Diana's death was still fresh in Michael's mind. In fact, we had spoken about their relationship the day before.

"Rat, we were very close. She used to call me at 4, 5 a.m."

"That shouldn't have been a problem for you," I commented dryly.

He chuckled. Michael was well known among his friends for calling at ungodly hours.

"What did you talk about?" I asked.

"Mostly her children and problems with the press. She needed to speak to someone who understood what she was going through."

Diana had been the object of overwhelming worldwide media attention. It began during the lead-up to her wedding, watched by almost 750 million people, and continued until her untimely death. Like Michael, she had become a celebrity of almost unequaled fame, and she was followed relentlessly by hordes of reporters and photographers. Articles about Diana, many unflattering or offensive, appeared almost daily in newspapers and magazines around the world.

"I know what it feels like to be hunted and trapped by the press," Michael continued. "I've had to deal with those slimeballs since I was young. I didn't have anyone to talk to, and that was hard for me, but I'm strong. She was nineteen, inexperienced, and very naive when it started. Rat, she knew that she could talk to me. We could relate to each other."

"Do you think you helped her?" I asked.

"We cried on each other's shoulders, and I coached her. I told her not to listen to the lies and to rise above it all. I said she needed to be determined and strong. That way nobody could hurt her."

"What did you think about the way she died?"

"I pray I am not next! I've been chased that same way."

I didn't know it then, but a few years later, I would be outside Paris in a car with Michael and with paparazzi chasing us. Our experience was eerily similar to Diana's, but we were lucky and got away unscathed.

"Did you ever meet her kids?"

"She really wanted me to, but I never did. I respected the way she brought them up."

Michael's son Prince had been born seven months before, and I knew he was concerned about being a good father. "A good example for you with Prince." I responded.

"Of course, Rat. But she didn't care just about her kids. She cared about all kids, the way I do, and it wasn't a show. Diana was a wonderful person with a good heart. She was like Mother Teresa. Her spirit will shine on forever."

Michael had ended the conversation by sharing a funny story about his London concert in 1988. He knew the Royals would attend, and he didn't want to offend the Princess with the song "Dirty Diana" since it was actually about a groupie.

She likes the boys in the band
She knows when they come to town

"When I met Diana before the show, she asked if I was going to do 'Dirty Diana.' I couldn't believe it! I answered, 'No, no. I took it out of the show out of respect to you.' You know what she said then?"

"I can't imagine."

"She told me it was her favorite song."

He he he...

He continued, "I said, 'Are you serious?' Play 'Dirty Diana' with you in the audience!?!'"

I started laughing.

"Did you do the song?"

"No. It was too late to change the set, but I would have."

"That's when we knew we were connected in a special way," Michael added as his smile faded, and he got very quiet. I could see tears in his eyes and I changed the subject.

I was shocked back into the present moment when I heard an explosion as a space capsule appeared on the Jumbotron screen and magically materialized on stage. I watched the crowd's reaction as Michael exited the capsule. Scores of young girls were behind me pressing up against the barricades. Most were crying uncontrollably. I felt as if I were at a Beatles concert.

I left the security area and I went backstage to watch the rest of the show. Luckily there was a spot on the side of the stage in one of the wings close to the front where I could get a good view of Michael. Fifteen minutes into the show, Michael spoke his first words to the crowd, his patented "I Love You!" It sent the audience into near hysteria.

Song after song, his feet never stopped moving. He was in the zone: not thinking about what he was doing but being in the moment! "Billie Jean" was a showstopper. After the medley, Rock With You/Off the Wall/Don't Stop 'Til You get Enough, Michael went backstage for a quick change. Then in Chaplinesque fashion, he ambled back onstage in a white T-shirt, black paints, white socks, and black shoes, with a suitcase in hand. A single spotlight followed him to a table where he opened the suitcase. It contained his jacket, hat and one white glove. The music started, Michael donned the jacket, hat and glove and treated the audience to a dance clinic. It wasn't long before the hat came off in one fast flick of the wrist and his feet and head moved in time with the snap of the snare drum. But it was his trademark step – the moonwalk – that took the audience over the top.

I had seen Michael perform at Madison Square Garden in 1988 during his Bad tour. Dr. Somers had invited me to join him when his wife couldn't go. At the time, I was falling deeper into addiction. What I mainly remember from the concert was my reaction to "Man in the Mirror," my favorite Michael Jackson song.

I'm starting with the man in the mirror
I'm asking him to change his ways

Hearing the song then made me feel despondent. I couldn't face myself in the mirror, and I knew it. And I couldn't "make that change."

At this concert, Michael sang "Man in the Mirror" toward the end of his set. As soon as I heard the first few notes, tears welled up in my eyes. I was a different person now. I had "made that change," and it felt incredible to be clean and sober and to have that part of my life far behind me.

The concert ended with "Heal the World" and a stage full of kids. I was overwhelmed by Michael's performance and didn't know what to say to him backstage afterward. He saw how I felt and smiled.

"Glad you liked the show, Rat!" he said.

13

Me And My Shadow

"... I think for most people, under normal circumstances, eight hours. There are some people, though, myself included, in a category called 'short sleepers.' We can get by well on as little as four hours of sleep. It may be genetic."

Michael and I were in his suite discussing sleep, a subject that fascinated him. The first treatment had gone off without a hitch. He had felt good all day and had given the audience in Cape Town an outstanding show, but I could tell by his tone that he had something on his mind.

"Are there people who need more than eight hours a night?" he asked.

"Yeah, the very young and very old. Certain medical conditions can also cause people to need more sleep, but eight hours is the norm."

"What about people who can't fall sleep?"

"Sleep problems come in two types: People who can't fall asleep and people who can't stay asleep...."

"I can't do either!" Michael interrupted. "I can't fall sleep because I can't turn my mind off. It's worse before a show. I need *everything* to be perfect. I stay awake for hours, and when I finally do fall asleep, it doesn't last more than an hour or two."

Michael had told me repeatedly that his mind never stopped racing no matter what he did or what meds he took. I had suggested many possible treatments, from meditation to different types of psychotherapy. Michael meditated on a daily basis and had worked with a nutritionist, but he was not open to psychotherapy.

"When I am performing," he went on, "I need at least ten hours of sleep."

He was bargaining for longer treatments, but I wasn't buying it.

"Michael, I have been on the road with performers before, and they did very well on eight hours or less. Carl Palmer used to do a three-hour set with his arms, hands, and legs constantly moving, and he didn't need any more than eight hours of sleep."

"He wasn't like me. You don't understand how hard I work."

"All right, maybe," I replied.

"At tomorrow night's show, I want you to be my shadow. I want you to stand on the stage at the side and watch everything I do. Follow me every time I go to my dressing room. Every time, Rat! You'll see what I am talking about. You'll see."

"OK, looking forward to it."

There was no point in arguing. I didn't know if Michael worked harder than other performers, but he thought he did, and that was a problem. Still, I had no qualms about saying no to him. I had carefully analyzed Michael's medical situation and set a limit on the amount of medication I was comfortable using and the duration of each treatment. In my experience, more sleep would just make him tired, and I was concerned that more medication would have a cumulative effect, which would be counterproductive.

The next evening, Michael and I traveled to the concert together. I had never seen him so exhilarated. Of course, the fact that President Mandela would be coming to the show had a lot to do with his mood. When we arrived at the stadium, Michael walked me to the exact spot where he wanted me to stand, close to the quick-change room. I was directly next to the path he used to get on and off stage, and I had an unobstructed view.

Working with different groups, I had seen how difficult it is to dance and sing at the same time. That's why many artists lip synch. Not Michael. Even through his most challenging dance routines, he was able to maintain his vocals.

During the short breaks between songs, Michael stepped just offstage and made minor adjustments to his costumes. He also dashed into the quick-change room four times during the show for more extensive makeup and wardrobe changes. Each time, he made sure I was with him. By the second costume change, his white T-shirt had begun to look like he had worn it in the shower. During every change, I encouraged him to drink as much as possible. But to no avail. Two sips, and he was finished. That was it. No wonder he was so dehydrated.

Watching his makeup artist, Sylvia, and his dresser, Danny, work, was like seeing a Formula One pit crew in action: Michael barking orders, Sylvia feverishly fixing his makeup, and Danny, his fingers a blur, working the buttons and zippers.

The concert ended with an elaborate sketch coordinated to the song "What About Us?" Michael sprinted into the quick-change room with sweat pouring down his face, his makeup smudged and running. I handed him water as Sylvia attended to his face. He was utterly spent and out of breath.

"You see!" he managed to say. "You see what I am talking about!"

The music to his encore, "Heal the World," began, and Michael bolted out of his chair. Danny slipped a new jacket on him, and he rushed to center stage and began the number at full throttle. After it was over, Michael walked off stage for the night and collapsed onto a chair. He looked utterly emptied, but noticing me in the mirror, gave me a good hard look.

"Work with me, Rat," he said. "Work with me."

As affected as I was by the intensity of Michael's performance, I saw my job as making sure he was healthy enough physically and mentally to get on stage every night and do what he did best. As far as I was concerned, things were going well. I had no intention of changing the duration of the treatments. Michael wasn't happy about my decision, but he trusted me, and he had to accept it. That was the deal!

14

Mandela And Robben Island

AFTER the show, as we waited for the president to arrive, a palpable air of excitement filled Michael's dressing room. Mandela's personal assistant, Zelda LaGrange, a heavy-set, stern-looking white woman, entered the room first, clearing a path. Mandela followed with two burly South African security people trailing close behind. Tall and slender, "Madiba," as he was affectionately known, was dressed in a loose, long-sleeve, button-down shirt in a bright African pattern. A few other dignitaries and family members rounded out the entourage.

Jerry stepped forward and warmly embraced the president. I joined a receiving line of about ten people, including Michael's manager, the tour promoter, and key members of Michael's production team. The room hushed as Jerry led the South African leader to the far end of the line. Mandela spent a minute or two with each individual, shaking hands and exchanging a few words.

Waiting, I felt as if I were in the presence of someone extraordinary. Of course, this was the president of South Africa, which was special, but there was something else. A peaceful air surrounded Mandela, and his eyes projected deep inner wisdom. But it was his infectious smile that affected me the most.

When it was my turn, I introduced myself as Dr. Neil Ratner. President Mandela looked surprised to find a physician in the line.

He asked how I liked South Africa, and I told him it wasn't my first time here. He smiled and said I should keep coming back. As he walked away, he looked back toward me.

"Doctor, make sure you take good care of Michael!"

Michael watched from the front of the room as "Madiba" greeted each of us. When it was his turn, they hugged one another warmly and talked like old friends. Michael beamed as Mandela told him how much he loved the concert. Meanwhile, the photographers were snapping photos continuously, getting as many images as they could of the icons together.

I was soaking in the experience when Michael looked in my direction. He seemed to be motioning for me to come up front. I glanced around to see who was standing near me, and I heard him call my name.

He and Mandela were surrounded by a group that included Jerry Inzerillo and Prudence Solomon, Jerry's bride-to-be; Dan Ntsala, a close friend of Jerry's and our contact at Sun City; Grace Michele, Mandela's wife; and two of the president's daughters.

"Rat, come take a picture with us."

I felt honored. It was an incredibly special moment for me.

The president and his entourage left the dressing room. I walked over to Michael.

"Hey, Michael, thanks so much for that opportunity."

"I told you, Rat."

"Yeah, but I didn't expect you to call me up front for pictures."

He he he....

...

Meeting Mandela was all the more meaningful to me because I had taken a trip that afternoon to Robben Island, the former prison where he was held for eighteen years. Dan Ntsala, our Sun City contact, had joined me. At lunch beforehand, Dan, a large black man in his late thirties with a jolly face and contagious laugh, told tales about life under apartheid, including ones about friends thrown in jail or shot for no reason except their skin color. Blacks in South Africa had endured humiliating work rules, forced relocations, and arbitrary policing. They were required to use separate restrooms and carry their identity cards at all times. In many ways, apartheid was like the South before the Civil Rights era, but magnified and legalized across an entire country.

Dan had filled an important role during the apartheid struggle as a messenger for Mandela. To defeat the white regime, all of the major tribes and political parties had to unite—not an easy task, especially since many were virtually at war. Dan had the dangerous job of carrying information from tribal chiefs to Mandela, and by doing so, he won a permanent place in the president's heart.

As the boat approached Robben Island, the setting reminded me of Alcatraz, the notorious island prison in San Francisco Bay. Both were places of unspeakable misery and isolation in the midst of incredible natural beauty.

The tour was chilling and memorable. Our guide had been a political prisoner during Mandela's time. As we walked through the hallways, history replayed itself as he described how he and his fellow inmates used the hallway's good acoustics to talk to one another at night. That is, until the guards patrolled the corridor. Punishment for reading, writing, or talking could include loss of meals, solitary confinement, or both. The prisoners ingeniously spread a little sand on the floor so they could hear the guards coming in plenty of time to stop communicating and put away any contraband.

I peered into the concrete cell where Mandela spent eighteen years, trying to imagine what his life had been like. The space was 8 feet by 7 feet and contained nothing but a bucket for a toilet and a straw mat to sleep on. The bucket, or "ballies," also had a small space on top for water, and it was the only water a prisoner had for shaving and washing each day. He wasn't Nelson Mandela anymore; he had become a number: Prisoner 46664.

Contact with the outside world was limited to one letter and one visitor every six months. Inmates bent in the hot sun every day, year after year, breaking rocks apart in the limestone quarry. The hard labor damaged Mandela's lungs and eyes, yet he never lost his dignity nor his belief that one day South Africa would be different, and he would be free.

Serving so many years in prison transformed Mandela into a mature leader and an extraordinary person. In many ways, he was both the George Washington and Abraham Lincoln of his country, helping to end apartheid and bring South Africa into the world of democratic nations.

In the spirit of Gandhi and Martin Luther King, Mandela had adopted a philosophy of passive resistance and dignified defiance. Instead of resorting to anger and revenge, he relied on his intelligence, charisma, and his capacity to forgive to bring about permanent change for himself and his country.

My Robben Island experience left me a bit shaken. I found myself dwelling on the Lauerson case, and I had a strong premonition that the case would end badly.

Five years later, my fears came true when I was convicted of insurance fraud. I was sentenced to four months in a federal penitentiary. My sentence also included four months of home confinement with a monitoring bracelet, followed by three years' probation.

I was no longer Neil Ratner, but prisoner 53501-054. I only hoped that I could handle my sentence with a small measure of the dignity and grace that I had seen in the example of Nelson Mandela.

15

Here Comes The Bride

MOST of the 53,000 or so people who were in the audience at Greenpoint Stadium in Cape Town had already left by the time Wayne led our group out of the dressing room and into an idling van for the ride back to the hotel. We were still hyped up over Mandela's visit.

"Mandiba can't make it to the wedding tomorrow afternoon, but he wants you and your parents to come with us to his house in the morning," Jerry told Michael.

Michael's parents were flying in that night.

"Hey, Rat, you're coming to our wedding, aren't you?" Jerry said, turning to me.

"That's really nice of you to offer, but I don't want to put anyone out."

"Don't be silly," said Prudence. "We would love to have you."

"It's going to be great," Jerry added. "Michael is giving Prudence away."

Michael grinned. It wouldn't be the first time he escorted a bride down the aisle. In 1991, when Hollywood icon Elizabeth Taylor married builder Larry Fortensky, Michael not only walked his friend Liz down the aisle, but also hosted the wedding at Neverland Ranch.

Jerry had known Michael for almost twenty years. They had met when Michael was with the Jackson 5 and remained close. Shortly after Jerry had begun dating Prudence, he introduced her to Michael. Prudence, a former Miss South Africa, was a true beauty with light brown skin, a striking smile, medium length hair, and big brown eyes. She and Michael were sitting next to one another in the van, chatting and laughing. It was obvious that they had clicked.

Jerry had arranged for the wedding to be held at the home of the U.S. ambassador on the outskirts of Cape Town, and he told Dan and me that a driver would pick us up late the next morning. At the hotel, I said goodnight as soon as we returned. I wanted to make sure I got a good night's sleep before the festivities started.

The next day, a short ride brought us to a modest white Tudor house, where a large room was arranged for the ceremony and decorated with magnificent white floral arrangements. Out back, well-dressed guests mingled near a bar set up on the expansive lawn.

After a drink, we took our seats inside. As the musicians started, the crowd fell silent and all eyes looked toward the back of the room. The procession began with the groomsmen and bridesmaids, followed by the family members. Jerry walked down the aisle next, accompanied by his best man. Everyone was waiting for Michael and Prudence. Most of the guests knew Michael would be escorting the bride, but seeing the two appear in person drew wild applause, and many in the crowd scarcely kept themselves under control.

Prudence looked elegant in a simple low-cut sleeveless wedding gown, complimented by an expensive-looking diamond choker. Michael wore a black military jacket edged with gold trim and decorated with a silver coat of arms. He also had a white rose pinned to his lapel. Of course, his outfit included his black fedora and dark aviator sunglasses, but neither obscured his obvious happiness.

As Prudence and Michael walked down the aisle, my mind flashed to another wedding ceremony I had attended in Africa. Mine!

Leann and I had fallen in love with Africa the first time we set foot on the continent. It felt different from other places. The primitiveness of the bush, the wildlife, and the tribal culture all made me feel as if I had been transported to a timeless world.

With our twentieth anniversary approaching, we were looking for a unique and meaningful way to renew our vows. I wondered if it would be possible to arrange a ceremony in Kenya, and I called my friend Irene Mugambi to check.

Irene, who is Kenyan, had been our safari guide and was well known and respected in her country. She had introduced us to members of two fiercely independent tribes of semi-nomadic cattle farmers: the Samburu, who lived in an area in the northern part of Kenya close to the Somali border; and the Maasai, who were settled in a southern territory known as the Maasai Mara. I asked Irene about the possibility of having our ceremony in either a Maasai or a Samburu village.

The groundwork had been laid for a small clinic in the Samburu village and initially I thought that would be the best place for us to renew our vows. But Irene disagreed. The Samburu village was literally in the middle of nowhere and was quite primitive while the Maasai village was much easier to get to and quite a bit more organized.

A week later Irene called. I could tell from her tone the answer was "yes."

"The Maasai are quite honored," Irene said, describing how pleased the elders were that we would consider sharing such an important event with them.

"The ceremony will be Maasai," she continued. "It is important for them to conduct it in their traditional way and in their native dialect."

After I hung up the phone, Leann and I looked at each other and started to laugh. We couldn't believe that Irene was going to make our crazy idea into a reality.

I felt fortunate to still be married to Leann. The first twenty years had some tough moments, and I deeply appreciated the fact that she had stuck with me. She endured four years of living in Mexico, my brutal schedule as a resident, and the difficulties of starting a medical practice. And I couldn't imagine how hard it must have been for her to watch my descent into addiction. I was profoundly grateful that she stayed around and supported me through my recovery. We had forged a true marriage and were committed to making our union work for at least the next twenty years.

We arrived in Nairobi a few days before our ceremony and spent a night in the capital. Then we flew in a small plane to the Mara Safari Club, our accommodations in the territory.

Leann and I were elated, but we also felt a twinge of apprehension about not completely understanding what we had agreed to. My old friend from the University of Vermont, Chip Prosnit, had agreed to serve as my best man and flew to Africa from New York a few days ahead of us. In the Maasai tradition there isn't exactly a best man or maid of honor but in our case it didn't seem to matter. Ironically, on the day of the wedding, he looked more nervous than I did.

It was July 25, 1996, the day of our twentieth anniversary. We drove the short distance to the village. Along the way, we passed a herd of impala, a few warthogs bathing in a watering hole, and a solitary zebra, but I hardly noticed. The circular Maasai village, or Kraal as it was known, sat amid large open grassland. An acacia thorn fence, or boma, surrounded the settlement as protection against lions and other predators.

The chief was waiting for us, smiling broadly. He greeted us with a hardy "jambo!" the Swahili word for "hello," and escorted us to the spot where the head woman, his first wife, awaited Leann and Irene, who was serving as Leann's maid of honor.

She took them to her hut, one of about a dozen similarly round, thatched-roof structures. Each home was constructed of a compound of cattle dung and mud and had a fire pit in the middle of a dirt floor, as well as a hole in the roof for ventilation. The air hole wasn't especially effective. Chip and I had followed the chief to his hut, and as soon as we walked in, we were overwhelmed by smoke and the strong smell of burnt wood. It stung our eyes and made us cough and choke. Thankfully, after a few minutes, we adjusted.

The chief, who spoke English, told us to strip down to our underwear. He dressed us in typical Maasai fashion, wrapping a red-checkered cloth, called a shukka, around our bodies. He carefully painted stripes on our forehead and cheeks with red ochre, an ancient clay pigment. The Maasai mix it with animal fat and apply it to their faces and bodies as symbolic, ritualistic decoration. Some of the tribe, especially the young warriors, also apply large quantities to their hair as a dye.

After Chip and I chose simple leather sandals, the chief adorned us with a few beaded necklaces and handed us rungus, highly decorated wooden clubs that designate warrior status. We walked outside and met the women. Leann looked incredible, like an African princess. She was dressed in classic Maasai fashion with a shukka and sandals, and her face was decorated in red ochre stripes similar to mine. She also wore a long, elaborately beaded choker and an intricately beaded headband, complemented by long hanging earrings.

A bridal party of unmarried women, all wearing large flat beaded disc necklaces, had formed around Leann and Irene. As the group moved, so did the necklaces, showing the women's grace and flexibility. Leann's was similar, but the longest and most elaborate, indicating that she was the bride-to-be.

The warriors, or Moran, looked impressive with their robust builds and braided hair slathered in ochre. A boy becomes a Moran after he is circumcised, usually between the ages of fifteen and twenty.

Ours was quite a procession with the spiritual elders leading, followed by Chip and myself, the bridal party, and the warriors as the protectors of the village. As we wove through the Kraal to a clearing where dozens of curious and excited villagers had gathered, the atmosphere was celebratory, but with a serious air.

We sat down in a semicircle with the officiating elder directly in front of Leann and me. I felt as if I were in a movie. He began the ceremony with an explanation of the Maasai tradition of marriage, and Irene translated as well as she could. In Maasai culture marriages are arranged by elders without consulting either the bride or her mother and polygamy is widely accepted. Much of their traditional ceremony dealt with cattle, their most important possession and the cornerstone of their lives. At the time of the wedding, in addition to negotiating the bride price (number of cattle given in exchange for the bride) the bride is allocated a herd which will allow her sons to have herds of their own. Of course, none of that applied to us but as in weddings everywhere, the elder stressed the importance of the new life we had agreed to and the responsibilities to each other that went with it.

I conducted a mock negotiation with the head woman for the number of cows I would provide in exchange for Leann. In the end, I gave the village enough money to buy a new cow. They were thrilled and so was I.

The ceremony finished with the most senior elder spitting a special brew on our feet. The Maasai consider this an act of great respect. It cemented the bond between us.

Everyone cheered. The youngest of the school-age kids, led by their teacher, sang a song in Swahili in our honor. There is no celebration in Africa without singing and dancing, and this one was no exception.

The men and women formed separate groups. *Hummm.. hummmmm... hummmmmm.* The men started to hum in a low tone. *EEEEyoyoyo... EEEEEEyoyoyo.* The women joined in chanting, their voices pitched high.

The Moran started bending rapidly at the waist as if building up tension in a spring. Abruptly, a warrior let go and jumped as high as he could. The dance evolved into an athletic competition to see who could jump the highest. Considering they were jumping on dirt in sandals, it was amazing to see the heights they reached. Villagers encouraged us to join in, and I made a total fool of myself. We couldn't stop laughing.

The afternoon closed with a toast. We had brought champagne as well as soda and a cake. There wasn't enough wedding cake to feed everyone, so we served the kids first.

I had to hold back my laughter as I watched them attempt to eat the sugary treat. To my surprise, some reacted as if they had eaten a lemon. A few kids even spit their bites right out. When I thought about it later, I realized they probably had never had foods made with sugar. Their normal diet was milk mixed with calves' blood and an occasional piece of meat. Most didn't like the taste of the cake at all.

The sound of people around me applauding and cheering brought me back to the present. Jerry was kissing Prudence, and the ceremony was coming to an end.

We followed the wedding party to the back lawn for the reception. The weather was slightly overcast, but comfortable. A small band played, and Dan Ntsala and I went to the bar where I chatted with other guests, ate hors d'oeuvres, and had a couple of drinks. After about an hour, we were asked to take a seat for lunch. Wayne walked over to our table, and I assumed he was coming to join us.

"Come on, Ratner. Michael is ready to go."

"Now, Wayne? We haven't eaten."

Wayne ignored my comment and told me to follow him to the limos. Surprisingly, Jerry was getting into one of the cars.

"What are you doing?" I asked jokingly. "You're not leaving your own wedding, are you?"

"Yes, I'm coming up to Sun City with you guys. Prudence is flying up later."

Waiting for us on the tarmac was the G3 jet we had used to get to Cape Town. After thirty minutes in the air, mostly spent ribbing Jerry about abandoning his wedding, we arrived at the private airport across the highway from Sun City.

The drive to our hotel took us past a casino, golf course, amusement park area, and a few other hotels, all bustling with activity. The grand Palace Hotel, set atop the tallest hill in the resort, commanded the landscape. With its Roman columns and terraced walkways, it could have been a real palace.

Jerry had arranged an impressive reception. In front of the hotel, a line of young girls in full costume danced to African rhythms gyrating their hips as they moved to the music. Spectators from the hotel as well as local fans were also on hand to welcome us.

Michael was thrilled to be in Sun City, which was, after all, a sort of African Disneyland. We exited the vans, received an official welcome, and watched the performance. After that, the hotel manager and Jerry walked with Michael to show him his suite. I was ready to go to my room, but Michael motioned for me to come with them.

The King Suite overlooked a magnificent pool and commanded sweeping views of the resort. I was taking in the sights when Michael came over. He looked out and made a sweeping motion with his arms.

"Isn't it great, Rat? I love this place."

"Yeah, I can't wait to explore."

"Look over there." Michael gestured toward the distance.

"What are you pointing at?"

"That hill. I am going to build a house there one day. This is where I want to live."

16

A Children's Hospital In Africa

"THERE is an old African legend about an ancient civilization whose people were looking for a place to build a home for their beloved king. They came upon a long-dead volcanic crater brimming with incredible plants and animals. There they built a magnificent palace, which became the centerpiece of a great city that thrived for many years. Then an earthquake destroyed everything...."

Jerry Inzerillo was recounting the origin of Sun City.

"Sol Kerzner and I knew the legend and fell in love with this site, so we set to work recreating the fantasy of that lost African city," Jerry said.

"Look at the ceiling," he noted, glancing upward. I gazed up at the domed cupola about thirty feet above me in the Palace lobby. Each of its six painted panels showed intricately detailed scenes of African flora and fauna. I wondered aloud how the painters did it.

"You have no idea how hard that job was," Jerry answered. "We had to hire special artists able to work while lying upside down in the scaffolding, the way Michelangelo worked when he painted the ceiling of the Sistine Chapel."

The rest of the lobby competed equally for my attention with its frescos, hand-carved furniture, inlaid mosaic floors, and wooden columns shaped like elephant tusks.

"We tried to make the interior and exterior feel as lavish and authentically African as possible," Jerry added, looking befittingly proud. "Be sure to walk around and see the other pieces of art."

'Thanks, Jerry. I'll do that."

I strolled through the lobby and out toward a beautifully tiled Olympic-sized pool, where out of the corner of my eye, I noticed a walking path. It took me past lush foliage, waterfalls, and streams to the Lost City, a re-creation of rambling archeological ruins. I could hardly conceive of the planning that must have gone into this place. The detailing on the "ancient" amphitheater was so authentic that I needed to touch the walls to make sure they weren't real.

The Valley of the Waves, a water park, contained a lagoon-shaped pool with artificially generated waves cresting six feet high. I watched as the kids tried to bodysurf. It was easy to understand why Michael, a big kid at heart, liked this place so much. I was tempted to go back to my room and put on a bathing suit, but I continued on my way.

I was crossing the Bridge of Time when I heard a loud rumble and the bridge began to sway, startling me for a moment. Then I realized the mock earthquake was part of the attraction. I continued across the bridge to a pair of massive carved doors that could have doubled as the entrance to King Kong's lair. They were aptly named the Kong Doors.

I paused, reflecting on what Jerry and Sol had accomplished. I had been to many resorts, but none as all-encompassing and creative as Sun City. Most resorts offered a few activities, usually off-property. Sun City was self-contained and seemed to have everything, and it was in the middle of rural South Africa.

The entertainment center was an indoor mall with a large game room, rides, restaurants, a movie theater, shops, and a casino. It was also the site of the "Superbowl," a ten thousand-seat arena that had drawn top artists like Queen and Elton John. In1985 Steven Van Zandt, guitarist for Bruce Springsteen and The E Street Band, created Artists United Against Apartheid and organized more than forty singers and musicians to collaborate on the song "Sun City." Its principal lyric was *"I, I, I ain't going to play Sun City."* The song effectively stopped artists from performing in South Africa and spurred a movement that raised more than a million dollars for projects aimed at ending apartheid.

From 1991 until 1996 Jerry was the COO of Sun City. One of his responsibilities was reintegrating the resort into the international community following the end of apartheid in 1994 and his knowledge of the entertainment business plus friendships with artists like Michael and Stevie Wonder made the transition much easier.

On my way back to the hotel, I stopped to see the crocodiles at the thirteenth hole of the Lost City Golf Course. It was the only course in the world that featured an Africa-shaped green, surrounded by a water hazard filled with man-eating Nile crocodiles.

Back in my room the phone was flashing with a message from Leann. She would arrive in a few hours. Michael was thoughtful enough to have invited her, and she wasn't the only guest. His parents had flown in the day before and Lisa Marie was coming the next day. Michael had also invited Mohammad Ali, Elizabeth Taylor, and a few other celebrities. All were unavailable. Every day he came up with someone new for Wayne to call and each time he did Wayne got more and more agitated. It was difficult enough for him and his team to protect Michael and his present entourage without adding more celebrities. The last straw was when Michael told him to arrange for his infant son, Prince, who was less than a year old, to join us.

"Ratner, tell him no way can Prince come," Wayne was livid. "You're the doctor. He will listen to you. We can't have a little baby on tour!"

I agreed and, thankfully, persuaded Michael that this was a bad idea.

Every time we left the hotel Wayne would set up his team to clear the elevators and position themselves in a way that we could walk through the lobby to waiting vehicles unmolested. Wayne himself would always lead the way. We would follow with one or two security people trailing behind. Since Sun City was far from Johannesburg, or any other major city, it wasn't the kind of place fans could reach that easily and our movements through the hotel and around the resort were fairly easy.

Leann arrived just as Michael, Doo Doo and I were getting into a van to take us to the entertainment center. She was tired from her trip, but Michael convinced her to join us. I thought we would hang out with them for a little while, excuse ourselves, and go back to our room for a quiet dinner.

Michael loved video games and both he and Doo Doo were accomplished players. Before we even got to the game room, they began teasing each other and betting on who would win. I realized this was the part of Michael that many people didn't get: I felt as if I were watching two kids. That's how they related. As we were getting ready to leave, Michael turned to me.

"Hey, Rat," he said. "You and Leann come back to the suite with us and have dinner."

I had introduced Michael to Leann in New York the previous year, and they connected instantly. Both Michael and Leann were serious students of dance, and it wasn't long before they were talking about the old greats like Fred Astaire and Gene Kelly.

Another topic they had in common was plastic surgery. Leann had taken full advantage of my involvement with cosmetic surgeons, and she and Michael liked to swap stories.

The spread laid out for us in Michael's suite was like the buffet at an expensive wedding, with more mouth-watering dishes, roasts, and seafood than we could possibly eat. Nearby, a dessert table set with sumptuous treats beckoned. Michael had arranged everything earlier in the day. It was an impressive way to welcome Leann.

After dinner, Michael asked Leann to get up and show him some dance steps. I could tell she was embarrassed, but he could be charmingly convincing when he wanted to be. With a little coaxing, she did a short routine to his delight.

Leann had brought along a video that we had made on one of our trips to Africa. I had told Michael about our Maasai wedding and the fact that I had done some charity work in Kenya. I was excited for him to see the short film, and he got off on the fact that we made the video with the Sony camera he had given me.

My friend Chip, who, coincidently, was a TV producer by trade, had filmed our adventure, professionally edited the video, and added music. Although I didn't recognize some of the songs, I had never asked him their titles.

The film was broken into three segments. The first was devoted to the animals and our stay at a tent camp in Tanzania. Michael was amused that Leann and I would rough it and stay in a tent.

The second began with images of me giving medical treatment to members of the Samburu tribe. To match the images the music changed, and we heard a young girl speak:

"Think about the generations and to say we want to make it a better world for our children and our children's children. So that they know it's a better world for them and think if they can make it a better place."

Michael heard the words, jumped out of his chair, and started shouting. I thought something was wrong.

"Rat, Rat, that's my song. That's the beginning of 'Heal the World.'"

I felt embarrassed and realized I should have asked Chip where the music came from. As Michael watched the film and saw me kneel down to put a stethoscope on the back of a very old bare-chested Samburu woman, I saw tears well up in his eyes.

The third part of the video captured our African wedding ceremony. Michael laughed aloud to see me dancing and applauded when the film ended. He was blown away. Leann said goodnight, and I told Michael I would be back in an hour. He was still buzzing about the video when I returned and asked me to tell him more. I answered in detail.

"I developed an interest in indigenous cultures during my years in Mexico," I said. "After I finished rehab, I began therapy with a man named Charles Lawrence, a true modern-day shaman. Charles, who is part Native American, educated me about his beliefs, ceremonies, and rituals. That got me curious about other primitive cultures and helped to anchor me spiritually.

"In picking a destination for our first trip to Africa, it was important to me to go to a place where we could not only experience the wildlife, but also the tribal culture," I continued. "I explained my interest to Irene Mugambi, our guide, and asked about going to a local village. I told her, 'Irene, a real tribal village, not a tourist village.' For me, this was not about buying trinkets, but about experiencing the culture.

"'I do know a Samburu manyatta (the Kiswahili word for village), Neil, about a half day's drive from our camp,' she told me. 'I will speak to the people there.'

"The Samburu, who are similar to the Maasai," I continued, "are considered more traditional because they have maintained their culture and ancient traditions better than their Maasai brothers. They survive mostly off their cows and goats, although some tribe members have small herds of camels. They live in a remote desert-like area without good roads or many services and with little access to water.

"We had a long uncomfortable drive across a harsh landscape to what Irene called 'Adam's village.' Adam was a young Samburu who had educated himself and gotten a job as a cook in a safari lodge. Irene, who had befriended him there, was doing her best to help him and his community. She had set up a small fund to pay the school fees for some of the girls but had never brought a group to the village.

"The huts of the manyatta were made of dung, mud, sticks, pieces of paper, and anything else that might have been lying around. The only water source was the unclean Waso Nyiro River, more than a mile away. The women wore two pieces of cloth (either blue or red), one wrapped around their waist, the other over their chest. They were all heavily beaded with bracelets, cuffs, necklaces, and headbands.

"The young men wore a single cloth around their waist, kind of like a Scottish kilt. They, too, were adorned with many pieces of beaded jewelry. Children followed us everywhere, amazed by Leann's blond hair. I don't think they'd ever seen a blonde before, and they couldn't believe her hair was real.

"We were brought to a small area in front of one of the huts. The kids got excited, and we weren't sure why. Then two magnificent-looking young warriors with red ochre-stained braids and beaded jewelry led an adolescent cow to us and tied it to a stake. One of the Moran held a very small bow and arrow. Standing close to the cow, he shot the arrow into its jugular vein. The other warrior slipped an empty gourd underneath the wound to catch the blood.

"As soon as the gourd was filled, it went to a child who took a big gulp. He handed it to the next kid, and so on, until there was no liquid left. They all wore big smiles and had blood dripping down the sides of their mouth. The traditional Samburu base their entire diet on their animals and blood is a major component of it. Adam, who served as our guide through the village and spoke English quite well, explained that the Samburu have more than thirteen ways to prepare blood and that sometimes it makes up an entire meal.

"Witnessing the Samburu's way of life affected me deeply. I had seen tribal villages like this on TV, but seeing in person the scope of how difficult their lives were was completely different. Their life was a daily struggle, yet they seemed grateful for the little they had.

"Before we left we shopped in an area the villagers had set up. Leann bought a beaded necklace and a pair of earrings, and I bought an intricately beaded cuff made within the manyatta. We thanked the chief, and as Leann and I got into the vans, Leann started sobbing. As poor as she had been growing up, this level of deprivation was in a different category. Years later, she reflected on how much seeing the Samburu way of life shifted her perspective of her own childhood.

"We'd gotten into our vans and were ready to leave, when I noticed the chief had gone back to a hut and was now walking quickly to Irene with a young boy, no more than eight years old, in his arms. The chief and Irene began a heated conversation, and I left the van to see what was happening.

"'Neil, go back to the van,' she said. 'Everything is fine,'

"'Irene, obviously the chief is upset about something, and this kid doesn't look good.'

"'I told them you were a famous doctor from the States, but that under no circumstances would you be able to treat anybody on this trip,' Irene replied, looking agitated. 'I told them maybe you would come back in the future to help them.'

"'And now the chief wants me to examine this child?' I asked.

"'I told him, 'under no circumstances.'"

"'Irene, where is the nearest clinic?'

"'About eighty kilometers, and the doctor comes once every few weeks or so," she answered.

"'Of course, I will," I replied without thinking. As I said the words, I realized I might have made a terrible mistake. *How could I possibly help?* I had no tools, not even a stethoscope. Even if I could make a diagnosis, what would I use for treatment? I was a big-city anesthesiologist, not someone from Doctors without

Borders. I had one advantage though. During my training treating people in rural Mexico, we went out into the field with little more than a stethoscope, blood pressure cuff, and a supply of drugs.

"The chief laid the boy on a makeshift table, and I used my senses as my tools. I put my ear to his chest and heard what sounded like early pneumonia. Next, I felt his belly. It was tender with a slightly enlarged liver. He also had a fever.

"Malaria was a good bet, as well as intestinal parasites. OK, so I had made the diagnosis, now what was I going to do about it?

"This was my first trip to Africa, and I had brought a large supply of a various antibiotics. I knew I had enough at our camp to treat at least the pneumonia. Irene could get inexpensive medication in Nairobi to treat the malaria and intestinal parasites.

"I had a plan. Back at our base camp, Leann and I emptied all the antibiotic capsules. I knew the boy's approximate weight, and I used that to calculate a daily dose. I eyeballed the amount of powder necessary for each dose, and Leann wrapped it in a piece of paper. When we were finished, we had enough packets for close to three weeks of treatment.

"Irene had explained to the chief we would be back the next day with medicine. The following morning, with Adam joining us, we left camp and retraced the slow half-day's drive over deeply rutted pathways to the village. On one hand, I felt nervous and way out of my league. On the other, I was certain the antibiotics would help, at least over the short term.

"The chief was eagerly awaiting our arrival. Adam translated to make sure that he understood the instructions for the medicine. Since the village's water supply was from a dirty river, before I handed over the antibiotics, I had Adam tell the chief to boil the water before dissolving a packet's worth of powder into the liquid.

"I went to check on the child. I was pleased to see that although he was no better, he didn't appear to be any worse. As we were leaving, the chief grabbed my hand between his two hands, squeezed hard, and didn't let go for a long time. I walked away feeling very inadequate, not knowing whether I had done any good."

Michael was on the bed watching me with an expression of admiration.

"Six months later, an odd-looking package arrived at my apartment," I continued. "I was shocked to find the chief's spear. That was a very big deal. Back in the day, a boy became a man by killing a lion and decorating his spear with some of the lion's mane, as the chief had done with this one. There was a short note from Irene: 'Neil, the child is doing well, and the chief wanted you to have this as a token of his appreciation.'

"Being honored in that way was profoundly moving...."

"Rat! Rat, from now on I'm going to call you Albert Schweitzer," Michael interrupted.

I felt my face growing red. Albert Schweitzer was a medical missionary in Africa in the early 1900s. He traveled more than two hundred miles upriver to an inaccessible part of the continent that is now part of Gabon. Against all odds, he established a hospital there.

"Hey, man, thanks for the thought, but I am no Albert Schweitzer! I was just trying to do what little I could. As a matter of fact, I learned an important lesson shortly after receiving the spear."

"What happened?"

"I know this doctor, Kevin Cahill, one of the best infectious disease docs in the world, and I was excited to tell him the story. For a minute, he stayed silent. I knew when his expression turned sour that I wasn't going to like his response, and he didn't mince words.

"'So, Neil, what do you think you accomplished?' he said, looking me straight in the eyes.

"I was taken back.

"'What do you mean, Dr. Cahill?' I said. 'I helped to heal a sick child.'

"'Really? Is that what you think? If you went there today, what would you find? Did you do anything to change the conditions that created the illnesses you observed? Did you do anything to improve the water or sanitation?'

"'No, I guess I didn't,' I replied sheepishly.

"'Most importantly, Neil, did you create anything sustainable? Without sustainability, these efforts fall by the wayside and have very little overall impact.'

"Michael, I am telling you, I left that office with my tail between my legs. But I was more determined than ever to keep going back to the Samburu. Now my goal is to create a sustainable clinic, and I am happy to say that we are making good progress."

"Rat, we have to do something together. We must! We must do it for the children. Like Albert Schweitzer, we will build a children's hospital in Africa."

I knew how much charity work Michael did, and my goal was that one day we would do something together. Although he knew I was involved in helping people in Africa, I had waited until he saw the video to tell him the story of the Samburu child. His reaction was more than I could have hoped for, and I wanted to believe that together we could make the vision of a children's hospital come true.

"OK, Michael, we will do something together."

"Promise, Rat."

"I promise, Michael."

17

I Am Not So Bad After All

"RAT, you sit here."

Michael pointed to a folding chair on the side of the stage. He came back with a second chair, put it next to the first and disappeared again. This time he returned with Lisa Marie Presley, his now ex-wife. They had divorced the previous year, 1996, but remained friendly. Michael had invited Lisa and her kids to join him in South Africa. We were at Johannesburg Stadium for the first of two concerts scheduled there.

"Lisa, you sit here next to Rat."

That was it. He turned and walked away.

Michael knew Lisa wasn't fond of me, but he was confident that if she got to know me, it would be a different story. That's why he took it upon himself to put us together.

Lisa and I looked at each other, her cool demeanor dissolved, and we both laughed. This broke the ice, and we began to talk. She mentioned how great it was to be in South Africa with Michael. I told her it was my first time at Sun City, although I had been to Africa before on safari. She said she was looking forward to taking her kids on a game drive, so I told her a few stories about my safari experiences and a little about the clinic. She commented on how good Michael looked and how excited he was about doing a tour in South Africa.

"I'm doing my best to make sure he stays that way," I said.

Lisa nodded her head as if to say, "I can see that."

We continued to make small talk throughout the show, and by the encore, we had started a promising friendship.

"Hey, man, what were you thinking, sitting Lisa and me together?" I said to Michael after the show.

"Come on, Rat! You two should be friends. It worked out good, right?"

We laughed.

"Yeah. We had a good time. I like Lisa, and, at least, she has a better idea of why I am here. She knows there are no bad intentions. Listen, I understand why she would be wary of doctors. She just doesn't want you to end up like Elvis."

"I know. I know!"

I thought about taking the conversation a little further, but it wasn't the right time.

Although I hadn't seen Lisa Marie since the incident at the hospital a few years before, Michael knew I had been upset by the encounter, and I was glad he cared enough to make an effort to get her to see that I wasn't a bad guy.

A curious mix of Michael's friends, family members, business associates, and fans had come to South Africa, and quite a few were staying in Sun City, our base of operations for the concerts in Johannesburg and Durban. We took short flights to those cities on the private jet but came back to Sun City after each concert. Every time we left the hotel for a local activity, we moved with a large group that usually included Doo Doo, Michael's parents, Lisa, her two kids, their security, Jerry, Prudence, Dan Ntsala, and whoever else could convince Wayne they needed to be there.

One of the major nearby attractions was the Pilanesberg Game Reserve, which borders Sun City. The park provided a real photographic safari experience with healthy populations of lion, leopard, rhino, elephant and buffalo. All of the national parks in South Africa strictly prohibited hunting as did most private reserves like Pilanesburg. But there were a few that raised both predators and prey and for a price you could trophy hunt the animal of your choice.

In years to come, Pilanesberg would play an important role in my life. Early in 2000, Dan Ntsala presented me with a business opportunity, explaining that Pilanesberg Reserve was taking bids for a second company to run game drives for its visitors. He asked me to join him and Bernard Marube, a black South African working for the Parks board, in forming a safari company. I provided business knowledge, mentoring, and an investment. We received the contract, and Mankwe Safaris was born. Leann and I were very much against hunting for sport and the company was dedicated to photographic safaris only.

We were the first predominantly black-owned safari company in South Africa. Most black South Africans never got to experience the bush, let alone own and operate a safari company. Although I left the company after a few years, I am proud to say it continues to thrive today.

The story of Pilanesberg fascinated me. Decades of farming and settlements had left the area depleted of wildlife. In the early '80s, the South African government embarked on Operation Genesis, a plan to repopulate the area with native animals. It was the largest project of its type. Wildlife managers moved in more than 6,000 animals from other game reserves. At first they left out predators because the gamekeepers wanted to be sure that the other animals could survive on their own. They introduced lions in the early '90s, and with this, the park grew into one of the most popular in the country.

The morning after the first show in Johannesburg, Wayne had safari vehicles pick us up in front of the hotel for the ride to Pilanesberg. There were multiple land cruisers, with Michael, Wayne, Lisa and her kids, and Doo Doo in the lead one.

Pilanesberg stretches across magnificent countryside in one of the oldest and largest volcanic structures on Earth. As we drove across wide-open grasslands and rolling hills, past rocky outcrops and lightly wooded areas, we encountered herds of antelope, zebra, buffalo, and elephant.

What Michael wanted to see the most were lions in action. The game wardens had been tracking a few males that wore radio collars. They motioned Michael's vehicle to follow them off road. The rest of us stayed behind, and that was fine with me. Leann and I had once experienced lions in an unforgettable way in the Okavango Delta in Botswana. Our Bushman guide had spotted a large pride consisting of two males, five females, and many cubs, and we had spent several game drives tracking them.

We were in a tent camp in an unfenced area with East African Safari tents as our accommodations. Each contained two beds, a nightstand, a clothes rack, a sink and a mirror, and had an outdoor shower. The toilet was in a smaller tent similar to an outhouse about fifteen feet from the back of our sleeping tent.

Most nights we would have a few drinks and trade safari stories around the campfire. Then an armed security guard would escort us back to our tents. We'd settle in and lay quietly in bed listening to the African night sounds and hoping to catch the whoops of hyenas or the grunt of a hippo. What Leann most wanted to hear, though, was the distant roar of lions. She often drifted off to sleep disappointed.

On this particular night, however, we caught the roar of the males far off in the distance.

"Neil, I think they're coming our way," Lean said with a mixture of fear and excitement.

"Sure, Leann." I answered, placating her.

I wasn't ready to believe it, but after a while, the roars did sound much closer. Then Leann nervously said the absolute last thing I wanted to hear.

"I have to go to the bathroom."

"Can't you wait?" I asked sharply.

The nearing echoes made me tense. These were real lions and exiting the safety of the tent would leave us dangerously exposed. Many minutes dragged by in quiet. We waited even longer. Nothing.

"I can't hold it anymore."

We hadn't heard the lions in what seemed like a long time, and I believed they had probably moved off in a different direction.

I stood guard outside the toilet while she peed. I heard a rustling in the bushes near the tent. Swinging my flashlight around, I thought I saw a flash of movement, but peering into the darkness, I decided it was my imagination. Still I was shaken.

"Hurry up!!!" I yelled.

Leann nearly flew into my arms. We grabbed hands and raced to the safety of the tent. As soon as we were inside, I zipped up the flap, and we breathed sighs of relief.

We climbed into bed and turned off the lantern. Within minutes, we saw the lions' shadows stalking our canvas walls. The pride had crept into camp silently and seemingly surrounded our tent. In the bright moonlight, their fearsome shapes eerily receded and expanded across the fabric like a predatory shadow-puppet play.

Suddenly, the loudest roar I could ever imagine blasted the air. It literally shook my body as if I were on a vibrating bed. Leann totally freaked out, and I was not much better. The lions were now roaring so loudly we couldn't hear each other speak. She squeezed my hand as hard as possible and inched closer to my ear.

"I have never been so fucking scared in all my life!" she yelled.

Frightening, yes, but beyond that, thrilling. I only hoped that what we had been told about lions was true: that they would not violate the integrity of the tent. The episode lasted about 15 minutes, but it seemed like hours. The shadows finally faded, and the roars diminished. Still, it wasn't easy to sleep that night, not because we feared the lions would come back, but because of all the adrenalin coursing through our bodies. The next morning, we saw buffalo dung scattered around the camp and realized the lions must have been following a herd.

Michael's vehicle returned. They had found the males, but they were sleeping. This wasn't surprising since big cats can sleep up to twenty hours a day. But Michael wanted an up-close experience, and Dan knew where to go.

Nearby, Sundown Ranch had more than forty lions living within the bounds of its extensive fenced enclosures. Michael wanted to play with a cub, and a trainer brought him one. It was a handful of squirming fierceness, but MJ thoroughly enjoyed the experience.

We all got a turn. It was clear from the cat's oversized paws, huge teeth, and feistiness, that although it was soft and cuddly now, this feline would grow into a fierce predator.

Those were not the only aggressive creatures we saw that day. On the way back to Sun City, we stopped at a crocodile farm. It had more than seven thousand Nile crocodiles on its premises, including two that were twenty feet long and weighed over two thousand pounds.

Michael asked to feed them. After receiving careful instructions, he ventured onto a fenced wooden walkway overhanging a pool where the largest crocs sunned just under the water's surface. There he dangled a rope with a dead chicken tied to one end, well out of reach over the crocs' impatient jaws.

"It's so sad!" he said half-seriously.

As if getting ready to say a toast to the crocodile, he raised the dead chicken up, pointed at it, and gave a little laugh.

"That's a sad chicken!" he repeated.

He began lowering it toward the water, and when it was no more than half way down, a large croc raised its large head and snapped up the poultry.

The Michael I was seeing now was a different person from the one I knew in New York. Here he was much more playful, social, and talkative. It was obvious he was having a great time just relaxing and being himself.

I spent the late afternoon watching him and Doo Doo jet ski and parasail at the resort's man-made lake. They acted like brothers or cousins together. I never observed anything the least bit uncool, and I only wished the press paid more attention to the type of relationship Michael had with kids like Doo Doo, instead of printing suggestive photos with unsubstantiated information.

We met Lisa by the lake. She was with her two children from her former marriage to musician Danny Keough: Benjamin, five and Riley, seven. They wandered over, sat down next to me, and we talked for a while. Lisa even asked me a medical question about one of her kids. That was progress.

It seemed obvious to me that Michael and Lisa still liked each other. I could see it in their eyes; they were kindred spirits and Michael was also clearly fond of her kids. At times, they looked like a family, Michael and Lisa holding hands, Lisa's kids and Doo Doo by their side. I wondered if they were attempting to reconcile.

That evening, Michael and I talked about Danny Diaggo, the artist who sculpted many of the large, amazingly lifelike animal pieces placed throughout Sun City. A few days earlier, we had visited his studio where sculptures stood in various stages of completion. Michael thought it must take a form of genius to create such magnificent pieces.

"Rat, do you think a person is born with genius or can it be developed?"

"You mean nature or nurture," I asked.

"Yeah. Which is it?"

"I don't think it's an 'either-or' question. I think we are all born with some genius, and it takes nurturing to bring it out."

"Okay, but what about people like Mozart and Michelangelo? Don't you think they were born with something different than everyone else?"

"For sure, some people are born with very unique talents, and they *are* different. Their genius is unstoppable, and society gets the benefit. What I wonder about are the undiscovered Mozarts, all of the people who have nobody to help bring out their genius, so their gifts go unrecognized."

"Yeah. That's true."

I was curious about what Michael thought of himself. In many ways, I thought of him as a genius. Not that he was the best singer or dancer, or even that his songs were that much better than anyone else's, but the way he put it all together, this to me was the genius of Michael Jackson.

"How about you?" I asked. "Many people call you a genius. Nature or nurture?"

He he he....

Michael thought for a minute.

"I don't create anything, Rat. It comes through me. It's just there. That's one of my problems. It never stops."

"I know, Michael."

We had talked about the constant chatter in his head before. I wondered if this was a common trait among people called geniuses, with some of them being better able to grab and filter the information than others. The sad part was that the labels "genius" and "happy" were not locked together. Maybe all geniuses were tortured by that chatter in some way. Michael certainly was.

"Durban tomorrow," I said.

"Yeah, last show."

I could hear some sadness in his voice.

"I am sure you will come back here soon."

"You know I will, Rat. I *am* going to live here!"

"Michael, I know you will."

Not everybody went to Durban. Lisa's jet was unavailable, so we only had one plane. Leann, as well as many others in the entourage, stayed behind, but Lisa came with us. We arrived at the venue late. Michael went straight to his dressing room, but Lisa and I were hungry, so we went to the hospitality tent. As we entered, African drummers began an infectious beat, and a group of topless Zulu women in native costume began dancing to the rhythm.

This was the beginning of an amazing night and a fitting ending to an unforgettable time in Africa. After the show was over, Michael invited his large crew, one by one, into the dressing room. He thanked each person, shook their hand, exchanged a few words, and had a photo taken with them.

When we got back to the hotel, I said goodbye to Lisa. She turned to walk away.

"Hey, Lisa, so, I'm not so bad after all, am I?" I added.

She spun around and smiled.

"No, Neil, you're OK," she said.

I was pleased, and on a professional level, I felt I accomplished what I had set out to do. No shows were cancelled, Michael's health was good, and he was happy and satisfied. So was I.

The odyssey ended back in New York. My lawyer wasn't happy, and he thought I could become a target of the Lauerson investigation. His suggestion was to add another more powerful criminal attorney to our team. I felt I didn't have a choice, and the bills began to mount.

The wheels of justice turn slowly, and nothing much happened with the case for the rest of 1997. I went back to my life as an anesthesiologist and didn't hear from Michael for the next few months.

18

The Boy Who Wouldn't Grow Up

"RAT, what are you doing?"

I hadn't seen or heard from Michael since we had returned from Africa in October, three months before. It was 3:30 a.m.

"You sleeping?"

I could tell he was excited about something, so I roused myself.

"No, Michael. It's OK. What's up?"

"Do you want to come to Neverland this weekend?"

I wasn't surprised by the invitation. Michael and I had talked about Neverland a number of times, and the conversations had often ended with him saying, "You'll see when you come."

This wasn't about work. Michael hadn't asked Neil Ratner, M.D. to come to Neverland. He had invited his friend, Rat, to his house to hang with him for the weekend. It was January 20, 1998, the Tuesday before Super Bowl weekend, and I would have to get someone to cover for me on short notice. Michael sensed my hesitation.

"Come on," he coaxed. "You can do it. You can come out. I am going to have Christine arrange the flights."

A few of the anesthesiologists I worked with owed me favors, and I was pretty sure I could get one of them to cover for me.

"OK, Michael. See you late Friday night."

Less than seventy hours later, as the limo I was riding in approached the gates of Neverland, I saw a brilliantly lit Ferris wheel rising above the treetops. The illusion of a fantasyland continued as countless Christmas lights came into view, framing Neverland's buildings.

We continued up a long driveway past an artificial lake where rising and falling jets of water danced to the melody of Debussy's "Claire De Lune." Other fantastical sights and sounds gave the scene a dreamlike quality.

My driver took me directly to the guesthouse. My room had rich dark wood paneling, wide beams across the ceiling, and oriental rugs on the floor. The four-poster bed, covered with fine linens, looked comfortable and inviting. I noticed that the Neverland logo, a little boy wearing blue footsie pajamas sitting inside a crescent moon, was almost everywhere, embroidered on the towels, the bathrobes and even on the soap packages.

The room was immaculate. It even smelled great. A bowl on the dresser was filled with cookies and candy, and the bedding was turned down with a piece of chocolate on the pillow. The staff didn't miss a trick.

I unpacked, and Michael came by a short while later wearing a black baseball cap and a ski jacket over his patterned blue pajamas. It was after midnight and chilly.

"Hey, Rat, welcome to Neverland!"

"Thanks, Michael. I'm already blown away. The lighting is spectacular."

"You know, you can see Neverland from space."

"Really, how would you know?"

Michael chuckled and asked me about the room. It was his favorite, he said.

"I always give it to Elizabeth [Taylor]," he added. "It's her favorite, too. She loves to come here."

Why wouldn't she?

I walked him outside.

"The chefs come in at 6 a.m. and they will cook anything you want," he said, pointing to the main house. "If you get cold, there are extra hats and jackets behind the door. Sleep good, Rat."

I woke early to a bright, sunny morning. As I pulled back the curtains, I had to rub my eyes to make sure I was not dreaming. A few hundred yards away, a uniformed trainer was taking an elephant for a stroll. Another trainer was playing with an orangutan on a set of swings. In front of the main house sat a magnificent black carriage with a pair of gorgeous brown Clydesdale horses, and its driver in full costume. *Wow!!* I felt like I was on the set of a movie, and I wondered how much of this was for my benefit and how much was normal for Neverland.

I stepped outside to get a better view. Music was coming from speakers cleverly disguised as grey boulders and scattered throughout the property. There was something to see in every direction. On the lake, black and white swans swam lazily, and pink flamingos fed by the water's edge, while fountains behind them danced to the tunes of Fantasia.

I got dressed and went for a walk. In Africa I had encountered monkeys and baboons, but never any of the great apes. I went to the swings to get close up and personal with the orangutan.

Her name was Brandy. She was three years old and stronger than most adult male humans. Her trainer gave me a pack of Skittles and said I could feed her, but before I could take the candy out of the wrapper, Brandy gripped my arm. She was letting me know that I had better be quick about it. It was obvious from the intelligence in her eyes that she had a sharp mind.

I made a couple of more stops to say "hello" to a llama and get a good look at the Clydesdale horses, and I was ready for breakfast. As I entered the kitchen, I bumped into a larger-than-life statue of an English butler. Michael had a thing for life-like figures. They kept him company and he had them strategically placed around the house.

The kitchen was warm and welcoming, and three cooks were preparing food for the day. I introduced myself in Spanish. They looked at me with surprise until I told them I had gone to a Mexican medical school. One of the cooks was from Guadalajara, and we reminisced about the slower pace of life in Mexico while they served me huevos rancheros, tortillas, fruit, juice, and coffee. Michael came downstairs and joined me, and I told him about my experience with Brandy.

"They're like us," he said convincingly. I wanted to question him further, but Michael was already halfway out of the house.

"You haven't seen anything yet. Let me show you around."

Far out. I wonder how many people get the private tour.

I followed him into the garage where four of his five golf carts were parked. Each had its own motif, and Michael jumped in the one that looked like the Batmobile.

"This one is mine. Any time you want to go around the property, just use that other one."

He pointed to one that featured Michael as Peter Pan, the boy who wouldn't grow up. It was a theme I would see repeatedly.

Nobody wants to get old, but that's the way it is, and the faster we accept that fact, the better and more productive our lives become. Unfortunately, Michael was stuck in a childhood he never had, and he didn't want to leave.

"Cool," I said, joining him in his cart for the grand tour.

It was funny being in a vehicle with Michael driving.

"Where did you to learn to drive?" I asked jokingly.

"I can drive, but I only do it around here. Wayne taught me."

Our first stop was the train station. It was Victorian, but like everything at Neverland, it had a Disney feel. I especially liked the floral clock rising from the ground in front of the station's main entrance. It reminded me of a float in the Rose Bowl parade.

"This is Katherine Station; I named it for my mother."

I had watched Michael with his parents when we were in South Africa. He clearly liked and connected with his mother, but his relationship with his father seemed confined to a few words here and there.

He showed me the Katherine Steam Engine and talked about how much fun it was to take groups of kids on the train. Neverland was designed with children in mind, he said, which explained the pushcarts scattered throughout the property filled with ice cream, popcorn, and candy.

Michael parked the Batmobile in front of the theater. It was modeled on a classic small-town movie house. As you entered, posters displayed along one wall featured movies and coming attractions. I was surprised that Michael's theater was playing a movie that had just started showing in theaters in New York.

"Hey, Michael," I teased. "You must know someone to get films here so fast."

He laughed.

"I have copies of almost every DVD ever made, and I get new movies as soon as they are released."

Michael was a serious student of film. Often, late at night, we would talk about the old classics, how they were made, and how the studio systems created the Hollywood stars of the day. He was knowledgeable and obviously wanted to get into the business.

Inside the theater were about fifty plush red velvet rocking-chair-style seats. On either side of the stage stood two ten-foot-tall replicas of the Oscar statue.

"How did you get those?" I asked, knowing the image of the Academy Awards was trademarked.

He he he....

What impressed me the most by far, though, were the two glassed-in rooms where the theater balcony would have been. We walked into one, and Michael explained it was for the sickest kids.

"It's very important that they have a place to watch movies," he said. "Look, I have a hospital bed and places for the IVs."

I imagined how therapeutic it must be for an ill child to come to Neverland, and as I had seen in South Africa, Michael had a special way with sick kids. The care and planning that went into these rooms also impressed me and reinforced the idea Michael and I had talked about of creating a children's hospital in Africa.

The next building featured Michael's dance studio, a large space with a hardwood floor, a mirrored wall, and sound equipment.

"I come out here by myself to perfect new steps," Michael said as he popped his head and performed one of his signature moves.

Michael had studied the moves of many dancers, including the old masters from Bo Jangles, Steptoe and Son, and Hines, Hines and Dad, to Fred Astaire, Gene Kelly, and James Brown. On tour, he brought a small portable wooden floor that he would place in a corner of his hotel suite so he could practice.

The amusement park across from the theater included bumper cars, a Ferris wheel, and a magnificent carousel, among other rides. Michael walked to the carousel. All of its animals were one of a kind. He climbed on a particularly beautiful horse.

"Rat, this is the fairy horse. Look over here.... Can you see? Read this." He pointed to a drawing along the bottom of the saddle showing children of all races holding hands. Above their images were the words "We are the World," and above that was a touching inscription written by the German designer. It read, in part, *"What you have so unselfishly done for others is being returned to you in this magical carousel, which will become a source of new inspiration to you."*

"You know, Rat, I bring a lot of disadvantaged children here," Michael said. "You should see their faces when they ride this carousel. Come on. Pick an animal and let's go around a few times."

I hadn't ridden a carousel in years. A finely carved zebra caught my eye and I saddled up. Michael's song "Have You Seen My Childhood" played as the carousel turned. A few sentences in the second verse caught my attention.

It's been my fate to compensate,
For the childhood, I've never known.

It was obvious that this was what Neverland was about.

Michael insisted we go on at least one other ride. My history of motion sickness made me reluctant. His favorite was The Zipper, a vomit-inducing ride if I ever saw one, and it was out of the question. I picked a ride I thought I could handle, named Dumbo for the children's story about a little elephant with big ears. I have big ears, and as a child I was often teased and called Dumbo, so the ride seemed fitting. Michael got into the car in front of me. As the ride started to pick up speed, Dumbo began moving in directions I hadn't anticipated. Very quickly I became nauseated.

"Michael, stop the ride!" I shouted. "Stop the ride! I'm going to be sick."

He began to laugh hysterically. "You'll be OK, Rat. You'll be OK."

I wasn't OK.

"It's not funny. Not funny! Get me the fuck off of this now."

Michael hated cursing, but I didn't care. He saw I was serious, and he motioned for the operator to stop the ride. After I got off, I had to sit a few minutes before we went anywhere else. He was still laughing and thought it was the funniest thing ever.

The zoo was in the back of the property. We stopped and gave the elephant some peanuts and climbed a platform to feed the giraffe. Next, we checked out an aviary that included a pair of beautiful scarlet Macaws, and a reptile house with an albino alligator.

The tour ended at the Neverland firehouse. Sitting out front was an old, shiny red fire engine. Michael was clearly proud of it.

"Neverland is 2,700 acres," he explained. "Big enough to have its own fire company."

"How did you find this place?"

"Paul McCartney stayed here when we made the short film for 'Say, Say, Say.' I loved the tranquility and especially the privacy, so I bought the property."

On the way back to the house, we made one more stop in front of an old oak tree that had some handles built into it to make it easier to climb.

"Hey, Rat, did you climb trees when you were a kid?"

"Not so much. The neighborhood where I grew up was suburban."

"Too bad. You should. I love it, and this is my favorite. I call it the giving tree because it gives me inspiration and ideas. I have written lots of songs up in those branches."

"Really, like what?" I asked.

"'Heal the World' is one. I sit up there, and it comes to me. It just comes through me."

Michael invited me into the main house to see Prince. Katherine had arrived earlier and was inside with him. I made small talk with her as I played with the baby, and after a while, I excused myself. Michael walked me outside and told me to do whatever I wanted.

"Have some fun, Rat!" he shouted as I turned away.

As terrific as Michael's fantasy home was, it needed people. Part of what makes attractions like Neverland great is watching and absorbing the energy of other people having fun and sharing the experience with friends. In many ways, this struck me as a lonely place. Michael needed and enjoyed company; that's why he invited me, but he didn't trust many people. I got the sense that most of the time Neverland was a ghost town.

The weekend went quickly. We ate a few meals together and had a good laugh watching Adam Sandler in *The Wedding Singer*. On Sunday afternoon, I wanted to watch the Super Bowl, so Michael had the projectionist set it up for me in the movie theater. It was surreal: there I was all alone watching the game in Michael Jackson's movie theater at the Neverland Ranch. It was fun, but again, I missed the camaraderie of watching with friends, and I pictured Michael sitting all alone there with no one to talk to except the projectionist. As the game was ending, as if on cue,

Michael called and said I should join him for dinner in the main house.

The cooks had prepared chicken with rice and beans, and I jokingly told Michael that there was a time in my life when this dish was a staple for me.

"I couldn't get into an American medical school," I explained. "There were limited spots and lots of applicants. Although I had good grades when I went back to college after leaving the music business, I don't think anyone believed I was a good candidate. It was about choosing students with the best grades, not necessarily students with the most life experience. Funny enough, my school in Guadalajara had more American medical students than any medical school in the U.S."

"I heard you speaking Spanish. How was it to get by in another language?"

"It was difficult at first, but I was very motivated. Leann and I had just gotten married. The classes were in Spanish, and we were in a new country. To make matters worse, Leann didn't speak any Spanish.

"But instead of isolating ourselves by living where most of the U.S. students lived, we embraced the culture and rented in a middle class Mexican neighborhood. We made lots of friends, Leann learned enough Spanish to teach at a local dance academy and in the end, we were very sad to leave."

After dinner, Michael showed me around the main house. The living room had lush white carpeting, a white grand piano, and a large replica of a medieval castle. Next, we went into the library, where Michael, who loved books, had a collection of more than ten thousand volumes. Throughout the house, I noticed portraits of him, as a king, a general, Peter Pan, and the Pied Piper. Nice paintings, but a little too much self-glorification for my taste.

In his bedroom, I sat down in a throne-like chair across from his bed. Next to it was a huge flat screen TV and stereo. The room was cluttered with CDs, books, dolls, video games, and a few of the awards Michael had won over the years.

We wound up back downstairs, and he offered me a glass of wine.

"You know I can't go anywhere, so it's all here. Everything I love."

"And it's great that you share it with those who need it most."

Michael nodded.

"You know I was always touring and rehearsing," he said. "I wanted a place where I could create everything I never had."

"You did a great job," I commented, not adding that I wished he had more friends to share his world with."

19

Rock Doc

LIKE I got back from Neverland, events in my life started to move quickly. My new lawyer told me I was now a target of the federal investigation, and the feds planned to charge me with multiple felony counts, including conspiracy to commit mail fraud and insurance fraud. The mandatory federal sentencing guidelines were Draconian, and if I were convicted, I would face up to five years in prison for each count.

He added that because I was an insider, the federal prosecutors wanted my cooperation, and they were willing to make a deal. On the one hand, I felt it was time to come clean; on the other, I loathed the idea of being a snitch. Once, I had convinced myself that if we were caught, the consequences wouldn't be my problem. Now they absolutely *were* my problem, and my mistake was driving me to make the toughest choice of my life.

The feds forced my hand. My father had retired in his fifties after doing well in business. At the time, I needed someone to handle the insurance billing for my practice, and he was looking for ways to keep busy. He offered to help me, and we set up an office. After a little training, he became proficient at filling out insurance forms and going after payments. The feds were aware of his participation and threatened to prosecute him. No way could I let my father face charges. On top of my already guilty conscience, this left me with no choice: it was time to cooperate.

I instructed my lawyers to see what kind of plea deal we could make. Immunity was out of the question because the prosecutor had already given it to our embryologist in exchange for her testimony. The best I could get was a promise to leave my father alone, a lesser charge, and most importantly, a strong letter to the judge recommending no jail time.

In late May 1998, I pleaded guilty to a one-count felony of conspiracy to commit insurance fraud. Pending sentencing, I was released on my own recognizance. I had hoped to get a chance to talk to Lauerson and explain myself. We had been friends for years and had shared good times in and out of the office. Sadly, Lauerson's lawyers got to him before I did and told him about my deal. From that day on, we were enemies. I felt terrible that our relationship ended the way it did. I wasn't trying to hurt Niels.

On many occasions, both the embryologist and I had tried to persuade him to stop the fraudulent billing and switch to a fee-for-service model. He either laughed or answered indignantly that, "These are my patients, and I am going to bill any way I want." I wasn't blaming Niels for my problems. I had gone into the situation with my eyes open, but now I had to do what was best for me and my family.

Of course, this meant I was no longer working with Lauerson. I also began spending a few evenings a week with the feds preparing for the eventual trial. As difficult and uncomfortable as that was, I had a bigger problem. I had explained my actions to the other doctors I worked with, and most, including Tillman, reacted favorably. The catch was, an anesthesiologist I had employed was also in trouble with the feds and had decided not to cooperate. We worked in the same circles, and I began to feel some animosity, especially when I worked with Lee.

I had seen Michael two or three times at Somer's office in the three months since my visit to Neverland. Michael knew a little about my legal problems, but I had left the details vague, knowing it would be better to explain out of the office. Meanwhile, we were talking more seriously about music.

I had never lost the desire to be a part of the business, and by the early nineties, the itch had gotten stronger. Lauerson knew of my music experience, so when he started to date a woman who had a similar interest, he arranged for Leann and me to join them for an evening out.

Niels' new girlfriend was Denise Rich, the estranged wife of Marc Rich, one of the world's most successful commodities traders and a wanted man. He had been indicted in the largest case of tax evasion ever brought against an individual in the United States. To avoid prosecution, he had fled to Switzerland with his family in tow.

Denise felt trapped there and wanted out. She returned to the United States with her three kids and a bundle of money. (Rich was one of the world's wealthiest men at the time.) While she was in Switzerland, she had written the lyrics to "Frankie," which Sister Sledge had turned into a big hit. Now Denise was working hard to create a name for herself in the music business.

We spent time with Denise and Niels socially and joined them on a trip to Tucson, and from the start, she and I connected. She was from an upper middle class Jewish suburb of Worcester, Massachusetts, and had enjoyed a childhood similar to mine in the Five Towns area of Long Island.

Denise was easygoing and down to earth. She and Leann got along especially well and a short time after they met, Denise asked Leann to help her set up a home gym and be her personal trainer. Leann had changed career paths from a dancer to the new profession of personal trainer shortly after we moved back to the States, and she was one of the first woman in New York City to offer in-home private training.

When Denise was invited to see Biosphere2, a project in Arizona to demonstrate that a closed ecosystem could support life, she asked Leann and me to join her and Niels on the trip. Ed Bass, one of Biosphere2's financial partners and a friend of hers, thought she would enjoy touring it before the project was closed to the outside world for a two-year study.

Our private tour took us through the five fascinating sections that recreated a rainforest, an ocean with a coral reef, a mangrove swamp, a savannah, and a fog desert. In addition, we also saw the agricultural area and living habitat. The eight participants were already enclosed in the living area, so we had our own video audience with them.

One evening after everyone else went to sleep, Denise and I had a long talk about her career and my desire to get back into the music business. Although she had a manager, Stewart Wax, she admitted he needed some help. After a phone call and a face-to-face meeting, Stewart and I joined forces to create a company called the Dream Factory.

Our first move was to encourage Denise to buy a studio. She had been paying large sums to rent time at a recording studio on 48th street in Manhattan. We negotiated a good price for a studio that was for sale, upgraded the existing room, and built a state-of-the-art second studio across the hall. Once this was completed,

Stu and I worked on getting Denise good producers able to help her co-write songs and show off her work. Our lawyer, Mike Selverne, felt Denise should partner with a well-known producer named Rick Wake who was also a client of his.

Rick had ideas about starting a record label, something Stu and I had talked to Denise about as well. It made sense because we already had the studio and a small stable of producers that brought us talent. Rick and I spent weeks developing a good business plan and it was decided that Mike Selverne and I fly to Worcester, Massachusetts to present the idea to Denise's father, her business advisor. The meeting did not go well for me. Her father and I didn't see eye to eye, but I didn't think our differences were insurmountable. He couldn't understand how I could manage his daughter's music career and be a doctor at the same time. Denise, Rick and Stu went on to form the label themselves and had a fair amount of success. I was unceremoniously fired which left me very disappointed and depressed for a while. My only consolation was when I ran into Denise a few years later, she apologized, saying it was all a big misunderstanding.

During my time at the Dream Factory I met some great people including Gary Haase, a multitalented producer/writer who had been working with Denise. He had produced artists like George Benson, NSYNC, Michael Bolton, and Celine Dion. We became close, and after I left the Dream Factory, I began helping him out with management. I had told Michael about Gary before our South Africa trip, but Michael was only mildly interested. Then on the plane, he started playing a tape of newly released singles. A song came on that he liked, and he began to groove to the beat.

"Who produced that track?" Michael shouted to no one in particular.

I got up to look at the sheet of paper noting for Michael the names of the artists, writers and producers of each track that was included with the tape.

The producer was Gary Haase. I couldn't believe it and started shouting, "Michael, Michael, that's Gary! That's the guy I have been telling you about."

"Really? What's the name of the track?"

"'Come' by Martha Wash, produced by Gary Haase!"

"He's special, Rat. That's a great groove. When we get back to the States, I want to meet him!"

"Cool. I will make it happen."

In late June 1998, I did. Gary was scheduled to produce a Celine Dion track in Los Angeles, and Michael planned to be at the Beverly Hills Hotel that week. He asked me to come to LA to make the introduction.

Celebrities love the iconic Pink Palace, as the Beverly Hills Hotel is affectionately called. It has been a second home to countless stars for more than a hundred years. Those who want extreme privacy, like Michael did, stay in one of twenty-three bungalows spread amid acres of lush gardens. John and Yoko once hid out there for a week, and Howard Hughes camped out there as well.

I arrived the day of the meeting, checked in, and went right to Michael's bungalow. He answered the door, proudly holding his infant daughter.

"This is Paris. Here, hold her."

Before I could politely refuse, Michael handed me the three-month-old baby. Leann and I don't have children. We were career-oriented and never felt the need to raise a family. As a result, handling babies wasn't something I did frequently. I had learned how to hold an infant during my pediatrics rotation, but I had never felt comfortable doing it. I looked down apprehensively at the little child. Surprisingly, she didn't seem to mind me holding her. She didn't cry or squirm. I rocked her back and forth for a minute (seemed like what most people did when holding a baby) and passed her back.

Prince, just eighteen months old, was in another part of the room tossing his toys and yelling at a short, pretty girl whom I guessed to be about sixteen.

"Nicole, take Prince into the other room. I need to talk to Rat."

As soon as they left, Michael realized I didn't know who the girl was.

"Sorry. I thought you two had met. That was Nicole Richie, Lionel's daughter. I am her godfather. She likes to come over and play with Prince and Paris.

We talked for a little while and Gary arrived. I stayed about twenty minutes longer to make sure they were comfortable with each other, but I knew it was important that they had time alone. I had laid the groundwork and felt positive about it, and now it was up to Gary.

Later, Michael invited me back for dinner. I had heard from Gary that things had gone well, but I was eager to hear Michael's impressions. First, though, he ordered us a room-service dinner of fried chicken and mashed potatoes, one of his favorite meals. It was nice to see Michael eating well, and I hoped it was not just for my benefit. "Are you going to work with him?" I asked. "Maybe write a song or two?"

Michael thought for a minute.

"No. he's bigger than that," he said. "I have other projects I think he would be great for. Like films. His writing is on a bigger scale. I told him about two projects I want to do, Black Peter Pan and an animated film called *The Endangerables*."

"I am sure the idea of a film about endangered species spoke to him. He wrote a song with a similar theme called, 'The Poacher Man.'"

"Yeah. He said you helped him write a few words."

"One word," I answered with a laugh. "He needed to know the main species of tree in Africa. Acacia."

"Rat, you love music, don't you?"

"You got that right!"

"Why did you leave?"

"You know, I was at a dead end. I had worked my way up, but I was never the drummer. And that's why I got into the business in the first place."

"It must be hard to be behind the curtain when you want to be out front."

I knew Michael, the consummate performer, would understand what I was saying.

"As hard as it sometimes was, I had amazing experiences, and I am very proud of some of the work I did—like the Dark Side of the Moon tour for Pink Floyd."

"You were on that tour?"

"I had a full-service production company with state-of-the-art sound and lighting systems, trucks, road crews, and everything else a group needed on the road. Most bands used a variety of companies, so it was a new all-in-one concept.

"Pink Floyd had planned a massive tour to support their new album, and they didn't have enough of anything. Peter Watts, their head sound engineer, was a friend. He took me to their manager, Steve O'Rourke, and Steve and I made a deal for my company to partner with the band. You would have liked that tour. The production was way ahead of its time."

"Too bad I missed it. I was very young, and we were always touring. Are you ever sorry you didn't stay in the business?"

"Not really. I have a great career as a doctor, and I am in the music business on the side. I did the Dream Factory with Denise, and I still handle a couple of producers like Gary. As a matter of fact, years ago I came up with a good name for myself that fits even better now.

"What?"

"Rock Doc."

Michael laughed loud and long.

"You asked if I was sorry I didn't stay in Rock and Roll," I continued. "Actually, I was almost finished with my residency, and MTV had been in existence for a couple of years, airing mostly music videos...."

"You know the changes I brought to MTV," Michael interrupted.

"Yeah, you desegregated MTV and were one of the first to use longer videos."

"Not videos, short films. They are short films."

"Okay, I get it," I said.

I continued: "Major stations had medical correspondents. I thought, 'Why not MTV?' My experience made me exceptionally qualified to be the 'Rock Doc.' I planned to interview rock stars on health-related issues and create hip segments conveying important messages."

"Like what?"

"I started with a story about Jim Fixx, the famous runner who died during a race. He had looked like the picture of health, but the autopsy found that he had significant coronary artery disease. As part of the piece I needed to interview a rock star. I called my old friend Carl Palmer from ELP and asked him if he would be willing to participate. Carl was a very physical drummer, a black belt martial artist and someone who I knew was concerned about his health. He agreed, and we were both very pleased with the results.

"Doug Herzog, the head of programming at MTV, liked the whole Rock Doc thing and seemed impressed that I was able to get a rock star involved. The problem was MTV was still in its infancy, and they had limited money. Doug promised to put the show on the air if I could get a sponsor, which I tried to do for about six months with no success. What a bummer!"

"You would have been good on MTV."

Michael sounded sincere.

"I thought so. And we didn't stop there. Jack, my lawyer, suggested we go after mainstream media. He thought I looked good on camera and said I had the right personality. He brought me to see an old friend and client who happened to be the news director at WNBC in New York City.

"Jerry Nachman was like a movie character, fat and disheveled with suspenders, and the stump of a cigar forever hanging out of his mouth. Appearances aside, he was one of the best in the business. He agreed to give me a producer and crew to film a sample segment. I wrote one on anesthesia and filmed it in an operating room at Lenox Hill Hospital. Jerry loved it and gave me the job. Two weeks later, he left NBC to become the editor of the *New York Post*. That was the end of my media career. I gave up on Rock Doc and concentrated on developing a career in anesthesia."

"Rat, I have something to tell you," Michael said, smiling.

"What's that?"

"You are the Rock Doc."

I laughed.

"No, really. You *are* the Rock Doc."

20

Live From The American Embassy In Nairobi

I arrived home from work on Friday afternoon, August 7, 1998 and found Leann glued to the TV set. A smoking pile of debris dominated the picture, alternating with shots of rescuers who were trying to uncover survivors. The news ticker scrolling at the bottom of the screen read, "Live from the American Embassy in Nairobi."

The news was shocking. A new terrorist group called Al Qaeda had meticulously planned and carried out simultaneous suicide bombings at the American Embassies in Nairobi, Kenya, and Dar es Salaam, Tanzania. More than two hundred people were murdered in Nairobi and another dozen in Tanzania, and an estimated four thousand Kenyans suffered injuries.

All of those innocent victims! What I saw horrified me. Leann and I had spent time in Nairobi and had been impressed by the friendliness we encountered. On top of that, Kenya's economy was struggling and needed tourism to survive. This strike was bound to scare people away.

The bombers had driven up to the security gate of the embassy and yelled to the guards to open the gate. When they refused, shots were fired. One bomber threw a stun grenade and ran away from the truck before it exploded. The sound drew bystanders and office workers in a high-rise behind the embassy to their windows. That's when a massive, multi-ton bomb detonated, shattering windows and blasting weaponized glass, metal, and debris into the bodies of those watching. Most of the dead were in the embassy, with many of the wounded on the street or in surrounding buildings.

In the aftermath, I received a phone call from Ian and Oria Douglass Hamilton, friends who lived in Kenya and had an apartment on the outskirts of Nairobi. The Hamiltons had led pioneering work on elephant conservation; Ian was the first person to collar and radio-track elephants on their migratory routes. I had met the couple on safari the previous year, and we had discussed the possibility of working together on projects, including a more effective way to monitor sedated elephants.

The Hamiltons cared deeply about Africa's people. Ian had located his research camp on Samburu land and part of our conversation had centered on ways to help Kenyan tribal society. I too was very interested in the Samburu since the clinic project was also in Samburu Land, although quite far from Ian's camp. The clinic was progressing well. A hut had been constructed and Irene was in the process of trying to get a government nurse to commit to a visit once a month.

Oria was pleading with me to do something to help the injured residents of Nairobi.

"Neil, you have no idea how bad it is over here," Oria said. "There are so many wounded, and the hospitals are short of everything, including simple things like antiseptic solution, bandages, and gauze pads. We must do something!"

She agreed that cash donations, through one of the reputable charities already involved was probably the best and most immediate way to help. Then she segued into the U.S. news coverage of the incident.

"You Americans, all you seem to care about are your losses," she complained. "I never see anything about the people who live here. There are so many hurting!"

In a way, I had to agree. Whenever these tragedies happened around the world, the U.S. news media unduly focused on any Americans who were caught in the crossfire, instead of reporting in a more balanced way about the entire scope of an event. I promised Oria I would solicit donations and we would talk in a few weeks.

The next time we spoke, Oria explained that the acute injuries were no longer the main problem. Surgeons had taken care of the life-threatening wounds, but disproportionately large numbers of locals had sustained disfiguring injuries. She suggested a meeting with the African Medical and Research Foundation (AMREF), an African nonprofit she was involved with. An American cosmetic surgeon, Tom Rees, and an English general surgeon, Michael Wood, had launched the organization decades before as The Flying Doctors to bring medical care to isolated Kenyan communities. AMREF had since expanded into training health care workers and delivering health services throughout the country. Oria had spoken to them about the possibility of organizing a mission of American surgeons to help the wounded. I met with Oria and the head of AMREF in mid-September when they were both in New York.

We agreed the best way to help would be to assemble a volunteer team of reconstructive surgeons and anesthesiologists to travel to Kenya to operate on the more than three hundred survivors who had sustained moderate-to-severe physical injuries with extensive scarring.

I served as lead of the anesthesia team. Our volunteers included a few work colleagues as well as anesthesiologists that a friend in the Anesthesia Department of Hackensack Hospital had recruited. Not knowing what kind of medical setup we would find, we decided to bring our own equipment, medications, and supplies. I had outfitted quite a few office operating rooms and had good contacts with anesthesia suppliers and drug companies. When I explained our mission, most of the reps reacted generously and donated whatever we needed, including big-ticket items like monitors and anesthesia machines. My friend Bob Burke, who provided technical service for the anesthesia equipment in the offices I worked in, went even further, volunteering his time and coming to Kenya to help us. I appreciated his unselfishness and invited his wife and two sons to join us in Kenya for a safari experience after we had finished at the hospital.

AMREF, meanwhile, enlisted British Airways to fly the doctors and equipment, and persuaded a Nairobi hotel to donate rooms. They also got the cooperation of Kenyatta Hospital, the largest public hospital in Kenya, for the use of its operating rooms and the help of staff. The foundation also recruited American, Spanish, and Kenyan reconstructive surgeons and secured funds through USAID.

All of this, as well as making sure all of the doctors had temporary Kenyan medical licenses, took time. Our teams didn't arrive in Nairobi until the beginning of February 1999.

After we checked in, an AMREF welcoming group took us to the site of the attack. Large piles of rubble rose in front of the collapsed concrete building that had been the American Embassy. Behind it stood the now empty high rise with its blown out windows and charred sides. Standing in front of the site was a chilling experience, completely different from seeing the scene on TV.

The next stop was Kenyatta Hospital, where we would meet the U.S. ambassador. We were eager to see the operating rooms, make sure the equipment had arrived safely, and examine some of the patients on whom we would be operating.

The 1,800-bed institution was located on the outskirts of Kibera, Africa's largest slum. I had worked in public hospitals, but none like this one. Ward after ward was filled with patients, but there was scarcely a nurse in sight. Each ward had one large fan, not nearly enough to combat the heat of the African summer. The twenty-four operating rooms, although spacious, had little of the technical equipment I was used to seeing in American hospitals.

We met the U.S. ambassador, Prudence Bushnell, and some press in one of the wards. She personally thanked each of us, and we all took part in a few photo ops. Then we got down to the business of examining the patients. Our first was a fifty-year-old woman with a nasty, dark scar on her forehead. She had been typing at her desk in the office building when the explosion occurred. She told us she had not been able to look in the mirror since the blast and hoped we could make her face look better. The next patient, a secretary in the same building, was scarred from glass that had blasted into her face and chest. She complained about pieces of glass left in her chest making it very painful to wear a bra.

As we went from patient to patient, I was surprised by the severity of the physical scars, but more than that, I was moved by the emotional toll the scarring had taken. I had seen burn patients transformed by minor reconstructive surgery, and I was sure that we could make a difference for these individuals on more than just a physical level.

That evening, I paired each of the anesthesiologists with a surgeon for the next day. I remained free to supervise and help out if anyone ran into problems. We began at 8 a.m. and didn't stop until 8 p.m. Each team operated on as many as a dozen patients a day. I spent much of my time going from operating room to operating room making sure both the surgeon and anesthesiologist had everything they needed, but I also gave anesthesia every day.

One of the more serious cases was a brave thirteen-year-old who had nearly lost his jaw. He'd been operated on at the time of the tragedy, but the results were poor, and he could hardly close his mouth. David Furness, a surgeon on our team from the University of California, took a skin graft from David's groin and used it to tighten his mouth. It would take time to heal, but it was a big improvement.

Another patient, a fifty-five-year-old cab driver, had been standing across from the embassy when the bombs exploded. After losing an ear and large patches on his scalp, he had a humble desire: to get an ear reshaped so he could wear his glasses. We implanted a balloon device under the scalp to stretch the remaining skin. After healing, the would surgeons would be able to attach an artificial ear. When we visited him post-op, he was smiling and said the operation was the first good thing that happened to him since the attack.

On the weekend between our first and second weeks at the hospital, Ian and Oria Douglass invited Bob Burke and me to their home in Naivasha, a short ride from Nairobi. Oria's parents had been big game hunters who had walked throughout Africa and eventually settled around Lake Naivasha. There they built Sirocco House, a famous landmark known for its French Art deco style. The Douglasses had set up a clinic nearby for the surrounding area. We brought along a modest surprise for it: basic medical supplies and a machine to monitor blood pressure and oxygen.

By the end of the second week, our teams had operated on almost three hundred and fifty victims. At a dinner on our last day, we presented the hospital with all of the medical equipment and remaining supplies, a donation worth many thousands of dollars. In return, we each received a certificate of appreciation, beaded jewelry, and a small curved wooden table in the shape of an African animal (mine was a zebra). The evening was emotional and a little embarrassing because of how grateful everyone was.

Our friend, Irene, who also lived on the outskirts of Nairobi, was great. None of the anesthesiologists I had recruited had been to Africa, and Irene arranged for them to go out into the bush for at least a long weekend before going back to the States.

Leann flew over and joined Bob, his family, another anesthesiologist and her family, and me on safari for the following week. I made sure one of our stops was the soon-to-be completed clinic in the Samburu village. It was a great opportunity to spend a day treating the villagers and it gave me an opportunity to stock the clinic with medicines we brought from the states. Irene let Adam know we were coming, and we were swamped with patients from the surrounding area.

My first night back in New York, lying awake in bed, I felt humbled by everything I had seen and by the difference we seemed to have made. My problems seemed small compared to what most of these Kenyans faced on a daily basis.

The patients we treated at Kenyatta Hospital weren't from an isolated tribe without access to basic services; they were average urbanites working in a major city on what they thought would be a typical day. I felt what happened to them could happen to me or anyone else. Although Kenya was a world away from the United States, and at the time, I didn't see Al Qaeda as a direct threat, somewhere in the back of my mind I had an uncomfortable feeling. I knew what had happened in Nairobi was a wake-up call.

21

The Hiltons, Some Diamonds, And A Surprise Tour

I visited Michael in his suite at the Waldorf Towers a few weeks after I returned from Kenya. The Waldorf Towers is a special section of the Waldorf Astoria Hotel where celebrities, royalty, and heads of state stay. Its entryway is around the corner from the main entrance, and it has its own doormen, lobby, and private elevators. All of the rooms are suites offering maximum comfort and privacy.

Michael was spending a lot of time in New York City working on what would become *Invincible,* his first studio album of all new material since *Dangerous,* released almost ten years before.

Recording, like touring, gave Michael serious sleep problems. He told me the process of writing new songs increased the volume and intensity of the chatter in his head, and the all-night studio sessions disrupted any semblance of normal sleep. We spoke about the demands of the new record and the stress he was under. Neither I, nor any of Michael's other doctors, had figured out a permanent solution to his sleep problems. When he asked me to work with him on a limited basis during this recording period. I agreed.

Michael knew a little bit about my legal troubles, but I hadn't told him about the plea deal. Now I decided it was time to talk. The conversation went well, and he seemed to agree that I had made the best decision. His main concern was that there would be no jail time. I confidently explained what the prosecutors had told me: I should get off with probation and a fine.

"You know, I went to visit Marcel in jail," Michael casually commented.

"Marcel, the promoter? I didn't know that." Marcel Avram had been Michael's worldwide concert promotor for years and had gone to prison for tax evasion.

"The worst part was they wouldn't let him wear his toupee. Can you believe that?"

"If that was the worst thing that happened, I would say he didn't have such a bad time."

"He came out of it okay. Don't worry, Rat. It will all work out."

"You're cool with it, Michael?"

"Of course. Friends are loyal. We are supposed to support each other." Changing the subject, he said, "Rat, tell me about your childhood."

"Like what?"

"What did you get excited about as a little kid?"

Michael was a proud, caring, single parent and forever curious about all things kids. He had told me about how his dad always had him and his brothers in the basement practicing. He would look up through the windows at other kids running past and playing outside. Naturally, he was intrigued about how other people were brought up.

I thought for a minute.

"I grew up in the suburbs in Long Island, and we didn't have a pool. When the weather got hot, my parents put sprinklers on the lawn. My friends and I took turns running and jumping our way through the ice-cold spray, and we loved it."

Michael grinned, and I went on to tell him another childhood memory, this one relating to the Christmas holidays.

"We don't celebrate Christmas," Michael interrupted. "You know I was brought up as a Jehovah's Witness. No holidays and no birthdays either."

"Michael, you have kids now. I think you should change that. You know kids love presents and special days. Christmas doesn't have to be about religion. I was brought up Jewish, but I still loved the excitement of going to the city to see the department store windows, sidewalk Santas, and the big tree. Just make it a very special time for you and the kids."

He seemed far away, and I wasn't sure he'd heard me.

"How come there is no Children's Day?" he mused. "There is Mother's Day and Father's Day, but no day especially for kids. I want to create Children's Day."

"I think when you have kids, every day is Children's Day."

We left it at that.

...

Occasionally Michael would invite Leann and me to come have dinner with him at the hotel. One evening, two-year-old Prince joined us. He was quite the little man with his blond hair, dark eyes, shirt, vest, and tie. Michael insisted that his children dress properly, say "please" and "thank you," and show good manners. Paris stayed with the nanny in another part of the suite.

Room service delivered a feast of steak and lobster. Prince was being playful and threw a piece of bread at Leann. Michael reacted immediately.

"No, Prince, don't do that! It's not nice to throw things at people. How would you like it if someone threw something at you?"

When he heard his father speak, he put down the piece he was about to throw. I was glad Michael didn't just tell him to stop but tried to make him understand that what he was doing was wrong. Michael was surprisingly strict, but also caring and involved. After dessert, the nanny took Prince to bed. Michael excused himself and went into his bedroom.

Rat, Leann, come in here," he called a few minutes later.

Leann and I looked at each other wondering what could be in the bedroom.

Michael was near the corner, fiddling with the combination safe. He opened the door, took out a small black attaché case, and put it on the bed. I knew something outrageous was about to happen.

"Holy shit!" I shouted as he opened the case.

The sparkle from the diamonds almost blinded me.

"Don't curse, Rat," Michael reprimanded me with a big smile on his face.

The briefcase was filled with several absolutely stunning necklaces and bracelets set with an eye-popping collection of diamonds, emeralds, and sapphires. Leann nearly fell off her feet. Michael was thoroughly enjoying our reactions.

"Here, Leann, put this necklace on."

I could tell by her face that she wasn't sure if she should.

"No, Michael, really I couldn't. I really shouldn't."

I gave her a wink to let her know I thought it was OK.

"Come on, Leann. Here, I will do it for you."

With that, he placed a magnificent emerald and diamond necklace around her neck.

"Maybe I'll give this one to Elizabeth," he said.

Next, he lifted up a bracelet sparkling with diamonds.

"This is for Paris," he said as he put it on his wrist. "I am going to save it until she is old enough."

There were two more pieces. He put a diamond and sapphire necklace around his neck and handed me one made of emeralds.

"Rat, here this one is for you."

"No, Michael, not for me. I am having fun just watching."

"Okay, okay. Come on Leann."

He took hold of Leann's hand and walked with her to a full-length mirror. They stood there admiring themselves.

"Rat, did you know that there is a real Presidential Suite in this hotel," Michael said, looking at me in the mirror.

"That's not so unusual," I answered. "Lots of five-star hotels have one."

"Yeah, but how many Presidents really stay there? All the Presidents have stayed in this one. Let's call the hotel manager and go see it. They said I could anytime."

"Now?" I asked. "It's almost ten."

"Now, Rat, now."

Michael picked up the phone and called. He was used to getting what he wanted when he wanted it, and the Waldorf took pride in granting even the most difficult or unusual requests. The night manager said he would personally take us on the tour.

Leann moved to take off the necklace. She didn't feel comfortable wearing it out of the room. Michael stopped her.

"No, no, Leann. Keep it on." He was giggling.

The doorbell rang. Michael took Leann by the hand, and they went to answer the door. The night manager found himself standing two feet in front of Michael Jackson and an unknown pretty blonde, staring at hundreds of thousands of dollars' worth of jewels. The stunned look on his face was priceless.

It's funny to watch people try to act normal in abnormal circumstances, and I often saw their attempts during those years. The hotel manager did everything he could to keep it together as he led the way. Michael and Leann waltzed down the hall after him, arm in arm as if they were the king and queen going to the ball. I thought that any minute I would break out laughing hysterically.

The suite was something to see. Every president since Herbert Hoover had stayed there, and many had donated items. There was a beautiful claw-foot desk of Eisenhower's and a gold mirror that Ronald Reagan had donated. Michael stopped to admire it.

Reagan had awarded Michael a Presidential Special Achievement Award, and Michael told me the Reagans liked to visit Neverland, especially after Ronald's diagnosis of Alzheimer's disease. Nancy loved the peacefulness of the property.

Michael sat down in a rocking chair that once belonged to JFK.

"Rat, did you know that Jackie Kennedy and I worked together on my book, *Moonwalk?*" "I had no idea."

"You should read it. She wrote the introduction."

Back in the room, I asked Michael about the jewels. He told me they were borrowed and worth a few million. I knew Michael liked diamonds from an experience we'd had in Sun City.

He was in the market to buy a raw diamond. Not any diamond; he wanted one bigger than the one Richard Burton had given Elizabeth Taylor. (That rough stone was 240 carats, found in a mine near Pretoria, South Africa.) Dan Ntsala made a couple of calls, and Michael, Dan, Wayne and I were on our way to a secret destination. After an hour, we pulled off the side of the road, literally in the middle of nowhere. Within minutes, two cars pulled up and four large well-dressed black South Africans got out.

Wayne and Dan went first and signaled to Michael when he was sure the situation was cool. I was not invited, but I saw through the window that diamonds were being shown. Even from my vantage point, they looked incredibly large. Michael came back to the van and showed us one. Sure enough, it was ginormous. He went back to Wayne, Dan and the South Africans. They exchanged some words, shook hands and everyone went back to their respective vehicles.

"How come the only thing I have ever seen on your wrist is a red string bracelet?" I asked as Leann returned the necklace. I wondered if it had any religious significance to Michael since both Jews and Hindus have a superstition about wearing red string bracelets to ward away evil.

"It's a friendship bracelet. The fans tie them on. It stays on until it falls off by itself."

"Yeah, but you like diamonds and expensive jewelry."

"Sure, Rat. They are beautiful to look at, but I don't want to make people feel bad. They would get jealous. It's not right."

"Knowing you, it's probably better you don't wear jewelry."

Michael was famous for giving away expensive things.

"Yeah, if a child saw me wearing a pretty piece of jewelry and wanted it, I would have to give it to them."

I laughed.

"I guess you would, wouldn't you?"

Michael got thoughtful.

"Of course I would," he replied.

...

Another evening in April, I arrived at his suite just as Michael was saying goodbye to two pretty young ladies.

"Hey, Rat, this is Paris and Nicki Hilton.

I smiled, said hello, and went inside. Michael followed.

"I have known them since they were born. I met their mother Kathy when I was fourteen. We've been close friends ever since."

I chuckled to myself. I had a good Hilton story for him.

"I sat next to Kathy at the Hilton Humanitarian Awards luncheon earlier this year," I told him. "I happened to mention we knew each other. She got excited and went on and on about how much she loves you."

"Did she tell you about the pact I made with her and Latoya?"

"No."

"We made a pact that each of us would name our first-born daughter Paris."

"Really, so that's how Paris got her name."

"Yeah, Kathy had her daughter first. She named her Paris. I was next."

I was going to ask about LaToya, but I knew their relationship was on the rocks. I changed the subject and told Michael about my mission with AMREF and the two weeks at Kenyatta hospital.

"Coincidentally, AMREF was the recipient of this year's Hilton Humanitarian Prize," I added. "I was invited to attend the ceremony and receive an award for my participation."

"Congratulations, Dr. Schweitzer, you deserve it," Michael said, putting his arm around my shoulders.

"Come on Michael, stop with the Dr. Schweitzer! It's embarrassing."

I continued, "I will say I am proud of what we accomplished. It went much deeper than just making people look better."

"Rat, you can't be happy if you don't like the way you look."

Michael understood this well. That's why the plastic surgery had started; he didn't like his nose, and he hated being teased about it.

I believe Michael had Body Dysmorphic Syndrome, an illness characterized by excessive concern and preoccupation with a physical defect. To him, his appearance would never be right. The sad part was there would always be a plastic surgeon waiting in the wings, convinced he was better than the last guy.

"Rat, I am going to do a charity tour in late June and I want you to come."

This was the first I had heard about a new tour.

"When I created 'We Are the World' it was my dream to do a worldwide series of concerts. I wanted to raise funds for the suffering children around the globe. Now I am ready to start. I am going to do two concerts, the first one in Seoul followed by a second concert in Munich. We are calling it 'Michael Jackson & Friends, The Adventure of Humanity.'"

"When I was with Mandela, we talked a lot about giving," Michael added. "I couldn't stop thinking about the words, 'What More Can I Give,' and I have been working on a song with that title. I want to use it as a theme for the shows.

"We all have to give, and we all have to do what we can to help end the needless suffering in the world. You're already doing it, Rat. That's why I want you to come."

"Where will the money go?"

"The money will be split between the Nelson Mandela Children's Fund, the Red Cross, and UNESCO."

"Cool! I'm impressed."

"Rat, you know how much I love Madiba. He inspired me to do something before the end of the century. It's more than an opportunity; it's my duty. You know how much it pains me to think how little we do for children. We are going to raise millions!"

22

Michael Jackson And Friends

THE charity tour became a reality two months later with a show scheduled for Seoul, South Korea on June 25 and one in Munich, Germany on June 27, 1999. Billed as Michael Jackson and Friends, the "friends" in the title included Mariah Carey, Boyz II Men, Slash, the Scorpions, and Luther Vandross, among other artists. With a lineup like that, I knew the shows would be once-in-a-lifetime events, and I appreciated the opportunity to go.

Things were pretty quiet with the feds. The prosecutors were busy preparing their highly complex case and rarely needed to see me. A trial was still a long way away. Meanwhile, I had been permitted to keep my passport, and no one had restricted my travel. Still, my lawyers asked me not to flaunt the fact that I was leaving the country.

I was grateful to have a reason to get away and happy that Michael agreed to fly Leann to Munich for the second concert. Going on the road with Michael was a real treat for Leann and besides we had German friends coming to the show and it would be fun for the four of us to hang out together afterwards.

The prospect of testifying haunted me, and my anxiety about the outcome triggered a rollercoaster of emotions. Going on the road would be a good distraction from the Lauerson case, and knowing that Michael would be giving the proceeds to charity made me feel happy as well as hopeful for the prospects of the children's hospital we'd spoken about building.

I flew to LA to meet Michael for a commercial flight on Korean Airlines to Seoul. He was traveling with his kids and that was new for me. Prince was a little over two, and Paris, just over a year. Grace Rwaramba, a long-time employee and the children's new nanny, was with them, but they would be my responsibility should they fall ill.

We had the first-class cabin to ourselves. An hour into the flight, I noticed Wayne's brother, Skip, a recent addition to the security team, filling a coke can with wine and giving it to Michael. Skip saw me and smiled. Later, I asked what was going on.

He laughed. "You mean the 'Jesus juice.'"

"The what?"

"'Jesus juice' ... wine, Rat. He doesn't want people to know what he is drinking."

I knew Michael drank a little. We had wine together, and he never drank more than a glass or two. I also knew that because of his upbringing as a Jehovah's Witness and his status as a pop idol, he didn't want people to know he drank. Certainly, based on what I had seen, his drinking wasn't anything to be concerned about.

After fifteen hours, our jet landed and taxied across the tarmac. Wayne had flown to Korea two days before and met us there with a few South Korean officials. They led us into the main terminal, where the crush of police, fans, and press was unbelievable. Thankfully, we were quickly ushered into a private room to complete our paperwork.

Michael's new manager, Myung Ho Lee, a South Korean Michael had hired in the late nineties after Tarek Ben Amir was let go, had promoted Michael's arrival in Seoul as a mega-event, and he had the friends in government to make it happen. Hundreds of police and security forces had been deployed to accompany us out of the airport. I'd never seen anything like the mob scene I witnessed that day, not for a president, royalty, or even the Pope.

A fleet of cops on motorcycles, with sirens screaming, led our procession out of the airport. We sped past blocked-off streets and legions of people waving wildly. It was utter chaos. The crowd's exuberance and size amazed Michael, and he told Lee he hoped the audience would be this animated at the concert.

At the hotel, Michael asked me to stop by his suite before going to my room. He had something to tell me.

"Frank is flying in tonight to be my personal assistant."

"Frank who?" I asked.

Michael seemed genuinely surprised by my question.

"Cascio, Rat. The Cascios are like my other family. I have known Frank since he was four."

I was tired from the flight and we left it at that.

The next day's schedule included a trip to Tower Records, an afternoon at the amusement park, Everland, and a stop at a fabulous teahouse for a tea ceremony with Samsung company elite.

At Tower Records, once we made our way safely indoors, Wayne escorted two fans in to meet Michael. One was a "mini Michael," part of a growing phenomenon we had observed everywhere we traveled: little doppelgangers who not only had Michael's look down, but also his moves.

This little boy was about nine or ten and outfitted in a red military jacket, black pants, black shoes, and white socks. A small black fedora rested atop his head, and a black silk surgical mask covered his nose and mouth. He busted moves to "Billie Jean" and did Michael's signature moonwalk. I was mesmerized, and Michael was beside himself.

During our four-day stay in Seoul, Michael put aside time every day to spend with sick or disadvantaged kids. He took them to the amusement park, visited an orphanage and a hospital, and invited a group to dinner. Repeatedly, I witnessed Michael's concern for them and what they were going through.

A rehearsal was set for the day before the show. Mariah Carey and Michael were label mates and friends. He had been there for her when she divorced Sony head Tommy Mattola in 1997, and she had happily agreed to come to Korea and do her solo set and a duet with Michael. We arrived after the other acts had practiced. Wayne updated Michael that Mariah had just flown in and would be there shortly.

Mariah arrived with a large entourage but went into the dressing room alone. She apologized to Michael for showing up a day late and explained that she couldn't sing on the day she flew. This meant no rehearsal, and although she was OK about doing her solo set at the concert, there would be no duet. Michael was cool about it, but I could tell he was disappointed.

The show went off OK, not great. Later at the hotel, Michael, very much the perfectionist, obsessed over a few technical glitches. I told him the audience probably never realized the problems, but he insisted I was wrong; his fans could tell. Mariah came by the suite and told him how great the concert had been, and seeing her lifted his spirits.

The next day we boarded a chartered 747 jumbo jet for the eleven-hour flight to Munich. Michael, Frank, Grace, the kids, Skip, and I were in first class. (Wayne had returned to LA because of a medical problem, leaving Skip in charge of security.) Luther

Vandross, Slash, and The Scorpions were in business class. The rest of the performers including Status Quo, Vanessa Mae, and Spirit of the Dance, were in the back. I walked back a few times to see what was happening. People were having a good time playing guitars and singing in small groups throughout both cabins. Even Michael came out of the front cabin a couple of times. The scene was cool and reminded me of the old days.

In first class, Frank, a likeable young man of just eighteen, grabbed the seat next to me. His father, Dominic Cascio, had been the general manager at the Helmsley Palace Hotel where Michael frequently stayed. Over time, Dominic had virtually "adopted" Michael into his large family. Michael frequently hosted the Cascios at Neverland, and members of the family often joined him on tour. Frank had been on tour with Michael many times before, but never as a personal assistant. He peppered me with questions about my experiences working with rock stars on the road. I said not to worry; I would keep an eye out for him.

In Munich, the police had closed the street in front of our hotel, but large crowds had gathered in the Promenadeplatz, a small park opposite the Bayershof. It was the same hotel where a few years earlier Michael had held Prince out the window. When I asked him about it, Michael said he was angry that people thought he was being cavalier with his new son. He knew he had a strong grip on Prince.

Michael agreed it wasn't the smartest thing to do, and that his over-exuberance to show Prince to the fans got the best of him. But it seemed to Michael that the press, as usual, was particularly hard on him and he was hurt by the articles that claimed he was a bad father for doing it.

Michael exited the van, looking sharp in a jacket created by Andre Kim, a famous Korean designer. It was black with two large gold embroidered dragons running up either side as faux lapels. The design continued onto the collar in the back, and from behind, looked like a gold necklace. A small sound system had been set up, and the speakers were playing "Billie Jean."

As part of the promotion for the Munich show, hardcore fans from clubs all over the world had been flown in and were awaiting Michael's arrival. And he wanted to see them. He walked along the park's perimeter when suddenly, a crazed fan broke through the barricades and came at him. Security reacted quickly and pushed her aside. Unfazed, Michael kept moving. A few minutes later, another determined fan made a run at him, with the same result. Skip and Marcel, the promoter, hurried Michael into the hotel. I met him by the elevator.

"Rat, my suite has multiple bedrooms. Why don't you and Leann stay in one of them?"

Between the racket outside and the lack of privacy that would mean, I wasn't anxious to agree. I knew, though, that Leann would be excited about this when she arrived the next night, and I didn't want to disappoint her.

The room faced the street.

Michael!!... Michael!!... Michael!!

The noise went on twenty-four seven. Funny enough, no matter what country we were in, the crowds sounded the same. Many of his devotees seemed to be wherever we went: Cape Town, New York, Seoul, and now Munich. Wayne was hyperaware of Michael's fans. He made sure they were treated well and was on a first-name basis with some of them. Both he and Michael respected "fan power."

In fact, the subject of fans and marketing came up that evening.

"Rat, what do you think of P.T. Barnum?"

"I don't know much about him except that he started the circus," I answered.

"He was way more than that. He was a master at promotion. You know what he said? 'Every crowd has a silver lining.'"

I laughed. P.T. Barnum may have been good at self-promotion, but in contemporary times, I doubted anyone topped Michael.

He walked over to a large pile of books lying on a table in a corner of the suite and pulled out an old copy of *The Greatest Salesman in the World* by O.G. Mandino.

"This book is very important, but you have to read it the right way," Michael said, handing it to me. "There are ten scrolls. Read each one three times a day for thirty days. It should take you ten months. It's helped me a lot."

"OK. What is it about?"

"We'll talk about it when you're finished."

The book's title reminded me of Michael. Show business was about creating an image and selling it. The problem in Michael's case was that, as with many other celebrities, what they sold didn't represent who they really were.

The concert started in the early afternoon with Michael scheduled to close the show around 10:30 p.m. We went earlier so that he could introduce Andre Bocelli. Michael and I watched him sing from the side of the stage. We were amazed by his beautiful sound.

Just before he went on stage, Michael had his musicians and dancers gather for a prayer, as they did before every performance. Michael spotted me from the corner of his eye.

"Rat, come join us."

We held hands in a tight circle as one of the dancers, who was a preacher, led the prayer. It ended with an emotional call and response.

The set was going well. Michael had two numbers to go, "Earth Song" followed by "You Are Not Alone." "Earth Song" included an over-the-top production with an elaborate actual bridge that spanned the stage as the centerpiece of the number. This Bridge of No Return was meant to signify a bridge between North and South Korea and the bridge that potentially exists between all warring societies.

It was designed to break into three sections to much fanfare and fireworks. Michael would stand on the platform that made up the center section as the hydraulics raised it high above the stage. Underneath him, Slash would wail on his guitar. Then the middle section would be lowered with Michael still on it and reformed into a bridge, while a soldier with a rifle appeared. After he chased Michael off at gunpoint, a child with a flower would approach the soldier. He would take the flower, put down the gun, and hug the child. In Korea, the tech wizardry worked perfectly.

Not this time. I watched Michael rise high above the stage, and horrified, saw the middle section he was standing on come crashing down. Through all of this, Michael somehow managed to stay on his feet.

For a minute, I lost sight of him. Then I saw him climbing onto the stage from the broken bridge. The band, taking his cue, continued as if the mishap was part of the show. I could tell from Michael's expression that things were bad. When the number ended, Michael, pale and seemingly in shock, made his way off stage.

His make-up artist, Conchita, yelled at him to stop the show. Michael, the consummate professional, refused and, with microphone in hand, went back out and sang an abbreviated version of "You Are Not Alone."

Ending the song, Michael staggered and collapsed.

23

You Are Not Alone

As soon as I reached Michael, my training and experience working in a trauma center took over. One of my responsibilities as Michael's doctor was to be there should something occur, and now it had. I cleared the area around him and began to evaluate him as I would any other trauma patient.

Airway—was it clear? Yes.

Breathing—Michael was breathing, but his breaths were short and labored.

Circulation—did he have a normal pulse? As far as I could tell, it was normal, but fast.

I had to be careful in assessing Michael's condition. It was not uncommon to see patients walking and talking after severe trauma, only to find serious, sometimes life-threatening injuries when they were examined more thoroughly at a hospital.

Michael had no obvious signs of external bleeding, and he was able to move all his extremities. I didn't think he had lost consciousness, and he was oriented to time and place.

"Ooooh, it hurts! It hurts!"

Michael started moaning.

"Michael, what hurts?"

"Everything, Rat, everything."

I pushed on his belly to see if there were any obvious signs of internal injury. He yelled, but I didn't feel any resistance. That was good. He was stable enough to move to a hospital, but I was concerned and wanted to get him there as quickly as possible, and there was no ambulance immediately available. I told Skip to get the car ready. Anthony, the stage manager, carefully scooped Michael into his arms and ran through the maze of walkways under the stage to the waiting car. Frank and I followed, climbed in and took off.

The ride to the hospital quickly turned into a nightmare. After a few minutes, the driver announced in broken English that we were lost. He had no idea where to go. Michael was sitting with Frank in the back seat. I was in front with my hand on his wrist to monitor his pulse. All of a sudden, Michael began to cry out.

"I can't breathe! I can't breathe!"

I didn't detect any real change in his condition, and I thought his response was probably an emotional reaction to the pain.

"Michael, you *can* breathe. Calm down. Breathe slower. Try to breathe a little more deeply."

"I can't. It hurts! It hurts!"

"Where does it hurt?" I asked, wondering if he could have bruised or broken a rib.

He pointed to an area of his lower back and started to cry audibly. Although he landed on his feet, the force of the impact would have been transmitted to his lower back and spine. It's difficult to judge the nature of someone else's pain, and until the hospital did tests, it was impossible for me to know whether Michael was overreacting or if he had sustained real damage.

Frank and I calmed him down. We needed to find the hospital. As much as I didn't think Michael was seriously hurt, time is of the essence, particularly when you don't know the extent of someone's injuries.

After what seemed like forever, the driver spoke to someone who gave him the correct directions. We were ten minutes away.

An orderly wheeled Michael into the ER's main trauma room, and the medical team went into action, cutting away his clothes, attaching monitors, and attempting to start an IV. I introduced myself and described what happened.

Starting the IV was taking ages, and the head ER doc asked me if it were always so difficult. I said it was and showed him a few areas on Michael's hands and feet where I thought he might have success. Within a few minutes, he had one working.

After multiple X-rays, a CAT scan, sonogram, and battery of blood tests, the doctors confirmed nothing was broken and Michael had no internal injuries. The bad news was that he sustained a serious sprain to his lower back.

The doctors felt he could leave that night, but Michael insisted on staying. I knew why. He would get pain medication in the hospital. I didn't push him to leave, but I made sure the doctors were aware of his history of narcotics abuse. It was better for them to control the dosages of medications that night.

Michael was moved to a private room, and I was more than ready to go back to the hotel. Michael saw me preparing to leave.

"Rat, where are you going?"

"Back to the hotel. You're in good hands."

"No, Rat, I want you and Frank to stay with me."

"Here in this room?"

"Yeah, I told them to bring two cots."

"No, Michael, I am tired. I don't want to stay here."

"Rat, it will be fun, a sleepover. Work with me, Rat, work with me...."

There was no use arguing. I smiled, and so did he. The staff brought the cots, and we bedded down for the night, however, Michael didn't sleep for more than an hour or two. He was a little high from the painkillers, and all he wanted to do was talk.

"Rat, you know why I didn't break anything?"

"No, why?"

"Because my body knew to jump just as the bridge hit the floor."

"That was good, but why didn't you end the show."

"I couldn't disappoint the audience. I heard my father's voice telling me over and over that no matter what, the show must go on."

Later, in the wee hours as the medication wore off, Michael's mood grew darker, and he wanted to analyze and rehash every detail of the accident. By that time, I didn't want to talk or hear any more about it. I wanted to get a few hours' sleep, but Michael grew angrier. Bad enough there were technical glitches in Seoul, he said, this mistake could have killed him.

"I want to know who is responsible. I want someone fired for this! Frank, call Kenny Ortega *now* and find out." Kenny Ortega was the producer of the concerts and a longtime Jackson associate.

"Michael, it's three o'clock in the morning. Can't this wait a few hours?"

"No, Frank. I said to call him now."

"Do you want to talk to him?"

"No. Just find out who is responsible."

Frank left to make the call and I changed the subject.

"Hey, Michael, being here reminds me of an idea I wanted to talk to you about."

"What's that?"

There was a cardiac defibrillator on a cart in the corner of the room.

When someone has a heart attack, there is a short window of opportunity, especially if the heart is not beating correctly. Defibrillators can get the heart beating to a normal rhythm until professional help takes over, and the machines have proven to save lives. I thought we should start a campaign to place defibrillators everywhere large groups of people gathered.

I wheeled it over to him. What used to be a big, bulky apparatus that was difficult to operate, was now a small, easy to use device that ran on batteries.

"Do you know what this machine is used for?"

He laughed.

"Sure, Rat. Do you know the words to my song 'Smooth Criminal?'"

"More or less," I replied, puzzled.

He began to sing:

Annie, are you OK?

So, Annie, are you OK?

"Annie is Resusci Annie, the mannequin used to teach CPR. We have a defibrillator at the ranch. I took CPR, Rat. Resusci Annie was my patient and my inspiration for 'Smooth Criminal.'"

We started to laugh. I explained my idea. He liked it and said he would help, but it never got any further.

Frank came back. Kenny Ortega had explained that the crash had something to do with the hydraulics and he would find out the exact details and get back to Michael. That answer seemed to satisfy him, and his mood improved. A few hours later, I convinced Michael it was time to leave the hospital, and Skip came to get us.

When we got back to Michael's suite, I was shocked and upset to find two German anesthesiologists waiting for us. I didn't know them personally, but I knew the two had been on the HIStory tour prior to my arrival.

Michael had been pestering me to contact them. He liked the way they had administered propofol and wanted me to learn their technique. I couldn't imagine what they did differently, unless they were combining propofol with other medications like Valium or narcotics, something I refused to do. I didn't have any objection to talking with them, but I'd never made any attempt to get their number.

Michael had obviously contacted them. He saw by my angry expression that I was fuming, and he pulled me aside.

"No, Rat, you don't understand. You worked hard the last few days, and I wanted to give you the day off."

The anesthesiologists had all their equipment with them, and I could see that their plan was to treat him as soon as he arrived from the hospital. Michael wanted to be out for the day, and he knew that I would never sanction it. In my mind, it was completely unnecessary. There weren't any more concerts, and he was on pain meds.

I didn't want to make a scene in front of everyone, so I half-nodded tersely. Michael went into the bedroom. I stayed to talk to the Germans for a few minutes to learn how their technique differed from mine. Dissuading them seemed impossible.

At first they were friendly and asked about Michael's injury. I told them about his sprained back and the meds he was on. When

I brought up propofol, however, their attitude grew hostile, and they tried to change the subject. I persisted until they stated in no uncertain terms that they had nothing to say about propofol, sleep, or the way they treated Michael. I let them know I thought they were extremely unprofessional, turned my back to them, and walked away.

I not only questioned their judgment, I couldn't understand why professional-to-professional, they wouldn't discuss their treatment techniques. I was also angry with Michael; I didn't like being used. As a people pleaser, Michael would rather do something behind your back and lie about it, than try to make you see his point of view.

Leann was waiting for me in our bedroom, which was part of Michael's suite. She had arrived in Munich a few days before and had been at the concert with German friends. I hadn't spoken to her since the day before, when I left for the show. I could see she was also unhappy.

When she returned to the hotel after the concert, the local German security refused to let her into the suite, and we were all at the hospital and unreachable. No matter how much she pleaded, she couldn't get them to budge. Finally, after being forced to wait through most of the night in a corner of the hotel lobby, Teddy, the promoter's assistant, saw her sitting alone, apologized profusely, and escorted her to the room.

I felt terrible for her and apologized. I was also upset with myself for not checking in with her. I had simply assumed Leann had come in and gone to sleep. After hearing about my experience of the past twenty-four hours, including the episode with the German anesthesiologists as the icing on the cake, Leann understood and all was forgiven.

I don't know exactly when the Germans left, but they were gone the next morning. Michael and I spoke later that day.

"Hey, Rat, I'm sorry you got upset."

"You should be, man!"

"I didn't want to bother you. I needed to sleep after the hospital, and I knew you needed the time off."

"Did you even ask me about it? No. You just went and contacted the Germans! You knew I probably wouldn't have agreed to it, so you played me, man!!"

I let that sink in but eased up.

"I know, you're in pain. You thought it would be a good way to escape. Besides, we didn't really sleep in that hospital, did we?"

Michael could see I was cooling off a little, and he laughed, but I wasn't finished.

"Next time, talk to me first," I insisted. "If you do that again, it will be the last time I ever work with you!"

"Don't be angry with me Rat. I want you and Leann to come to Paris with me tomorrow. I have an important photo shoot there for the cover of the new album."

"What about your German friends?"

"*RRRaaattt,* I want you to come. Work with me Rat. Work with me."

"OK, OK, we'll come." Michael could be a real charmer when he wanted to be. I knew I was being manipulated but on the other hand, I sensed that Michael was really sorry for having upset me and wanted to make up for it in some way. That was one of the paradoxes of Michael Jackson; "I want what I want right now no matter how it inconveniences you but don't be mad at me." And it was always a delicate balancing act for me to determine what was necessary and appropriate.

Dan Ntsala had also come to Munich for the concert, and Michael mentioned he would be flying with us to Paris. It was news I was happy to hear. A few days in Paris with Leann and Dan would be a nice way to end the trip.

We checked in late the next morning at Plaza Athenee, one of Paris's finest hotels. Then Grace called and said Paris Jackson was not feeling well. She had nasal congestion and a mildly sore throat. I didn't think it was strep, but because I couldn't take a culture, I got a local pediatrician to look at her. It was nothing serious.

Michael finished his photo shoot early the next day and suggested that we all join him to see *The Matrix*. He had already seen it and was excited to turn us onto it. Michael, Skip, Frank, Dan, Leann, and I slipped into the back of the movie theater just after the feature started. Michael was in his typical attire and had made no attempt to disguise himself. Everything was cool until the end of the movie. As a few people started to leave the crowded theater before the movie finished, we heard a couple of screams. Michael had been recognized, and we had to make a run for it.

Skip grabbed Michael, Dan led the way through the lobby, and we took up the rear. As we ran out of the theater, a group of people was close behind yelling Michael's name. Leann dropped her scarf and wanted to go pick it up. *No way.* We had to keep moving. The cars were nowhere in sight and the situation was getting intense. Even passersby had realized it was Michael. In a minute, we would be completely surrounded.

Skip noticed the doorman of the Moulin Rouge, Paris's famous nightclub, waving his arms frantically. He had watched the scene unfold, and now we ran towards him. He moved us quickly into the club and led us to its kitchen. Skip contacted our driver and the car met us a few minutes later at the back entrance.

Unfortunately for Leann and me, it wasn't the van we had arrived in, and we had to wait another twenty minutes for a car back to the hotel.

The next day, Michael's fame led to an even closer call when we went out into the countryside to look at a chateau. Michael loved Euro Disney, and he wanted to buy a place in its vicinity. Skip ordered decoy vehicles to wait in the front and back of the hotel, while we snuck out a little-known side entrance and departed in two cars. Beyond the city, paparazzi on four motorcycles began to follow us closely.

We sped up and tried to shake them off with no success. They kept speeding, getting closer and closer. Things got dangerous when we turned quickly off the main road and onto a narrow two-lane country road. As we made the turn, pairs of the motorcycles, each bearing a driver and a photographer, came up on either side of our cars, effectively blocking any traffic coming from the opposite direction. The paparazzi were yelling, snapping pictures, and driving very recklessly. An oncoming vehicle was directly in front of us approaching rapidly. My mind flashed to Princess Diana's fatal crash, and I thought we were all going to die in a head-on collision. Our driver couldn't turn without hitting the motorcyclists. He didn't know what to do. Only at the last moment, did the motorcycles peel off onto the grass, letting the oncoming car skirt us without incident.

After that, the paparazzi followed at a distance to the chateau. We passed through the gates and up the driveway. The paparazzi caught up and gathered outside the gates. Even before our vehicles had fully stopped, Skip and Atila, another member of the security team, were out the doors, running back to the paparazzi. I don't know what was said, but that was the last we saw of our harassers that afternoon. But just to be sure, Skip arranged a police escort back to the hotel.

The incident rattled us. All I could think of the rest of the afternoon were Michael's chilling words when we had discussed Princess Di's accident: "I hope I am not next."

We were lucky that day, but Leann and I were ready to go home. I had been away from my practice long enough, and we both knew it was only a matter of time before the Lauerson case heated up again.

That evening we stopped by Michael's suite to say goodnight.

"Rat, come with us. We are leaving tomorrow for Euro Disney and then South Africa."

"Not this time, Michael. We have to get back to New York. Maybe we will catch you in Joburg later this summer. We are going on safari for my birthday."

"You really love South Africa, don't you?"

"I do."

"Maybe you'll live there someday. Wouldn't it be cool if we were neighbors, Rat?"

"Yeah, Michael, that would be cool."

24

Fifty Years Old And A Time For Reflection

THREE weeks after returning from Paris, Leann and I left for Africa. On July 30, 1999, I would be fifty, and there wasn't a place on Earth I would rather be. Safari was addicting, and Africa had become a second home for us. Leann loved it as much as I did, and the time we spent together in the bush had strengthened our relationship.

We stayed at the Michelangelo Hotel in Johannesburg on our way to a safari camp in Zimbabwe. Michael was also at the hotel that night. After we'd left Paris, he had continued on to Euro Disney and then to South Africa where Frank's family had joined them for Mandela's eighty-first birthday. Now they were on their way back to New York. I found Michael racing down the hallways with the younger Cascio brothers.

"Hey, Rat, what's your room number? I'll come over in a few minutes."

He arrived out of breath and without shoes. Michael was more vibrant, more alive, and very much at ease when he was in Africa. He jumped onto the bed and made himself at home.

"You should have come with us!" he said excitedly. "It was great to be with Mandela and his family. I surprised him with a birthday cake."

I had to laugh to myself. When I met Michael, he didn't celebrate birthdays because of his upbringing. Now he was bringing birthday cakes to his friends.

"Wow, it sounds amazing. I still hope to meet him again someday. You know I never got a copy of that picture from the concert."

"I'll get you the picture, Rat, and you will have a chance to meet him again. That's one of the things I want to talk to you about.... I want to give you a birthday present."

"Really? You don't have to do that."

He he he...

"I want you and Leann to come back here with me in September to give Mandela a check for the money we raised at the concerts, one million rand." That was about $150,000 at the time."

"Sounds great! Where?"

"Sun City, at the Kora awards. They are the African version of the Grammys. I'm getting a lifetime achievement award. It's a good time to give Madiba the check."

"Very cool, man."

"Oh, and one more thing. No work. I don't want you to bring any medical equipment. This time, Sun City will be a vacation. I want you two to have fun."

"OK, twist my arm. No work."

Most of the time when Michael and I got together, it had nothing to do with work. Treatment was reserved for those unusual times on tour when sleep was a pressing issue. This would be friends going on vacation together, and I couldn't wait.

The next morning, we flew to Harare, the capital of Zimbabwe. After a night in a lodge where we slept on a mahogany four-poster bed surrounded by lion-skin rugs, we took a small plane to an airstrip not far from the Zambezi River. Our guide set up camp on the banks of the river, notable for the world's largest concentration of crocodiles and hippos.

Day one was a canoe trip, and as soon as I sighted the two small canoes by the riverbank, I flashed to summer camp. As a kid, I spent my summers at sleep-away camp in Pennsylvania, and I loved it. We often went canoeing on the camp lake, and once each summer we went on an overnight down the Delaware River. For weeks before the trip, we practiced paddling and emergency procedures. Every day when we least expected it, a counselor would tip a canoe. One by one, we would go under water and come up in the air pocket formed by the upside down canoe. We learned how to get the canoe righted and climb into it from the water, not an easy task even when you know the right technique. That training had served me well for my Delaware adventures, but that was decades ago, and this was the Zambezi.

Each guide packed a small pistol. I wondered what good they would do should an angry, three thousand pound hippo attack. Encounters between hippos and canoers were rare, but memorable. An oft-told story involved a marketing guy for one of Africa's biggest safari companies who went down the Zambezi with friends. As experienced as he was, he inadvertently canoed across the top of what he thought was a boulder. A now-furious hippo rose up behind him and tried to snap his canoe in half from behind. The massive jaws just missed him, and the impact threw the man into the water. He managed to scramble back, grab onto the wrecked canoe and paddle himself, and it, back to safety. Only when he got the wreckage onto dry land and saw how close the bite marks were to where he had been sitting did he realize how lucky he had been.

Relaxing around safari campfires, Leann and I had heard other hippo-versus-paddler stories where the victims were not so lucky.

As we canoed further down the river, crocodiles slithered into the water from the embankments, while multiple sets of hippo eyes at water level followed our progress. We paddled through twists and turns and saw colonies of beautiful little colorful birds called carmine bee-eaters nesting in the sandy banks. The calmness of the river contrasted with the dangers that surrounded us. It was easy to get lured into a false sense of security and we were both relieved when the canoes pulled up to the riverbank close to our camp.

From Zimbabwe, we flew to Kenya to see one of the greatest wildlife spectacles on earth. Twice a year, more than a million wildebeest, four hundred thousand zebra, and two hundred thousand gazelle travel between the Serengeti, in Tanzania, and the Maasai Mara, in Kenya, in search of the best grasslands.

Leann and I were on a private tented safari with a guide nicknamed "Piggy," and a Maasai warrior, Joseph, who would function as our spotter. Early on a beautiful morning, with the mist rising and lions roaring, we set out in an open jeep. We stopped on a small hill overlooking the vast plains of the Mara. Holding his spear and sitting regally atop the back seat, Joseph, the young tribesman of about eighteen, embodied his people's proud traditions.

Piggy took a cassette out of his bag, put it into the jeep's tape deck, and turned up the volume. As soon as I heard the violins, I recognized the theme from *Out Of Africa*. There is music designed to stir your emotions, and this was one of those pieces. The migration was spread out in front of us with zebras and wildebeest numbering in the thousands, and as we rode down the hill into the multitude of wildlife, a pathway magically opened for us.

I don't cry frequently. It probably has to do with growing up in a household where I was taught not to show feelings. Neither of my parents expressed much emotion, and they didn't approve of public displays, but this time, there was no way to stop the tears. To be in the middle of a spectacle as intense as the migration was unlike anything I had experienced. The raw beauty of what was before me unleashed all of the pent-up emotion from the stress of the impending trial, the tours with Michael, and the Kenya mission.

I was turning fifty, and I reflected on my adult years; the six I'd spent in the rock-and-roll business working my way up from road manager to tour management to owning a successful production company; the ones I'd spent going back to university, the first step in the long road of becoming a physician. Finding and marrying my soulmate, Leann, the love of my life; the four years in Mexico where I gained the medical education I needed and important life experiences; and my residency, one of the hardest things I ever did, starting with surgery and ending with a certificate in anesthesiology. I had created a successful career and, in addition to everything else, I was working with Michael Jackson, the King of Pop. Now it was all in serious jeopardy, and I was scared.

I turned to see Leann sobbing. The magnitude of nature's display had affected her too. I knew the case had been hard on her. She had married a doctor and thought the rest of her life would be relatively smooth. Instead, I was facing a possible prison term and the loss of my career. But more than that, she was worried about me. Leann was very perceptive. She knew I was strong and could take a lot, but as strong as I pretended to be she could sense my underlying fear and it frightened her.

The hoof beats and grunts were louder than I could have ever imagined, and the pungent smells propelled me back into the moment. I looked at Piggy and he, too, was wiping away tears. Even Joseph was visibly moved.

We arrived back in New York in the middle of August, and within a few weeks, we were on a plane again, bound for Johannesburg to join Michael and his kids for the Kora Awards. They had flown to South Africa from LA and arrived a few hours after we had checked in. Michael had arranged an elegant room for us at the Palace Hotel, and we were in the bar, relaxing, when he called to tell us to meet him in his suite.

"Rat, you know there is a fashion show tomorrow, and they are going to give out awards for the best African designer. Leann, you'll like that, right?"

"Of course, Michael, you know I'm a clothes horse," Leann answered happily.

Whether offstage or on, Michael wore pretty much the same outfit. He didn't like fancy clothes except onstage and, for that, he had his fabulous jackets. When we were in Sun City for the HIStory tour, he didn't have enough room in his closet for all the jackets, and he gave me a few to hold. Leann couldn't help trying them on and posing. Most were heavily sequined, and we were awed by how much they weighed and how much time it must have taken to make each one.

"Rat, I have something else to tell you."

I had no idea what was coming.

"I'm going to do two concerts for the millennium."

"On New Year's Eve?"

"Both will be on New Year's Eve in two different cities."

"C'mon, you're joking!"

"The first show will be in Sydney on December 31. Then we will fly across the international dateline to Honolulu for the second concert, also on December 31. It will be the first time it has ever been done, and, Rat, I need you to be the Millennium doctor."

My first reaction was, "Great, can't wait," but I considered the timing. The prosecutors had recently said they thought the trial could be early in 2000, which was only a few months away. But with nothing set in stone, I thought it was better not to bother Michael.

"I'm looking forward to it!" I said with as much confidence as I could muster.

Leann had often mentioned wanting to be at a runway fashion show. Granted this wasn't Paris or New York, but the fact that it was Africa lent its own unique excitement, and we had seats right up front. Accompanied by music, much of it Afropop, six African designers showed their collections. The crowd rose to their feet, dancing and cheering as each model sashayed up and down the runway.

Dance and movement are a major part of African culture. Whether it's to convey sadness at a funeral or joy at a wedding, Africans dance. I think that's one reason Leann and Michael related to Africa so well. As Leann joined in the dancing, a small circle formed around her, its members applauding and encouraging her. It was a great evening.

Mandela would be arriving the next day and would be meeting with Michael and his kids privately mid-afternoon. When Dan Ntsala told Leann and me that we were invited, I felt extremely grateful. It was far beyond anything I had expected.

We met at Michael's suite. Prince was dressed up in black patent-leather shoes, black short pants, white shirt, and a white cardigan sweater. He also had a black necktie tucked into the top of the sweater. Paris was wearing a white frilly dress with short white socks and black patent-leather shoes. I'm sure they had no idea who Nelson Mandela was, but Michael must have told them something because they were quiet and well-behaved.

Michael had on a baseball cap, aviator sunglasses, and his usual red shirt and black pants. He asked Leann to take the kids as he walked ahead with Dan. Leann wasn't used to being with children, and she looked a bit awkward with Prince holding her right hand and Paris, her left.

The door to the African suite opened. Michael ran in and gave Mandela a big hug and embraced Graca Machel, Mandela's wife. Then he presented his kids. Mandela had met Prince, but it was his first time meeting Paris. His expression said it all: He was a man who loved children, and these children were special to him. Mandela took a seat. Prince immediately climbed up on his knee, and the two played a little game. Michael brought Paris over. She was shy but within a minute, Mandela had her smiling and on his lap as well, Prince counting for him while Paris fought for his attention.

Mandela looked over at me and said, "So, Doctor, you did come back."

I chuckled and answered, "You remembered."

"Rat, tell Madiba about the work you do in Africa," Michael said.

I talked about the Samburu child and the clinic, and I made sure to include the lessons I learned from Dr. Cahill. Mandela seemed impressed. We spoke about the cycle of poverty and the importance of sustainability. He told me South Africa welcomed outside help and that there were many international social welfare organizations working hard in the country to better the lives of the people. A photographer came over, and we posed for a photo.

"Doctor, I hope you will consider creating one of your worthy projects for our people here in South Africa," Mandela said, taking my hand.

"President Mandela, you can be sure I will," I replied, looking in his eyes to convey my sincerity.

Nelson Mandela's aura was incredibly powerful, and an inescapable positivity surrounded him. What impressed me most about him, however, was his humility and lack of bitterness. His was an example I hoped I would be able to follow regardless of the outcome of my situation with the feds. We said our goodbyes, and as we walked to the elevator, I thanked Michael.

"I told you, Rat. I told you I would arrange it. Isn't he a beautiful man? I adore him."

"Yeah, Michael, that was something else. Thanks! I won't ever forget it."

When we got back to the room, Leann started to cry. She and Mandela had exchanged only a few words, but the experience had deeply moved her.

"I never thought something like this could happen to me," she said, smiling. "I feel like Cinderella."

Leann was raised by a woman she called her grandmother, although they were not related. Grandma Gasky was a friend of her mother's who cared more about Leann than her own mother did. But even with Grandma Gasky pitching in, things were tough. Leann was made fun of in school for being poor and left home for good when she was seventeen, creating a life for herself in New York City out of little more than her desire to dance. I could only imagine how she felt that day with Mandela as she reflected on her own path.

I, too, felt emotional, but inspired. I was not going to let the Lauerson case ruin my life. I had reinvented myself as a rock and roll manager and as a doctor. If I had to, I would do it again. If Mandela could spend twenty-seven years in prison and become the president of South Africa, I could at least take the ominous situation that I was facing and turn it into something positive.

That night, the Super Bowl arena in Sun City was filled beyond capacity. I don't know if the crowd was more excited to see the King of Pop or their beloved, former president. Certainly, seeing them together must have been unforgettable.

The entertainment was terrific. From Angelique Kidjo to Miriam Makeba, the talent kept coming. The highlight was Femi Kuti, the son of the late Fela Kuti, an icon of Nigerian music and an early AIDs victim. Femi performed with a large ensemble including horns, a variety of African percussionists, and dancers in native dress. The house rocked. Michael was on his feet, and even Mandela was moving his body to the music. Next came the moment everyone was waiting for. The master of ceremonies introduced Michael, who was wearing his Andre Kim jacket and dark aviator sunglasses, and presented him with the award.

"Africa, I love you!" Michael yelled to the audience.

Finally, it was time for Mandela's introduction. The MC went on and on, and Mandela walked onstage before he was finished. The crowd broke into song and dance, and Mandela loved it. Michael gave him the check for a million rand, and Mandela spoke about the lack of caring for children that exists in the world.

"This contribution from Michael Jackson, I hope, will inspire people not only in our country, but throughout the world to follow his example and to bring a measure of happiness to our children," he added.

Michael was beaming. He grabbed Mandela's arm, and they left the stage together. The crowd went wild.

The next day we flew with Michael to Frankfurt. We were meeting a friend and going home to New York. Michael had business in Germany and would be going to New York a few days later. He had rented an apartment on the Upper East Side of Manhattan and was planning to spend a few months in the city while he worked on his new album, *Invincible*.

Michael sat in first class on the way there, and we were in business. A short time after takeoff, he came strolling back looking for me. You can imagine the expressions of shock and surprise when the other passengers saw Michael Jackson in the aisle of the plane.

"Here, Rat. You wanted pictures!"

He handed me a plastic bag with all of the pictures from the afternoon with Mandela. I was flabbergasted.

He watched me open the bag, saw my surprise, turned, and walked back up to first class.

He he he....

I could hear that laugh trailing off in the distance.

25

Rebbe Michael

"Secret Neverland: Jackson in Manhattan renting for $75,000"

With headlines like this one in the *New York Observer*, Michael's presence in New York was no secret. The article went on to report that the amount equaled the highest monthly rent ever paid for a townhouse in New York City. According to Wayne, the $75,000 was a bargain. Michael's hotel bill was easily $3,000 to $4,000 a day, and he rented a suite for weeks or even months at a time, whether he was there or not.

The townhouse, a six-story brownstone on East 74th Street, accommodated Michael, Frank, Grace, and the kids comfortably. Frank was now firmly entrenched as Michael's right hand man and often took care of Prince while Grace was busy with Paris. A room on the fifth floor had been converted into a game room with a pool table, video game consoles, fully stocked candy counter, popcorn machine, and movie projector.

Frank bought a variety of mannequins similar to the ones at Neverland and scattered them around the first floor. They included an English butler, a French maid, and a few cartoon characters. Dominating the second floor were two oversized paintings by a French realist named William Bouguereau. Worth millions, both paintings featured angels. Going from the sixth floor to the second floor was a bit strange, with games and toys on one and the irreplaceable art on the other. In many ways, this captured the paradox of Michael, an adult with a taste for high culture and an irrepressible desire to play.

Grace didn't stay around long. Michael desperately wanted to be a good father, and he knew that meant spending time raising his children. He felt the situation in New York allowed him to be more of a full-time parent, so he sent her back to LA shortly after he and his family had settled in Manhattan.

Prince was turning three and Paris was close to two. They could be a handful, but that is where Frank came in. Michael treated Frank like a brother, and the kids loved him. When he and Frank had to be somewhere without the kids, a host of friends, like the Hilton sisters, filled in.

The first time I visited the townhouse after we returned from Europe was in mid-September. I noticed a mezuzah on the doorpost. A mezuzah is a piece of parchment containing inscribed verse from the Torah. Usually placed in a small, tubular metal container attached to the right side of a front door, it designates a home as Jewish and symbolizes God's presence.

"Michael, what's with the Mezuzah?"

He he he....

"You're funny, Rat. Shmuley gave it to me."

"Who?"

"Rabbi Shumley. He's a good friend of Uri Geller."

"The psychic?"

"Yeah. He is a friend. I wanted to meet him, and Mohammad Al Fayed introduced us."

I wasn't surprised that Michael knew Uri Geller. Michael had told me of his interest in magic and illusion. We had never discussed Uri's talents specifically. Our discussion focused on Michael's fascination with the difference between illusion and reality. The topic had come up earlier in the year when we watched magician David Blaine entomb himself underground in a plastic box for what turned out to be an incredible seven days.

Michael's connection with Mohammad Al Fayed had to do with Fayed's ownership of Harrod's department store in London. Michael loved the store, and Fayed would open it for him to shop alone late at night.

"Uri Geller and Shmuley are writing a book together called *The Psychic and the Rabbi*," Michael continued. "I like Shmuley, Rat. You know I like Jewish people."

I knew he did, but much of the public wasn't so sure, especially after the lyrics he had written in "They Don't Care About Us" on the *HIStory* album.

Jew me, sue me
Everybody do me.

Michael had offered a public explanation at the time that read, in part: "The song, in fact, is about the pain of prejudice and hate and is a way to draw attention to social and political problems." It was hard for me to believe Michael was anti-Semitic considering the number of Jewish friends and business associates he had and the way he acted toward me.

"When I was young, I was tutored by a Jewish woman named Rose Fine," he said. "From the time we first started touring until I was eighteen, she came on the road with us. She gave me the love I have for books. Every new city we were in meant Rose and I had a new bookstore to visit."

Even as an adult, one of Michael's favorite pastimes was to browse bookstores the world over for whatever volumes caught his eye.

"So that's where the bookstore thing started."

Michael laughed.

"She changed me."

He became pensive.

"Rose isn't well now," he added. "Janet and I are making sure she's taken care of.

"That's great, Michael."

"She was like our mother when we were on the road. It's what you're supposed to do."

"You're right, but, unfortunately, many people have short memories."

"Rat, I forgot to tell you," he said, changing the subject. "I am going to temple with Shmuley and Uri Geller. You're Jewish. You should come with us."

Michael going to temple? I was surprised, but when I learned it would be the Carlbach Shul on West 79th Street, known the world over as a place of music and dance, I understood. Although it was Orthodox, all were welcome, and I agreed to go.

Rabbi Shmuley Boteach hadn't picked just any night. We were going Saturday evening, October 3, to celebrate Simchat Tora, the most festive night of the Jewish calendar. The holiday marks the completion of the annual cycle of Torah readings and is filled with song and dance. Michael had been to a service before when he went to the bar mitzvah of the son of friends in South Africa, but this would be different. The Orthodox Jews at Carbach Shul practiced a strict form of Judaism. The service would be almost entirely in Hebrew, and the men and women would sit separately.

After my own bar mitzvah, I lost interest in Judaism, I didn't believe the supernatural stories, and I felt all human beings were chosen people, not just those of any one religious group. I practiced my own form of spirituality, encompassing many principles of Buddhism and I hadn't set foot in a temple for years. Having said that, I was born Jewish and am proud of it. Many of the things I believe in, like healing, helping others and redemption, are embedded into the cultural and spiritual traditions of the Jewish people.

A few days before the service, I stopped by the townhouse to find out the details. Shmuley happened to be at the door getting ready to leave. He was short and stocky and wearing wire-rimmed glasses. A black yarmulke covered his head. He smiled through his full, unkempt beard, and as Michael introduced us, we shook hands. When I mentioned I was Michael's doctor, his warm, open expression flashed into one of suspicion. Obviously, he must have assumed I was some "Dr. Feelgood." I feel bad that I never had a chance to dispel his misgivings.

On the night of the service, Michael and I met Uri Geller and Shmuley in front of the synagogue. Michael was wearing a dark shirt and a beautiful red necktie with a diamond tie pin. I think it was the only time I ever saw him in a tie. He had his signature black fedora, but no sunglasses.

As we entered the building, Shmuley handed Michael a prayer shawl. Men were seated to the left and women to the right. It is a small space, maybe accommodating a hundred people or so, but the synagogue was filled to capacity. Most of the men were dressed in traditional Orthodox clothing: a black suit, white shirt, and either a black fedora or a skull cap, and all had "payot," or side curls, a tradition based on a biblical injunction against shaving the sides of your head.

The service had begun, and the congregation was on its feet. Shmuley led us to a pew in the middle of the floor, amid the animated and almost ecstatic praying. It took a while for the people around us to realize who was in their midst. Once they did, it was hard for many to control themselves, especially the teenagers, who couldn't stop giggling and pointing at Michael.

Shmuley handed Michael a prayer book and told him to follow as well as he could in English. The highlight of the service came with the removal of two Torahs from the Ark. That was the signal for a few men to join the rabbi in a procession through the temple aisles.

Those within reach, as is the custom, tried to touch the Torah with a part of their prayer shawl and kiss that part of the shawl. Women reached out and touched the Torah with their prayer book and kissed that. This is a measure of respect and bestows a blessing. As the procession reached us, all eyes were on Michael. He and I hadn't talked about what happens at these services, and I hoped Shmuley had briefed him. Happily, Michael had the edge of his prayer shawl ready to go. By the gratified expressions around us, the congregants deeply appreciated his gesture.

As the Torahs made their way back up to the pulpit, the singing and dancing reached a fever pitch. Michael was absorbed and on his feet with the rest of the congregation, as if he had been attending the services for years. The energy was infectious.

Although my parents weren't especially religious, my grandfather was. He emigrated from Russia as a penniless twelve-year-old in the early 1900s, but eventually launched a successful business and started a synagogue. When I was young, my family spent Passover Seder at his home in Brooklyn with my relatives. We would gather around the table while my grandfather led the service. My cousins knew every word of every song. I listened, snuck a little wine and learned a bit about Judaism. That part of Jewish tradition and culture I liked; it was the dogma that turned me off.

The Simchat Torah service was ending and it was time for the Rabbi to make a short speech. He thanked "Rebbe Michael" for coming and explained that "Rebbe" or rabbi is a term of great respect and denotes a religious or spiritual leader. Michael was radiant. He nodded his head in thanks and put his palms together as a gesture of respect, humility, and gratitude.

On the way back to the apartment, he reflected on the service.

"That was great! You know I am not religious, but I am very spiritual, and there was a special feeling in that room. You felt it, didn't you?"

"Of course. But it was a little hard for me in that setting; I'm not sure I approve of that type of extreme Judaism. Having said that, however, I always appreciate a high level of spiritual energy."

"Rat, it has nothing to do with religion. It's about feeling connected to a higher source. I have that, and that's how I write songs. They come to me even fully written. I dance like that, too. I become a part of the music and my feet move. When I perform, I become one with that spiritual energy."

I believe Michael had access to a higher level of consciousness, especially through his ability to sing and dance. The problem was, he hadn't been able to tap that connection to solve his problems.

"Rat, it's a God-given gift. I want to use the talent God gave me to give people a sense of escapism. All I want to do is to be honest and make people happy."

"I know, and I also know from personal experience that you have to make yourself happy first. If you are not comfortable in your own skin, it's hard to project a positive feeling to others."

"Rat, are *you* comfortable in your skin?"

"Most of the time. That is, if I am not pretending to be someone else."

He laughed.

"It took lots of work and honest personal reflection," I said. "Eventually I was able to see myself for who I was and, over time, make changes in the things I saw that I didn't like. Michael, throughout my life, I've searched for spiritual meaning, read many books, and experimented with drugs, philosophies, and religions. I even practiced a form of Buddhism for a number of years."

"Like Tina Turner," Michael commented.

"Funny you should mention that because it *was* Nichiren Shoshu Buddhism, just like Tina practiced. Now I work with Charles Lawrence, a modern-day shaman who has introduced me to ritual and ceremony as a way to deepen my connection to spirit."

After my drug addiction and rehab, I was lost spiritually, and I needed to fill the void I felt. Indigenous cultures have a deep bond with the Earth and learning about their ways helped me get out of my head and into my heart.

"Yeah, Rat, you told me about Charles."

"I want you to meet him one day. I think you would find him very interesting. He began his own personal journey when he met and worked with Joseph Campbell, author of *The Power of Myth*."

"I'm familiar with Campbell.

"After years of study and working with indigenous peoples, Charles got it. He understood the connection between ritual, ceremony and spiritual enlightenment. I think that's what we felt in the synagogue tonight."

"Hey, Rat, I want to give you something to read."

I had to laugh, "There's that Rose Fine influence again."

At the townhouse, Michael picked up a thin, used paperback from among a large pile of books on a table in the living room.

"Here, Rat, do you know it?"

The book was *Creative Visualization* by Shakti Gawain. I was familiar with it.

"Read it! It has helped me a lot. I use it for meditation."

"Thanks, man. I will."

26

You've Got A Friend

A FEW weeks later, Michael asked me if I knew a good dermatologist. The burn he had sustained on his scalp years before while doing a Pepsi commercial had caused painful scarring. He was self-conscious about it, and Conchita made sure to style his hair so the scar was never seen. No hair grew in that area, and Michael wanted a new dermatologist to take a look.

I called Stu Schwartz, a good friend. He saw Michael and thought he could do a procedure to help with the problem. We scheduled it for the following Friday afternoon.

I hadn't realized the severity of the burn until, when during the procedure, I saw the substantial area of nasty-looking, contracted scar tissue. As he was wrapping up, Stu injected a long-acting local anesthesia to dull Michael's pain for a few hours. We both knew he would have discomfort for several days, and Stu wrote him a prescription for painkillers.

I had agreed to look in on Michael periodically during the weekend. The phone rang early the next morning, and I wasn't surprised to hear Michael's voice.

"Rat, it *really* hurts. Can you come over?"

After the procedure, I had asked Frank to hold onto the pain pills and give them to Michael only if he really needed them, and then, no more than the prescribed amount. I wanted to make sure Michael didn't abuse the pills.

"Did you take anything?" I asked.

"Yeah, Frank gave me a few pain pills, but they aren't working."

I talked with Frank. He'd given Michael two pills an hour before. However, Michael had a low threshold for pain, and this left me between a rock and a hard place, not an uncommon spot for a doctor.

No one wants a patient to suffer, but at what price? Opioid abuse is rampant, in part because doctors don't pay enough attention to their patients' profiles and their potential for addiction. Also, formulations are stronger than in the past, and some doctors prescribe too many pills to be taken over too long a period of time. Even in cases in which pain medication is necessary, I knew from experience that managing its use appropriately is a delicate balance.

"OK. I'll be there in a little while."

I didn't rush; I wanted the effects of the pills to wear off before I arrived. When I got to the townhouse, Michael answered the door in his pajamas. He had a pained expression on his face.

"Why does it hurt so much?"

"Schwartz said it would be a little painful for a while. Let's go upstairs. I want to change your dressing and take a look."

"I need something for the pain!" I could tell that Michael was really uncomfortable by the look on his face and the sound of his voice, but I needed to see the wound to properly evaluate what was going on, and I knew it would be easier to examine if I took the edge off of his pain.

I gave him a deliberately small amount of Demerol. The wound was healing well but the area we operated on was large, and I could understand Michael's need for more pain meds.

We were in the bathroom. He was sitting with his head bent. I was standing, and we were facing the mirror. I focused on the glass and started to laugh.

"Busy mirror today."

I could barely see myself because it was covered with words. Written in big letters in dry erase marker were messages like "Heal the World!" "Make It a Better Place," and "Look Beyond Yourself." Multicolored Post-it notes with reminders about people to call and things to do took up the rest of the space.

He he he....

"You know me."

To distract him, I had brought a surprise get-well gift that I had been waiting for the right time to give him. I handed it to him in the bedroom.

"What's this?" he asked as he tore away the wrapping paper.

His face registered happy surprise when he saw a framed, autographed copy of the first Jackson 5 single ever released.

"*Raaaaaat.* This is great! I don't have a copy."

It was a 1968 song called "Big Boy." It had some regional success, but never went national. I had come across it by accident in the window of an autograph store.

Michael paused and looked at me.

"How did you know about this song?"

"Hey, man, you know I do my homework."

We talked for about an hour. Michael took a phone call, and I got up to leave. He motioned for me to wait and hung up quickly.

"Where are you going?"

"Home," I answered.

I could hear in his voice he wanted me to stay.

"Come on, keep me company until Frank comes back with the kids. Work with me, Rat, *work* with me!"

I laughed and took off my coat. I didn't mind staying longer. Michael liked to have company around, but his distrust got in his way. The extent of his loneliness may be hard to grasp given his popularity, but Michael was shy as a child. When celebrity hit, he was overwhelmed, which caused him to isolate even further. Sure, there were managers, record company people, publicists, and the ever-present security personnel. But most of them weren't friends, and many were only there for what they could get for themselves, without great regard for Michael.

Sometimes I believed Michael thought he wanted to be Howard Hughes. He read books about him, studied the way he lived his life, and in many ways, emulated him. That's where the black fedora came from. But Michael wasn't a recluse. He needed that human connection.

"Rat, which of my songs is your favorite?"

"Man in The Mirror," I answered without hesitation.

"Oh, yeah, of course. That's my mother's favorite too...."

"When you were on the Bad tour and played Madison Square Garden, Somers took me to the concert. You gave him VIP seats. We were right next to Janet. At the time, I was a functional drug addict. Somers didn't know, because I came to work every day.

During high school and college, and while I was in the music business, I experimented with drugs. Once I became a physician, I stopped. Yes, I smoked a joint occasionally, but that was about it. After I was an anesthesiologist, a colleague encouraged me to try a little Fentanyl, assuring me it would improve the boredom of long, drawn-out cases. At first I used it only occasionally and never during work hours, but as time progressed, so did my addiction and my ability to rationalize my behavior. The desire to escape from hours of doing little but watching beeping monitors coupled with the strength of the drug itself drove me deeper and deeper into the abyss of addiction.

"You know, Michael, I'll tell you how arrogant I was. There was a junkie who lived outside on the street not far from Somers' office. I walked past him every day and said to myself, 'Well, at least I can control my habit. I am an anesthesiologist! I understand these drugs, and I would never let myself get to that point.' I couldn't have been more wrong. It took another year or so for me to go to rehab, but that song was always lurking around in the back of my mind."

At that point, I stood up, pointed to Michael, and in my best Michael Jackson voice sang, "Maaaaake that change."

"Powerful words, right?"

"For real."

I hoped he would make the connection to himself.

...

The Millennium concerts were cancelled—I heard the logistics became too expensive—and Michael moved back to LA. I was happy he was out of New York. The trial date was set for mid-January, two months away, and I began going downtown to the federal prosecutors' offices three or four nights a week to review the case and my testimony.

At first we talked about the scheme and how it worked. The problem for the prosecutors was that to laymen, the medical procedures would seem quite complex and difficult to understand, a point the defense would try to use to confuse the jury. The feds hoped that by questioning me and other medical experts, they could get the jury to understand the fraud. They also knew the defense lawyers' strategy would be to go after me personally. Because I was an insider, the jury needed to be convinced I was a liar in order to acquit Lauerson.

An anesthesiologist who worked with me had decided not to cooperate with the government. She was indicted with Lauerson, and she knew intimate details about my history of drug addiction. It wasn't public knowledge because I had gotten help voluntarily, completing a program run by the New York State Medical Society, which was supposed to keep my records sealed.

I was extremely distressed that I would have to tell my story in court. I had successfully addressed my substance abuse eleven years earlier, and that part of my life had nothing to do with this case. Exposing the gory details was solely a way for Lauerson's team to ruin my reputation and distort the jury's impressions of me. Of course, I wasn't proud of my story, but I owned it and had shared it many times in rehab and recovery to help myself and to encourage others to get past their addictions. It would be painfully different in the courtroom.

On February 2, 2000, we wrapped up the evening sessions with a rehearsal in the courtroom I would return to the following day. The room was imposing, with high ceilings and stately windows. Constructed wooden enclosures for the judge, witness, and jury dominated the room. Chris, the lead prosecutor, and I ran through the questions and answers until she was satisfied, and next she played Lauerson's lawyer. She was tough, but thought I handled myself reasonably well. By the end of the session, we both felt I was ready.

I didn't want Leann or other family members present when I testified. The emotional strain was hard enough on them without this added pressure. But I did want some support, so I asked my teacher and friend, Charles, to attend. He and I had been working together for years and had been focusing on my emotional state during this stressful time. I had a tendency to let my anger get the best of me and that was something I couldn't allow to happen on the witness stand.

That night I didn't sleep much. As prepared as I was, I felt incredibly nervous. I arrived at the federal building early, dressed conservatively in my best three-piece suit. The courtroom was packed. I stood outside the room with my lawyer until I heard, "The prosecution calls Dr. Neil Ratner to the stand," and the big double doors to the courtroom swung open.

I took a deep breath and walked down the aisle to the witness box, scarcely noticing a couple of reporters in the back. I got nasty glares from a few of the young women who had worked in Lauerson's office and downright evil looks from many of his patients. I tried to keep my gaze focused straight ahead. As I approached the bench to be sworn in, there was one stare I couldn't avoid. As if they were laser beams tracking a target, Niels' eyes followed my every move. As much as I didn't want to, I gave him a quick glace and saw him shake his head as if to say, "How could you! Go fuck yourself!"

I was on the stand the entire day testifying for the prosecution. The questions and answers went pretty much as we rehearsed, and the drug stuff came out quickly and was only a small part of my testimony. All in all, it felt pretty painless, and the feds were satisfied I had done a good job.

Court wasn't in session the next day. I was at work giving anesthesia for a breast augmentation in a plastic surgeon's office. The receptionist's voice came over the intercom in the OR, "Neil, pick up for Leann. She said it's an emergency." I grabbed the phone.

"The satellite trucks are here," she said sounding frantic. "They're looking for you. I don't know what to do."

"What are you talking about?"

"The concierge called from the lobby. There are three TV trucks in front of the building with reporters looking for Dr. Neil Ratner."

"Oh fuck! Tell them I am not home, and you don't know when I will return. I'll figure something out and call you back in a few minutes."

I had never thought about, nor discussed with the prosecutors, the possibility that any of the reporters might write about me. Stupid on my part. Lauerson was a colorful figure, and he had already used the press to take his side of the case. After all, he was Geraldo Rivera's friend, the "Dyno Gyno."

Calm down and devise a plan.

I called Isis, an anesthesiologist who worked with me. She was off and agreed to go to my apartment and get Leann and my car. They could leave through the underground garage, so no one would see them. Isis would finish my case, and Leann and I would escape to the Hamptons, where we had a small weekend house.

It was all set. As I was waiting for them, a colleague faxed me a page of that morning's *Daily News*. The headline shocked me:

"Doc crocked for 10 years. Stoned even while in O.R."

The New York papers were feasting on the story. Typical of the press, the articles were filled with half-truths and misinformation. Of course, they got most of the bad parts right, and I did almost accidently kill myself in an operating room of a doctor's office. But what the story didn't say is I went to rehab three days later, participated in a three-year doctors' recovery program run by the State of New York, and spent years in individual and group therapy to recover and continue on substance-free. Most importantly, there was no reference to the fact that this was ancient history.

By the time we arrived at the Hamptons, there were phone messages from every surgeon's office informing me that I had been fired. The only saving grace was that no one had my picture. My life was crumbling before my eyes. I was in a total state of despair, and I felt helpless to do anything about it. I was also embarrassed and ashamed. It wasn't so much that the story was out, but the fact that I didn't have a chance to explain it to my friends and colleagues first.

I called my lawyers. They said to sit tight. It would pass. I had one more call to make. Over the past few weeks, I had been worried Lauerson's team would question me about my relationship with Michael. Lauerson knew that I had been on tour with Michael and I was concerned that his lawyers would try to get me to breach patient-doctor confidentiality and disclose details of his treatments, which they would try to use against me. I had made it clear to the prosecutors that testifying about Michael had nothing to do with the case and was not going to happen. They told me not to worry.

I hadn't spoken to Wayne since the beginning of the year. I called.

"Hey, Rat, what's happening? You OK? You don't sound too good."

"No, Wayne. I am not OK. The trial started, and I began my testimony yesterday."

"How did it go?"

"Terrible. The TV trucks are sitting out front of my apartment building, and I am all over the news."

"What!?"

"I told you about the details of my past drug addiction. It all came out in court yesterday."

"I am sorry, Rat. Is it just local or did it go national?"

"I don't know. All I have seen is local."

"I am going to have to tell him."

"I know. Michael knows some stuff. He knows I am in trouble. But I'm worried that when I am questioned by Lauerson's lawyers, they will try to talk about my relationship with him."

"You may have to talk to one of his attorneys but let me tell him and see what he says."

"OK. I hope he is cool with all of this."

"Don't worry, Ratner. He likes you."

Fortunately, the house in the Hamptons was difficult to find and there were no unwanted visitors. Leann and I were left alone.

It was hard for me to see how it would all end. I didn't feel like crying; I just felt hopeless. Would any surgeon ever take me back?

If not, what then? How was I going to redeem myself in the court of public opinion, and how would I make a living?

Chris called. She had seen the newspapers. She knew I would be brutally attacked on Monday when cross-examination began and was worried. She insisted we have a meeting over the weekend and agreed to come out to the Hamptons.

I was screening my calls. Most of the press left messages on my city phone, but a few found the Hamptons' number. Wayne called me back.

"Ratner, he's going to call you in a few minutes, so answer the phone."

I was ready to talk to Michael. I thought he would understand, but I was concerned that I wouldn't be able to prevent his name from being dragged into court.

"Hey, Rat, how are you doing?"

"I've been better."

"Yeah, I know. Wayne called me."

"Yeah, it's bad, Michael. I never told you I almost accidentally killed myself in a plastic surgeon's office. That's what made me realize the need to get help. The story is out and in the press and the worst part is they made it seem like it happened yesterday. Shit, it was more than a decade ago.

"Rat, you know the press. Look at what they have done to me."

"The problem is that because of the bad press, no surgeon wants me in their office. I spent the last fifteen years creating something from nothing. Now, in one afternoon, it's gone."

"Somers, too?"

"Yeah, him too."

"It's OK, Rat. People forget over time. You'll get work again. Somers will take you back."

"I don't know, Michael. Maybe."

"I won't desert you, Rat."

"You don't know how much I appreciate hearing that."

"You are going to find out who your real friends are."

"Yeah, I guess so."

"With me it's all about loyalty. Look at my fans. It's their loyalty that gives me the strength to do what I do, and I give it back to them. That's why when they say, 'I Love you,' I say, 'I love you more.'

"That's how I am with my friends too, Rat. I want my loyalty to give them the strength they need when times are hard. Look at my relationship with Elizabeth. I am there for you too, Rat, and I am not going anywhere. Our journey together has just begun."

I was finally starting to feel a little better and had stopped pacing around the bedroom. Michael's words were in earnest and his tone was comforting. If anyone understood being viciously attacked in the press, it was Michael. I was glad he was around to talk.

"Thanks, Michael, but there is one more thing."

"What's that?"

"I am afraid they are going to attack our relationship in court and try to imply that I am with you only to give you drugs. Don't worry, no matter what, I am not going to say anything. Believe me, I value our friendship too much, and that would break doctor-patient confidentiality. I hope to prevent any discussion at all."

"I'm not worried."

We talked for more than an hour. Then it was time to meet Chris. "Michael, I have to go meet the prosecutor. I'm breathing a little easier, and I really do feel better. Thanks for taking the time to calm me down."

"That's OK, Rat. Stay strong. Remember they can only hurt you if you let them."

27

Witness For The Prosecution

"Doctor Ratner, what drugs are you on right now?!"

Ted Wells, Lauerson's attorney, demanded an answer as he shook his index finger in my face.

Standing mere inches from the witness box, Wells cut an imposing figure. He was a tall, light-skinned black man of about 6'3", who sported a bold mustache. He knew I had been drug free for years and hoped to throw me off balance by shouting and demeaning me. All he succeeded in doing was making me angry. I was prepared to be asked whether I currently used drugs, but I never expected the lead defense attorney to begin his cross examination this way, and it certainly put me on the defensive.

That first morning, Wells focused his entire questioning on drugs beginning with the first time I tried pot at age seventeen. He built a year-by-year chronicle of my usage. At one point, he zeroed in on how I could afford to buy drugs while I was in college. This made me particularly uncomfortable. Although I had earned money on the side playing in a band, my parents by and large had supported me while I was an undergraduate. Wells made it seem as if I was taking my parents' hard-earned money and throwing it all away on drugs.

Hour by hour, he lit into me mercilessly, exploiting the substance use disorder I had struggled with years before, and labeling me a drug addict, a cheat, and a liar.

Since I was cooperating with the government, the prosecutors functioned as my lawyers. They objected vigorously to Wells' line of questioning, but the judge consistently overruled their objections.

Cross-examination went on for days, and by the third session, I was having a lot of trouble controlling my emotions. I was angry and frustrated and wanted to explain things from my point of view. But I was a witness and that was not to be. I could answer questions with only a "yes" or "no." It would be up to the jury to decide which picture of me was correct: the one sketched by the prosecutors or the one painted by Wells and his team.

Before I took the stand on my final day of cross-examination, Chris and I had a long discussion about Michael Jackson. I asked what she would do if Wells brought up my relationship with him. She told me she would object, and that she felt this time the judge would agree with her. Bringing Michael Jackson's name into the court was not only irrelevant and a big distraction, she added, but it was also a violation of patient-doctor confidentiality.

I made it clear to her what I would do if her objections failed. I felt bad enough about testifying against Lauerson. I would not betray Michael and answer questions about him, even if it meant that I was charged with contempt of court.

Each day of my testimony, the court had been filled to capacity. Now it was standing room only. Lauerson had taken his usual seat with his team on the left side of the courtroom. With a mocking smile, Niels, as usual, locked his sights on me.

Without missing a beat, Wells strode toward me, paused for effect, and asked if I knew Michael Jackson. The courtroom audibly hushed. Chris jumped to her feet.

"Objection, your honor! Irrelevant!"

"Overruled."

I hardly had time to give Chris a dirty look.

"Would you give Michael Jackson drugs?" Wells interjected.

"What do you mean by drugs?" I snapped back before the judge

had time to admonish me for not keeping my answers to "yes" or "no."

"You're the anesthesiologist," Wells jumped in. "You tell me."

I looked at Wells and then turned to the judge.

"I'm not going to discuss a patient's personal medical condition," I stated.

Chris sprang to her feet and requested a sidebar conversation. I couldn't hear what the lead attorneys were saying, but it was obvious from their body language that both were presenting passionate arguments. The conversation went on and on and grew increasingly heated.

It looked like the decision could go either way. By now I was extremely anxious and sweating profusely. At one point, I thought I might pass out. It was hard to conceive that I could go to jail for refusing to betray my friend, but I knew that what I was about to do was serious, and I prepared myself for the consequences.

Chris smiled at me on her way back to the prosecution table. I felt a little better, but still held my breath as Judge Pauley announced his decision. Mercifully, he ruled in favor of the prosecution: there would be no more questions about Michael Jackson.

I went home from court that day utterly relieved. It didn't last long. The headline in the next day's *New York Post* screamed: *"Jacko Drug Stunner in Gyno Trial."*

Chris had told me what went on during the sidebar, but I never expected the details to be leaked and become public knowledge. The article went on to say Wells had told the judge I was Michael's personal pusher and gave him drugs on tour. Chris had shot back that my medical relationship with Michael was confidential information and had no business in the trial, nor did it have anything to do with the case. Wells countered that I was engaged in illegal activity and therefore it was fair game. Thankfully, the judge didn't buy Well's argument.

I was grateful and relieved that my part of the trial was over, but as much as I had tried to keep Michael's name out of court and the press, I had failed. Fortunately, Wayne said that when he showed Michael the article, MJ just laughed it off.

For the moment, my criminal problems were over, but a new set of problems were beginning. The New York State Medical Board had contacted my lawyer and demanded I voluntarily surrender my medical license. They weren't concerned about my guilty plea in the Lauerson case. It was all about the story in the press about my drug addiction. The board knew, but didn't care, that eleven years earlier I had successfully completed an extensive three-year program for impaired physicians, which they sanctioned, and I had remained drug free ever since.

The main reason to revoke a medical license is if a doctor, by continuing to practice, poses a threat to the community. The Medical Board is responsible to the public, and bad headlines about doctors always cause the board to try to take quick action, often without investigating first. Clearly, I was not a threat. During the trial, many of Lauerson's patients were witnesses, and they were asked about their anesthetic care. As much as they might have wanted to come down on me for testifying against

Lauerson, not one patient had anything negative to say about the care I had given. As a matter of fact, most praised their anesthetic experience. The prosecutors felt the Board's action was politically motivated, and they thought I should fight them.

I had my lawyer tell the board that I would not voluntarily give up my license, and if they continued to pursue any action against me, they could expect a legal battle. That was enough to make them back off, at least for the moment.

I waited impatiently for the trial to end, and when it did, the jury took weeks to deliver a verdict. Finally, Mike, the FBI agent, called. I could hear that something was wrong.

In criminal trials, the jury must render a unanimous verdict or the trial is declared a mistrial. And that's what happened. A lone female juror refused to convict Niels. In a way, I was relieved. As bad as the fraud was, I didn't want to see Lauerson go to jail for an extended period.

Then Mike dropped the other shoe. The feds were pissed. They were suspicious that Lauerson's team had somehow gotten to the holdout, and there was no way they were going to let Lauerson off. They were determined to make an example of Niels and had immediately petitioned for a new trial.

What would that mean for me? I had done my part. The agent informed me that my deal didn't end until there was resolution of the case. This meant I would have to go through the whole nightmarish ordeal again.

The weight that had been lifted off my shoulders after testifying crashed back down on me. The invasive, humiliating experience would never get easier, and the fact that I had gone through it once was no consolation.

I had to get back to work. The bad press, the trial prep, and the trial had made earning a living impossible, and my financial situation was looking grim. Although I had been a witness for the prosecution, I still had multiple lawyers; a criminal lawyer who negotiated with the prosecution for my plea deal and advised me during the trials and a special lawyer who dealt exclusively with state medical licensing issues. By this point, I had accumulated exorbitant legal bills. Luckily, many of my colleagues had more cases than they could handle. Once I put the word out in the anesthesia community that I was available, I began getting calls. Over time, even some of the surgeons who had fired me hastily after the bad press, relented.

The retrial was set for November 2000, four months in the future. Lauerson, I learned, also had a new lawyer, Gerald Shargel, famous for representing Mafia Boss John Gotti. The same judge, William Pauley, would be presiding.

This time, when I was called to testify in December, I was less nervous and more prepared. But once I got on the witness stand and the questioning began, I was just as uncomfortable as I had been almost a year before.

The courtroom was packed to the rafters, and it seemed Lauerson's supporters had turned out in even greater numbers. Shargel's manner was different than Wells'. Whereas Wells was tough and imposing, Shargel was intellectual and tried to charm the jury. The questions covered the same topics but were worded in such a way that I might answer them differently. Judge Pauley was no kinder, and over the objection of the prosecutors, he permitted Shargel to delve deeply into my past.

As I left the courtroom for the last time, one of Lauerson's old girlfriends followed me out. Leann and I had spent time socially with her and Niels, and I had really liked her. She came up to me, grabbed my hand, and said, "You did what you had to do." It made me feel good that at least one person recognized that I meant no malice towards Niels nor anyone else.

The trial lasted seven weeks and continued into the New Year. This time the jury deliberated for two short days and delivered a verdict of guilty.

I felt greatly relieved the trials were over. Now it was all about the sentencing. I had pled guilty way back in 1998 but would have to wait until Lauerson was sentenced to learn my fate. I had done my part and fully expected to escape prison. Still, I felt bad because I knew Niels was probably going to prison, and with the mandatory sentencing guidelines, his sentence could be up to ten years.

Unfortunately for Lauerson, a few months later while out on bail, he was caught trying to obtain a Danish passport. He was jailed, and his sentencing was delayed until mid-September 2001. Bad luck for me. I would have to wait even longer.

28

Michael, Movies, And Christmas

IN the summer of 2000, in between the two Lauerson trials, Michael unexpectedly invited me to spend a weekend at Neverland. Al Scanlan, or Big Al as he was known at the ranch, was waiting for me when I got off the plane. At six feet tall and about three hundred pounds, the former carny was easy to spot.

We talked through the hour-long drive to Neverland. Big Al had worked for Michael since 1990 as director of maintenance, responsible for the grounds and the attractions. Before, he had traveled from one small town to another fixing carnival rides, sometimes clocking more than three hundred days a year. Now a good portion of his time revolved around the trains at Neverland. He told me he was one of only two of Michael's employees capable of starting up the big steam engine.

"I run the trains from one end of the property to the other," he said, proudly. "Mr. Jackson loves to hear their sound. He says it adds to the magic. My favorite time is when sick and inner-city kids come for the day, and I believe Mr. Jackson is the happiest on those days."

We arrived late. Neverland was dark and strangely quiet. It was after 1 a.m. I said goodnight to Big Al and went to sleep.

I didn't hear from Michael until early the next afternoon. He wanted me to meet him in the theater where he and his friend Mark Lester were hanging out.

Mark Lester, a former British child star, rose to fame as the lead character in the 1968 musical *Oliver*. He and Michael were close, and Mark was godfather to Prince and Paris. When I told Mark I was a doctor, he explained he had stopped acting at age nineteen and became an osteopath. It was interesting to talk to someone who had made a similar career change.

As *Oliver* came on, Michael carefully analyzed each scene. He was surprised when Mark said Peter Sellers, Dick Van Dyke, and Peter O'Toole had all turned down the role of Fagan. Michael added that Elizabeth Taylor had told him she was offered the role of Nancy. Mark topped that by mentioning that Director Carol Reed had considered Shirley Bassey for Nancy, but the studio bosses thought the public wouldn't be ready for a black Nancy.

After the movie, we said our goodbyes to Mark and walked back to the main house.

"Rat, I am getting ready to do a film."

I had read that Michael was going to play Edgar Allen Poe in a major new film.

"The one about Edgar Allen Poe?"

"It's called "The Nightmare of Edgar Allen Poe. It's a great story about the pain he went through writing his stories and about how the characters haunted him before his death."

"Right up your alley," I said, making him laugh.

"Quoth the raven, nevermore," I added as we walked into the living room.

Michael pointed out a glass case sitting on a pedestal. In it was the Best Picture Oscar for *Gone with The Wind*.

"I always wanted this."

"And you paid a lot for it," I replied.

I had read Michael won a bidding war at auction, paying a whopping one and a half million dollars. He smiled slyly. The fact that he showed me an Academy Award wasn't lost on me. Michael wanted to make movies, and he intended them to be very successful.

...

Michael was busy with his album and I was rebuilding my practice, so we saw very little of each other the rest of the summer and fall. But the week before Christmas, he was in New York and invited Leann and me to his hotel for dinner.

When Frank opened the door to the suite, I couldn't believe my eyes. There was a large, magnificently decorated tree, beautifully wrapped presents, a new bicycle, and a working train set. To top it off, Prince and Paris were running around the room chasing a cute golden retriever puppy. The scene was right out of a Christmas movie.

I'm sure I wasn't the only one who talked to Michael about making a memorable Christmas for his kids. However it happened, it was great to see. Leann added the presents we brought to the boxes under the tree.

Prince wanted to show me the puppy.

"Wat, Wat, look, look!"

I bent down.

"Wat, why are your ears so big?"

"No, Prince," Michael said taking him by the hand. "Don't say that. You're not supposed to ask people questions like that."

Prince looked at Michael, gave me a shy smile, buried his head in his father's legs, and ran away.

"Sorry, Rat," Michael apologized.

He tried hard to make sure his kids did the right thing.

"Don't worry about it, man. He'll learn. At least he is observant. I do have big ears. Look!"

I moved my hair away and wiggled my right ear. Not up and down, but back and forth.

...

Michael delivered his new album in June 2001. I received a call from California shortly thereafter.

"I need you to come help me."

"What's up?"

"I'm making the first short film for *Invincible,* and I want you to come for a week."

"Maybe I can do a few days, not a week."

I was working hard at developing new clients, and I didn't want to be away long.

"Come on, Rat."

The film was being shot at Universal Studios, and by the time I arrived, the filming had stopped, and everything was on hold. Michael had walked off the set when the director wanted to darken his skin and fill in his nose with putty. Frank said he was in his room, inconsolable and unwilling to speak to anyone.

One of Michael's most crucial concerns was the way he looked. Although he was never satisfied with his appearance, he was extremely sensitive to critical comments by others.

I told Frank to let Michael know I had arrived and went to my room. Five minutes later, the phone rang.

"Rat, can you believe what they wanted me to do! They think I am *ugly!*"

Michael's voice was shaking, and he was on the verge of tears. I had never questioned him about his reasons for having plastic surgery. I knew it had started with his unhappiness with his nose, and I could only imagine how upset he had gotten when the director suggested changing it.

"What do you care what they think. In the end, it's your film."

"Rat, they think I'm a freak!"

"Yeah? So, are you? I said jokingly.

That got a little laugh.

"Fuck them!" I added.

He he he....

"Don't curse, Rat."

I could hear the hurt in Michael's voice, and I wanted to say something to cheer him up a bit. "Michael, you know beauty is in the eye of the beholder, and millions of people around the world think you are a beautiful person. So what do you care about what some stupid director said?"

"You're right, Rat. I shouldn't let things like that bother me."

"What's most important is how you see yourself."

Michael didn't say anything for a long time. I changed the subject and started talking about myself.

"So, I'm going back to South Africa in a few weeks."

"Really, Rat? How come?"

"It's our twenty-fifth wedding anniversary, and Leann and I want to celebrate in a special way."

"Another wedding?"

"Not exactly Michael. This time we will meet with Credo Mutwa, a renowned Zulu Shaman. My work with Charles has gotten me more interested in shamanism and traditional healing. After I read a book about Credo, I realized how special it would be to have him renew our vows. Besides, I want to talk to him about his methods of traditional healing. The best part is Dan knows Credo and is arranging everything. You should come."

"I wish I could, Rat, but I have to start getting ready for the concerts."

Michael was talking about the concerts celebrating his thirty years in show business. David Guest had organized them for early September at Madison Square Garden in New York City. Two star-studded concerts were planned a day apart and would include a reunion of the Jackson 5. Preparations were under way. I knew Michael was worried. He hadn't done a concert in the states in a long time. We spoke about it a little. Michael asked me to work with him during the few days of the concerts and I agreed.

The rest of my stay at Universal was uneventful. Things calmed down on the set, and the short film got made. I was excited about going to see Credo. After the two trials and all that I had been through, I needed some spiritual support and a morale boost.

29

Triumph And Tragedy

"I must give you an African name."

Credo Mutwa lowered his head and closed his eyes.

"You will be called 'Lembay,' a word that means battle-axe," he continued after a minute or so. "Like an old battle-axe, you have gone through much. I am afraid more is to come. Another seven years of turmoil. Although you may get nicked a few more times, you will succeed in the end."

Credo knew virtually nothing about me or my life. For him to have been perceptive enough to sense what I had been going through was quite impressive, and the name definitely fit. I didn't like the part about seven more years, but I was happy that he, at least, saw a light at the end of the tunnel.

He had just turned eighty years old. Even so, he was striking, weighing more than three hundred pounds and dressed elaborately in a long, purple robe covered at the shoulders by a powder blue shawl. Two necklaces hung around his neck, the larger made of copper with an enormous heart-shaped piece of jade suspended from the center; the smaller, a simple Coptic Cross, hung almost to his waist.

In 1976, a front-page piece in the *Wall Street Journal* had described Credo as "the Pope of all Zulu witch doctors."

We found him living on a small tract not far from our base at Sun City, where he was working with his companion and assistant, Virginia, to develop a model cultural village where tourists could experience Zulu tribal life. Sculptures he had created, depicting a secret African mythology and said to be prophetic, dotted the property. Dan made the introductions, and we stepped into his home.

Leann and I settled on a couch facing the shaman, who eased into a big cushioned chair. I had read that Credo believed alien forces controlled the world, and he was certain he had been abducted. This still didn't prepare me for the large wall mural in front of us that Credo had painted, depicting extra-terrestrial life and aspects of his abduction. He looked at me for a long time, and I could feel a palpable energy emanating from him.

After naming me, he designated Leann "Leenda," or "one of patience." An appropriate title considering all she had been through. He talked to us about marriage as a spiritual union. As such, he said it was crucial to honor and respect the commitments we had made to each other and ourselves.

Our conversation turned to HIV and a plant, *Suderlandia Fructosate* that Credo passionately believed could cure AIDS. He felt it was essential for him to spread the word about the plant, although I never really understood whether any clinical trials had been conducted.

I had invited Charles Lawrence to come with us to South Africa. He knew of the Zulu holy man and appreciated the chance to meet him. Charles presented Credo with a ceremonial Hopi blanket, which humbled and honored him. They talked about a Native elder who was a mutual acquaintance and of Hopi prophecies. As they spoke, a force seemed to fill the room. It was as if, in addition to the conversation we could hear, there was another one going on: a nonverbal energy exchange taking place between the two shamans.

Our ceremony ended with a blessing, and Virginia spread rose petals along our path as we walked outside. However one described it, Credo's vibrations affected Leann and me, and after the ceremony, we both felt a sense of release and calm. Somehow, we knew that eventually everything would be OK. I was sorry Michael hadn't been able to join us.

Charles returned with us to Sun City feeling unwell. The doctor recommended bed rest for a few days, which meant he would miss our safari. Since his spot was paid for, we invited Dan to join us.

Under apartheid, safari was for whites only. Most black South Africans never saw an elephant or a lion unless it was on TV or in a zoo. Dan had gained some limited wildlife experience while working for the Parks Board, but he had never slept in a tented camp deep in the bush.

Mandela sent Dan to the States a few times a year on personal errands, and when he came to New York City, we invited him to stay in our apartment. It was his first time staying in the home of white people, and it worked out so well that from then on, he used our apartment as a base. We told him about the United States, and he taught us about South Africa, not the South Africa that most Americans knew from CNN news bites, but the South Africa Dan had grown up in and still loved.

Dan, Leann, and I took a commercial flight to Maun, Botswana. There we were met by a small aircraft and flown to a grassy clearing close to Xakanaxa Camp in the Okavango Delta, the premier safari location in Botswana. Our first night turned out to be exciting. A young female leopard had been stalking the camp, and that night, the rangers baited a trap to catch her.

Dan had the tent next to ours. The tents were zipped up tight, but we were able to converse through the window screens.

Whooop, whooop, whooop.... I could hear a hyena calling in the distance.

"Lembay, Lembay, did you hear that?"

Dan sounded nervous.

"Just a hyena, Dan. Don't worry, they only eat white meat," we said, laughing.

Later, Leann and I heard the leopard's rasping sound, as if a piece of wood were being sawed. I called out to Dan, but he was asleep.

In the morning, we saw the long beautiful feline pacing back and forth in the cage. I felt bad for her. It was obvious from her skinny frame that she was hungry. The rangers planned to feed her and release her far from humankind.

Dan went home after two nights. I would see him in September when he came to New York for Michael's anniversary concerts. Although Leann and I continued on safari for another week, I was anxious to get home. My efforts to rebuild my practice had been successful, and I was getting busy again.

We got back to New York mid-August, a few weeks before Michael's 30th Anniversary Concerts. Wayne and Michael had become increasingly at odds. None of the financial deals he and Michael's manager were trying to set up had clicked, and Wayne blamed it on Michael. To make matters worse, about nine months prior, Michael had fired Skip, Wayne's brother. Michael thought things didn't run as smoothly with him in charge of security. That may have been true, but I thought Michael was being a little hasty.

Wayne was OK with Michael letting Skip go but firing him the day before Christmas was not cool. About a week before the first concert he called me with distressing news.

"Ratner, I'm quitting."

"What?"

"I have had it with him and his nonsense! And it's not just about Skip. I can't work with him anymore. He isn't the same. I don't like his behavior."

I couldn't believe I was hearing this. I knew Wayne had been unhappy for a while, but I never thought he would walk away. He was super-loyal and as close to Michael as anyone had ever been. Michael had changed in recent months, but I thought it was just the additional stress, and I tried to convince Wayne of this.

"He's just freaked out with the new CD and the concerts."

"No, Ratner, it's more than that."

Obviously, this had been building up in Wayne for a long time. I liked both of them, and I knew each would be unhappy if Wayne left. I could go just so far with Wayne. He hated when I asked too many questions. but I had to try one more time.

"Are you sure, man? You two have been together a long time."

"Ratner, I told you I'm quitting. He will have my letter of resignation before the shows."

I could hear in his voice Wayne was getting angry with me, and I let it go at that.

There was no point trying to reason with him. He was strong willed, and when he made up his mind that was it. But in my heart, I hoped he would reconsider. I felt sorry for them both. Michael was losing one of the most professional and loyal people who ever worked for him, and Wayne was losing the life he had led for twenty-five years.

Two days before the first show, Wayne resigned and called the next day to tell me. The timing seemed intentional. Wayne knew the news would throw Michael off balance and affect the quality of the shows. Wayne, like Leann, was a Scorpio and, although I don't put that much faith in astrology, both could be vindictive at times.

"Ratner, I don't work for that man anymore."

"I hope it's what you want, Wayne."

I could tell he wasn't really listening to me.

"You know what he had the nerve to do? He had Elizabeth Taylor call me. She was trying to convince me to go back with him. Can you believe this shit?"

"That's because he really cares, Wayne."

"Ratner, when I'm done, I'm done."

And he was. Looking back, I think things would have been different and much better if Wayne had stayed around. He was a strong, stabilizing force in Michael's life, and he had always had Michael's back. But Wayne did what he had to in order to keep his own peace of mind.

The day before the first concert, Dan arrived at my apartment. I called Michael to confirm our session and to tell him Dan was in town.

"Rat, why don't you Dan and Leann come to the hotel late in the afternoon before I go to the MTV Video Music Awards?"

The awards show was that night at Lincoln Center, and Michael was going to make a surprise appearance and sing with NSYNC.

"OK. But let's confirm our start time for 11 p.m."

I wanted to make sure he got back quickly so I wasn't waiting around until 1 a.m. or 2 a.m.

We arrived to find Michael seeming weirdly distracted. It wasn't just about Wayne leaving. Michael was tuning out the conversation and, at times, staring off into the distance. Dan and Leann noticed it as well. I hadn't seen Michael much for a few months, and he was definitely different. What I found out many days later was that Frank and members of the Jackson family were worried that Michael had fallen back into a prescription opioid addiction. They had tried a mini intervention a few days earlier, but it had done nothing but annoy and anger Michael.

I didn't question his mood, and after Michael returned from the Video Music Awards, his disposition was improved. We laughed about his performance.

"You looked good dancing to Justin Timberlake's beat boxing." I told him.

"He's great, Rat. I like him a lot, and they all idolize me and always want me to show them some moves."

The treatment I gave him went well, and Michael slept through the night. When I left in the morning, we exchanged a few words. Although it was almost 10 a.m. and he needed to be dressed and ready in an hour or so, he said he was still sleepy and didn't want to get up right then. I knew he was nervous about the show, but Michael was a true professional. I was sure he would work it out and be great.

About 4 p.m., I got a frantic phone call from Frank.

"Rat, I don't know what to do! I can't wake him up."

"What?"

"He must have called the house doctor to get a shot of Demerol. Now he won't get up."

"Oh shit! Is he breathing?" My first thought was a possible overdose.

"That's not the problem. He has to start with makeup and get ready for the show."

Frank was extremely agitated.

"Throw him in the shower, get him some coffee, and force him up, Frank."

My mind was racing. I kept Michael away from narcotics because I knew of his weakness for painkillers, but other doctors didn't.

"OK, OK. I'll call you back."

I thought about going to the hotel but realized I would get angry and make things worse. Frank called back an hour later. Michael was slowly getting it together, and they would be very late.

I knew Michael was uptight about these shows and I understood why. Whoever the group, the pinnacle of the U.S. concert scene was playing at Madison Square Garden. Besides that, he had not played in front of a U.S. audience since the Bad tour in 1989. As nervous as he was, I didn't think he would try to sabotage himself. He had done it before, but not since I had been working with him.

Demerol was his go-to drug when his feelings of fear and discomfort overcame him. Zone out, escape, cancel the show, and tell the world you were sick. I was upset and discouraged that Michael was slipping back into that bad place. I wasn't sure what I could do to help. I had already decided that the propofol treatments would be ending after these concerts, and I had never been effective at stopping him from getting Demerol from other doctors.

I knew how hard it was to stay clean, and I felt bad for my friend. He just didn't get it, and no matter what I, or many others said, he refused to face his demons and get professional help.

Frank gave us great seats in the first loge, not far from the stage. The concert was disappointing. Marlon Brando was there to do I am not sure what, and he bored the crowd. They were tired of waiting for Michael to perform. And when he did, he was good, but not as polished as he could or should have been. We didn't go backstage. I knew it would be crazy, and I hadn't yet decided how I wanted to handle the Demerol episode.

I worked with Michael the evening of September 9, 2001, the night before his second Madison Square Garden concert. Dan was going home the next day and came with me to say goodbye to Michael. Now that he had one of the two concerts under his belt, Michael was more at ease. He and Dan talked for a while. I went into the bedroom to set up. When Dan left, Michael came in and sat on the bed.

"Don't you love Dan, Rat?"

"You know I do. He and I just started a safari business together. I wouldn't have done that if I didn't really trust him. But I don't want to talk about Dan."

"Rat, you sound angry."

"I am! Why *the fuck* did you call the house doctor before the show?"

"Don't curse, Rat."

"Don't tell me what to say, Michael. That was bullshit!"

I was livid and close to losing control. I felt betrayed, and I wanted him to know it.

"It was the pain," he interrupted. "I was afraid my back would give out, and I wouldn't be able to do the show."

"You know what, man. I'm going tell you something you once told me 'Lies run sprints, but the truth runs marathons.' I am really disappointed in you! You didn't have to do that. Did the Demerol make anything better?"

I didn't wait for an answer.

"No. It never does. I was there, Michael, and I know how hard it is."

"I'm sorry, Rat. I'm sorry."

"Forget it. I said what I had to say. Let's talk about something else."

Before I put him to sleep, we needed to calm down. I would have more to say at a later date, but right then it was important that he be in a good frame of mind. We talked about the concert. I could tell Michael had a crush on Britney Spears by the sly little laugh he gave when I told him how hot the two of them looked together.

We ended our conversation in the usual way prior to a treatment, with a creative visualization and a positive affirmation about the next evening's concert on September 10. Before I left in the morning, Michael and I had a short conversation, and I knew from his positive attitude that the show that evening would be much better, and it was.

I was tired, and Leann and I went right home after the show. Dan's visit, working during the day, and staying up all night to monitor Michael had taken its toll. I was glad my schedule would be light for the next day or two.

...

September 11, 2001 was a beautiful, late summer day. Sunshine filled the clear blue sky, and I had only two cases. Both were at Steve Pearlman's office on 60ᵗʰ and Park Avenue and our starting time was 9 a.m. It was 8:15, and I had plenty of time, so I walked there. As I approached the entrance, I waved to the doorman. He was standing outside with a puzzled look on his face.

"Morning, Doc. Strangest thing just happened."

"Good morning. What happened?"

"A plane crashed into the World Trade Center."

"Huh. That is strange, but I think it's happened before. Probably some small private plane."

"No, Doc, they think this was a commercial flight."

"Really?"

That didn't seem right. I went into the office.

"What are you doing here so early?" the office manager asked.

"Nine o'clock case." I answered.

"Ten o'clock" she snapped. I didn't know who made the mistake, but I was irritated and let her know it. She returned a snide remark, which I ignored. I left the office and started toward a coffee shop on Lexington Avenue. A block away, I tried to call Leann. Nothing. No signal. Something was seriously wrong.

I returned to the office. The TV was on and the second plane crashed into the World Trade Center. We watched the third plane hit the Pentagon, and I canceled the cases. I was able to reach Leann on the landline.

"You should come home *now,*" she said anxiously. "There are a few people here watching the news and the smoke from the towers."

"I'm on my way."

I walked out into the street a little after 10 a.m. I couldn't see the Trade Center, but clouds of black smoke poured into the sky from downtown.

As I made my way home, I became aware of people covered in grey ash walking uptown. They looked like zombies—literally covered in ash from head to toe. It was unnerving. I got to my building at about 10:45 a.m. The concierge told me they had just watched the towers fall. Everyone was in a complete state of shock.

I lived on the 40th floor of our building with unobstructed views of the World Trade Center. All I could see now was billowing black smoke. We watched TV for the next few hours as friends and family from around the world called to see if we were OK.

I called the downtown hospitals to volunteer, only to be told they had an abundance of doctors, but no patients to treat. The implications were beyond anything I could imagine. There were thousands of people who worked in the towers. Could they all have died? I was horrified.

One of the first phone calls was from Dan. He had just arrived in Johannesburg.

"Lembay, you OK?"

"We're fine, Dan. Unbelievable, right?"

"Shaaaa. It doesn't seem possible. When I arrived, my phone was filled with messages. People on this side didn't understand. They thought because I was in New York, I must have been killed."

"Who knows what will happen next," I said half to myself.

"Lembay, you and Leann take care of yourself. I have to go. I will try to call again in a couple of days."

The next few days were tense. It seemed as if everything had stopped. Watching fighter jets patrol Manhattan was particularly unnerving.

Charles held a gathering for his spiritual group and invited us to attend. It was a way for people to express themselves after experiencing such an unimaginable tragedy.

He began with a few words. There were fifteen of us sitting in a circle in his living room. We all held hands and spent a few moments in silence. Charles brought out a talking stick. People spoke of where they were when they heard the news, what the past few days had been like, and what effect the attacks had on them. All of the stories were quite poignant and emotional, but nothing compared to the words of Ann Roberts.

She and Charles had been friends for a number of years and had met as a result of Ann's work with Native American causes. Ann was about ten years older than me and was quite unassuming. She traveled the subway, wore a backpack, and had a real down-home way about her. We liked her a lot.

What many people didn't know, and would never have imagined, was she was the daughter of Nelson Rockefeller, the former governor of New York and former vice president of the United States. That made her a member of one of the wealthiest and most powerful families in America.

The talking stick passed to Ann. She began to speak about the idea for the buildings. Her father was governor and her uncle, his brother David Rockefeller, was a real estate developer who later headed Chase Manhattan Bank. The two were determined to get the World Trade Center built and stepped on many toes to get it done. As the two towers began to rise over the skyline, they were called "David" and "Nelson," affectionately by some, sarcastically by others.

As Ann told her story, she began to get agitated.

"I told them not to build those buildings! It was wrong. I told them not to do it. I told them not to do it."

Ann was now beside herself. She covered her face with her hands and began sobbing uncontrollably. I couldn't begin to imagine what it must have been like for her to oppose her father and uncle, two of the most powerful men in America, only to now be proved right. The circle grew silent except for Ann's sobs. Charles got up, walked over, and put his arms around her. The events of 9/11 had left me numb until that moment. The tears came, and as I looked around the room, I wasn't alone.

Michael called a few days after the attacks. He was in New Jersey at the home of Frank's parents. He was a mess.

"Rat, I was supposed to be there. I had a 9 a.m. meeting at the towers."

"This is the one time being late probably saved your life," I said, trying to lighten his mood.

"Rat, I haven't slept in days. All those people! All those people!"

"I know Michael. It's horrible."

We talked for a little while. He wasn't sure how long he was going to stay in New Jersey. By the end of the conversation, he was reflecting on the concerts, the attacks, and all that had happened in the past few days.

"What a week. Right, Rat?"

"Yeah, Michael. You capped off thirty years of success with two wonderful, sold-out concerts at Madison Square Garden, a real triumph. Only to wake up the next morning and experience the greatest attack our country has ever seen. Triumph and tragedy... Triumph and tragedy!"

30

Welcome Back My Friends
To The Show That Never Ends

It had been two weeks since the 9/11 attacks, and New York was an eerie place. The realization that we had been attacked and thousands had died had now sunk in. It was time to pick up the pieces and attempt to get back to life as it was. But that was never going to happen. New York City was a different a place, and we were all changed in some way by what we had experienced.

I wasn't surprised when Christine called to ask me to come to California for the weekend. I had spoken to Michael a few times since 9/11, and he wasn't doing well. He was sleeping less than usual and was more worried than ever about the success of his new album. The fact that he was supposed to have had a meeting at the Twin Towers on the morning of the attack had also really shaken him up.

Invincible was now slated for a late October release, and plans were moving ahead to shoot the videos for the album, or "short films" as Michael called them. He was scheduled to film that weekend, and from the sound of Christine's voice, he needed moral support.

When I mentioned to Leann I was thinking of going to California, she asked about coming along. With New York still on edge, she didn't want to stay there alone. When I asked, Michael said he understood and thought having Leann join us was a great idea.

When I went to medical school in Mexico in the '70s, it was common to see National Guard troops with automatic weapons at airports, but seeing armed soldiers on alert at JFK airport felt disconcerting. What's more, the plane was virtually empty. Not surprisingly, most people weren't ready to fly again.

By the time we landed and arrived at a packed Beverly Hills Hotel, it was evening. I went over to Michael's bungalow after dinner.

The first question Michael asked was, "How's New York?" I could see real concern in his eyes. Michael loved the city. He had many friends living there and spent as much time in NYC as his schedule allowed.

"Very strange," I reflected. "It's like something out of a bad science fiction movie. I don't know if things will ever be the same. New York is grieving and, yet, everyone is on guard. Sometimes I feel like I'm in an armed camp."

"I've been thinking constantly about what happened," Michael said. "It made me rewrite my song, "What More Can I Give." I want to bring us together as a world, and the best way I can do this is with a song."

The strange odyssey of the number that would eventually become "What More Can I Give" had begun years before when the acquittal of the police officers in the Rodney King case had sparked the 1992 LA riots. The episode inspired Michael to write a song tentatively titled "Heal LA." But he put it on hold for a later date.

Then, in 1999, when Michael and Mandela discussed the concept of giving back, it gave Michael the inspiration he needed to finish "Heal LA." But now the title didn't fit, so he changed it to "What More Can I Give." Although Michael had wanted to premiere the tune during his charity tour, he ended up shelving the project for a second time.

Now it was the right time. Deeply affected by 9/11, Michael was motivated to make his song happen.

I wasn't surprised by his resolve. Michael had a heart for the world, and I had figured he would respond in a meaningful way.

"Let me know if I can help in any way."

Since the tragedy I had been looking for a way to do something to help. I remembered the Kenya bombing and how good it felt to be able to volunteer. Now all I felt was frustration at not being able to help alleviate any of the sadness and sorrow. What's more, the thought of all the doctors sitting around the ER waiting for the injured who never arrived still haunted me.

"Rat, the filming is cancelled. I'm in the studio tomorrow, and that's it until Monday. Let's go to Neverland on Saturday for the rest of the weekend. But I have a surprise for Friday night. Be ready at 6:30 and make sure you and Leann dress up!"

When I got back to the room and shared our plans for the weekend with Leann, she could hardly contain her excitement, especially about going to Neverland. I knew she envied the fact that I had been there a few times, and I felt bad I hadn't been able to bring her. It would be great to share the experience and a perfect way to get our minds off the terrible events of the past few weeks.

The Friday night surprise was a mystery. Since Michael could be quite the prankster, I had no idea what he was up to, but I suspected it was something cool.

Late Friday afternoon, Michael's security called: He was stuck at the studio and had pushed our plans back to 7 p.m. The time passed, but by 7:45, we were getting antsy. By 8:30, I didn't care what the surprise was. I was angry. As a road manager and a doctor, I had learned the value of being on time, and I didn't appreciate waiting.

Michael was one of those people who was never on time. I don't think he did it intentionally. He would get distracted by one thing or another forget about the time and keep you waiting. He didn't wear a watch and time in general didn't seem very important to him. But his hurry up and wait way of doing things would drive me crazy since I am an impatient person to begin with. The funny thing was that Michael was very concerned about other people being on time and on a few different occasions had said to me, "Punctuality, Rat, punctuality. It's very important." *Right,* I thought to myself sarcastically.

Leann and I decided to change into casual clothes and get something to eat. I was pulling the door shut when security called again.

"Be downstairs in five."

We quickly changed back into our nicer clothes and left the room. As annoyed as I was, I knew I would be sorry if we didn't go.

We met Michael and the kids in the elevator and continued down to the garage where two amazing limos were idling. Michael pointed to one.

"That's yours, Rat."

The limo was a 1999 Rolls Royce Silver Seraph. That in itself was extraordinary, but what made it really amazing was the interior with its white leather seats surrounded by rich, dark wood paneling. A painted design framed in gold graced the ceiling. Dark blue velvet curtains framed the windows and an antique clock stood on a small table among expensive bottles of alcohol.

I had ridden in plenty of limos, but none decked out like this. It seemed as if we were in a cozy apartment in eighteenth century France, not the back of a Rolls Royce.

The limo Michael climbed into wasn't shabby either. It was a 1990 Silver Spur II with darkly tinted windows and white curtains.

After a short ride to the Hollywood Hills, we pulled into a large circular driveway. It was dark and difficult to see the property. The front door was already open, and Michael and the kids were inside the house by the time we got out of the car.

An attractive blonde was standing in the doorway. As we approached, she extended her hand. I recognized her and was dumbstruck.

"Hi, I'm Angie Dickenson."

At close to 70, the actress, known for her seductive TV and film characters, still looked great. Her personal life had been as interesting as the roles she had played. In her younger days, she was rumored to have gone out with both Frank Sinatra and John F. Kennedy.

I still didn't know whose home we were in. I looked around the living room and saw the pictures of Gregory Peck. And there he was, standing in a corner of the room talking to Michael. It was as if he had stepped right out of a movie screen; Tall with dark glasses, dark hair, great presence, and that distinctive voice.

We were introduced to Gregory and Veronique, his wife of many years. She was elegant and spoke with a slight French accent. Their daughter, Cecelia, son-in-law Daniel, a writer and producer, introduced themselves and their two-year-old son, Harper. He was named after Harper Lee, author of *To Kill a Mockingbird*. Gregory famously played the lawyer Atticus Finch in the movie version of Lee's book.

We had arrived more than two hours late, and dinner was served immediately. The kids went to eat in an adjoining room. There was a conspicuous empty seat at our table.

"Where is Elizabeth?" Michael asked no one in particular.

"Oh, Michael, she waited as long as she could," Veronique answered. "You know Elizabeth. She wasn't feeling well and went home. She knew you would understand."

Of course, they were talking about Elizabeth Taylor. I couldn't believe we had missed her. I could see Michael was upset.

The buffet featured fried chicken and mashed potatoes, one of Michael's favorite meals. Nothing fancy. That was the way he liked it.

It was very important for Michael to have friends like the Pecks. He could be himself with them and let his guard down. He also cherished the idea of an extended family, especially after he had kids, and the Pecks were family to him.

Michael was highly protective of Prince and Paris. I thought it was misguided that he would cover their faces in public, and I told him so repeatedly. He was only trying to protect them, but I felt it increased their isolation. So to be with a family like the Pecks, people who fostered a close atmosphere where the kids could be kids, meant a lot.

When the others found out that Leann and I were from New York and had been in the city on 9/11, the conversation turned to the attack and its aftermath. Gregory had tears in his eyes as we told him of our experience that day. Michael sat quietly and nodded when Veronique asked if he really was to have been at the towers at 9 a.m.

Michael added how he was fearful for his fans, many of whom had traveled great distances to get to the concerts and were stranded. He said he had arranged for a group to be picked up and taken to a hotel in New Jersey until airports opened and they could fly home.

The conversation lightened up when Angie and Veronique began dishing about old Hollywood. Michael loved the stories and peppered the pair with questions between bursts of laughter. Gregory didn't say much, but every now and then he would add an interesting fact.

He sat directly across the table from Leann and me. It was hard to look at him and not see the great characters he played, from Captain Ahab and Atticus Finch to General Douglas MacArthur.

Leann was right at home, and I could see she was having the time of her life. It didn't seem like we were in the house of a Hollywood icon. It was more like a casual dinner with old friends. I knew Michael didn't invite many people to dinners like these, and it meant a lot to know he was comfortable enough with Leann and me to include us.

Before the evening ended, Michael and Gregory went into the bedroom and spoke for about 15 minutes. Michael later told me Gregory was someone he often went to for advice.

After we said our goodbyes, and as I walked back to the limo, Michael tapped me on the shoulder.

"The night isn't over yet, Rat."

"What do you mean?"

"I feel very bad about Elizabeth. I want to go to her house and apologize."

Soon we arrived at a ranch-style home set on a hillside.

The maid, accompanied by a small, white Maltese, answered the door and let us in. The downstairs was tastefully furnished with antiques, plush white carpeting, and a large collection of Impressionist art. In one corner was a bookshelf filled with photos and awards, including a few Oscars. An impressive collection of crystals scattered throughout the downstairs area caught my attention.

The maid said Elizabeth was upstairs in bed.

"Rat, you and Leann wait here with Prince and Paris. I am going to say hello."

Paris kept trying to pick up expensive pieces around the room, and Leann had her hands full making sure she didn't break anything. I kept an eye on Prince. Michael came down after 20 minutes, and we returned to the hotel. Leann and I walked Michael to his bungalow.

"Michael, this was an unbelievable evening! I don't know what to say."

"Rat, Gregory Peck is like a second father to me, and Elizabeth is one of my best friends. I'm sorry you didn't get to meet her. She would have liked you."

"Maybe another time." I shrugged.

"Yeah, there will be another time. Goodnight, Rat." Michael gave Leann a hug and walked inside.

The next morning, we woke up early for the trip to Neverland; the kids couldn't wait to get there. At the guesthouse, Leann was visibly blown away. I could see Michael was enjoying her reaction.

"Rat, you know where the carts are. Take one with Leann. I will meet you at the zoo in about an hour. I want to show you something there."

After we got settled, I brought Leann to the garage where we picked out a Peter Pan golf cart. I drove her around on a quick tour of the grounds before we wrapped up at the zoo.

Michael met us in front of a cage containing two large impressive-looking Bengal tigers, Thriller and Sabu, who were lying together in the corner. Leann and I had seen the big cats of Africa: cheetah, leopard, and lion. But we had never seen tigers close up. There are no tigers in Africa, and we hadn't been to the parts of Asia where they still exist in the wild.

Michael was standing about 10 feet from the cage. As he approached, Thriller stretched out his long, feline limbs, rose, and lumbered over to investigate.

"Leann, come closer," Michael said. "Look at how beautiful they are!"

Leann edged in cautiously. I followed. I thought Michael was going to reach through the bars. Thankfully, he didn't. The tigers were something magnificent to see. It was sad to think that only about 3,000 of these animals remained in the wild. Although Michael said these two were bred in captivity, I noted to myself to raise the question of whether this was the best home for them. But I never got the chance.

Michael showed Leann the reptile house and the aviary, and then went off to play with his kids. We spent the afternoon by the pool and then joined Michael and his kids for dinner. Unlike previous visits to Neverland, that night none of the outside lights were lit. We used flashlights to get from building to building. I was a little bummed because the lights were so beautiful, and I had wanted Leann to experience them.

"What happened to the lights?" I asked Michael.

"We had to go dark, Rat." Michael explained. "The government asked us. Neverland is easy to spot from the air, and after 9/11 they were afraid we could be a target."

After the kids went to bed, the three of us talked late into the night. Michael had an amazing collection of coffee table books on the life and art of the old masters. This brought up a conversation we'd had many times before.

"Rat, were they born geniuses?"

"Nature or nurture again, right?" I answered.

He laughed, "You always say that."

"Whatever it was, either God-given or developed, and I think it was a little bit of both, they created amazing work."

"I never get tired of looking at these pictures," he commented.

It was almost 3 a.m., the help was gone, and we were hungry. Michael was like a little kid.

"Rat, Leann, come on! Let's raid the kitchen."

Leann is a good cook, and I knew she would whip up something tasty.

"Michael, how about eggs, bacon, and toast?" she asked with her head in the refrigerator. "Turkey bacon," he yelled back to Leann. Although not a strict vegetarian Michael ate very little red meat. We feasted, and it was reassuring to see Michael not only eat well but care about what he was eating. We all went to sleep satisfied.

The next morning, as we approached the main house for breakfast, I noticed lots of equipment on the back lawn. I couldn't tell exactly what it was until we got closer. Then I started to laugh.

"What?" Leann asked.

"A couple of years ago, I had a conversation with Michael about sprinklers, and how we loved to run through them as kids," I recalled. "Look over there in the backyard. There must be ten different types."

Sure enough, sprinklers were set up all over the lawn. Spaced between them were water slides. It was like a mini water park. The kids saw us and came running out while Michael followed closely. They were screaming and yelling.

"Wat, Wat, come on, come on!" Prince called to me. He wanted me to run through the sprinklers with him.

"Later Prince," I said with a laugh

"Leave Rat alone, Prince. You and Paris go play!"

With that, the water came on and the kids went frolicking through the sprays.

That evening, Michael wanted to eat in the dining room. It was just the three of us. The table was set beautifully, and we had a nice bottle of wine. It had been a terrific weekend, and this was a great way for it to end.

Afterward, Michael walked us back to the guesthouse. Our suitcases were by the door. I went to grab them, but Michael insisted on carrying Leann's bag to one of the waiting cars. He and the kids got in the other car and we drove back to L.A.

By the time we all returned to the Beverly Hills Hotel, it was quite late. Leann and I were on an early morning flight to New York, so we said our goodbyes as we got out of the car.

"Michael, this was one of the best weekends ever," I said. "Leann and I really needed this after all that's gone on."

"You know, Rat, so did I. The attack affected me just like you, but maybe even more because I was supposed to be there. Neverland was the right place for us to be this weekend...

"But, wait! I have to get something in the bungalow for you and Leann. I'll come to your room."

"OK." I couldn't imagine.

He knocked a few minutes later and handed me a commemorative booklet that had been sold at the thirtieth anniversary concerts.

"Here, I want to write something." He flipped to a page in the back and inscribed,

> "To
> Leann and Ratner
> Our journey
> Has been amazing.
> Let's not forget

We are destined
for a higher
source.
Keep believing
And reaching.

Love and friendship
Always in
Loyalty

Michael Jackson

31

What More Can I Give?

A few days after I returned from California, Michael called to say he was organizing a star-studded 9/11 tribute concert called "United We Stand: What More Can I Give," which would be held at RFK Memorial Stadium in Washington D.C. on October 21, 2001.

"Rat, it's going to be great. We are going to raise *a lot* of money for the families of the victims. You should be there. You said you wanted to do something to help."

I didn't reply. Michael had told me earlier that he had no plans to tour for quite a while, if ever again, once he completed his 30th anniversary concerts. This was fine with me because I was finished with giving him the propofol treatments. I had meant them to be temporary, and they had gone on long enough. Unfortunately, there was nothing to replace them with, and now Michael had an important concert, leaving me very much on the fence.

He took my non-answer as a yes, and a few days later Christine called.

"Hi, Neil, I want to book your flight to Washington."

I didn't respond right away.

"Neil, are you there?"

"I'm here, Christine. It's just that I'm not sure I'm going to come this time."

"Oh no, Neil. You have to come! He is really bad, and we are very concerned that he will not make the show."

The tone of her voice surprised me. Christine was always business-like and rarely interjected her feelings into the conversation. I was not going to get into a discussion with her about what she meant by "bad." Michael was a very private person and as one of Michaels doctor's, I was very conscious of doctor patient confidentiality even when speaking with his personal assistant, Christine. Besides she seemed to have disdain for most of his doctors, and I was sure she wasn't fond of me. However, she was aware of the fact that Michael had never missed a show when I was around.

It was a difficult decision for me. During the years that I had been working with Michael, I expected to be able to transition him into a more natural eating and sleeping pattern especially before concerts. But it never happened, and I was worried that if I didn't go and help him get through this show, Michael might make some choices he would later come to regret.

So I decided to go and help him one last time.

The night before the concert, Michael stayed at a private home in an upscale D.C. neighborhood. I arrived late Saturday evening, and found him there with Frank and Frank's brothers, Eddie and little Dominic, and one more guest, the 21-year-old actor, Macaulay Culkin. I wasn't surprised to see Culkin. Michael spoke of their friendship often and told me how the two looked out for each other. After all, Macaulay was Michael's kids' godfather.

Michael led me upstairs to one of the bedrooms.

"Hey, Rat. How are things?"

"Slowly getting back to normal. You OK?" I asked.

"I'm tired. I haven't slept much for weeks."

To me, Michael didn't look any worse than he had when I'd seen him a few weeks before in California.

"What have you been taking to sleep?"

"Oh, you know, the usual stuff."

I knew he meant Ativan.

"Anything else?"

Michael never told me when he went to other doctors and got Demerol. I didn't expect a positive response, but I wanted him to know what I was thinking.

"No, that's it, and you know those pills don't really work for me anyway."

"Yeah, I know. I really hope you're not taking anything else," I continued. "You know, Michael, at some point you're going to have to deal with your sleep problems in a different way: without pills, shots, or propofol.

He just looked at me.

"We've talked about it before. The propofol treatments are not a solution for any time you have a show. I came tonight because I want to help you get through this concert if your insomnia is still a problem, but this is it."

"OK, Rat, but let's not talk about it now. Tonight, the most important thing is that I get some rest and prepare for the show."

Early the next morning, I went to a nearby hotel where the band, security, and crew were staying. After sleeping a few hours, I went to the gig. I spent most of the evening by the side of the stage watching the acts. Macaulay Culkin joined me. We spoke about a variety of things, and I was impressed with how interesting and personable he was.

Michael came out of his dressing room and joined us to watch Destiny's Child. As Beyoncé left the stage, she saw MJ, gave a wave, and called out, "Hi, Michael." Michael turned and smiled. He and I often compared notes on different acts, and later in the dressing room, I mentioned I didn't think Destiny's Child was so good.

Michael let me have it.

"You're wrong, Rat! Beyoncé is fabulous. One day she will be a very big star!"

It was well into the evening by the time Michael took the stage. He was wearing an unbelievable jacket that his dresser, Michael Bush, had made for him. Covered entirely in sequins, it featured on its front an amazing design of a bald eagle stretched across the chest area with a full-color American flag overlay against a background of silver sequins. Both jacket arms were blue striped with white stars. The outfit was finished off with Michael's signature armband done in bright red sequins.

After an emotional version of "Man in the Mirror," Michael made a speech while the music continued softly. He began by asking everyone to look at the person next to him or her and join hands.

"Now, I ask you for a moment of love and silence. I love you, and tonight We All Stand United and ask, 'What more can I give?' When we leave here tonight, let us take this love and give it to all the people everywhere in every corner of the Earth. And that's what we can share, and that will make the difference, and that will make the change. It's very important!"

Michael usually never said more than a few words at his performances. This was well thought out and from his heart.

"To the families of the victims of September 11 that are here tonight, you are not alone," he said, wrapping up with, "You are in our hearts, you are in our thoughts, and you are in our prayers."

Michael called all the performers to the stage, and the concert ended with the first and last-ever live performance of the song "What More Can I Give."

I saw Michael in the dressing room after the show.

"Hey, man, I am proud of you. That was really good!"

"We had to do it, Rat."

I stayed for a while, chatting and watching other visitors come in and out of the room. Neither I nor anyone else that night knew it, but this would be Michael's last live performance. "What More Can I Give" was the last song he ever sang on stage and, for a variety of reasons mostly related to the executive producer of the project, Marc Shaffel, neither the video of the concert nor the record was ever released.

...

The last time I saw or spoke to Michael Jackson was at the office of Dr. Stu Schwartz in April 2002, about a week before my scheduled sentencing. We spoke before his procedure.

"Hey, Rat, you're nervous, aren't you?"

"Yeah, of course, I am."

"But they said no jail time. Right, Rat? So don't worry."

Michael was trying to comfort me.

"I finished the *Greatest Salesman in The World*," I said, changing the subject. "When you turned me on to Og Mandino, you didn't say much about him or his books. They were deep. I liked him so much I read three others."

"I knew you would. What message did you get out of it?"

He was curious.

"For me, one of the most important lessons was in the first book, 'I will persist until I succeed. The slaughterhouse of failure is not my destiny.'

"But right now, with the turmoil in my life, there's a stronger lesson for me in another of his books: 'Search for the seed of good in every adversity.' I have to keep a positive outlook. Whatever poison comes my way, I am determined to turn it into medicine. One of the things I have learned in life is that the difficult times are the ones that provide the best opportunity for personal growth."

"You'll be OK, Rat."

"What did you get from him?" I asked.

"That I have to be the best at what I do. When I commit to something I will work like there is no tomorrow. I am a salesman. I sell my projects, and, most importantly, I sell myself. Og gave me some powerful tools."

Schwartz poked his head through the door and said he was ready. I turned up the volume on the headphones and gave Michael anesthesia for the last time.

32

Thirty Days In The Hole

ABOUT a week before Michael's concert, Judge Pauley finally sentenced Dr. Niels Lauerson. Whether it was personal hostility, or he just wanted to make an example out of Niels, Pauley was merciless.

"You were a medical doctor at the top of your profession and a public figure at the apex of New York society," U.S. District Judge William H. Pauley III intoned contemptuously. "Your fall from prestige has been Faustian in its dimensions."

Wrapping up, he sentenced Lauerson to serve more than seven years in federal prison. In addition, he required the rash and once-arrogant gynecologist to pay the insurance companies restitution of $3.2 million, which was the amount the prosecutors had calculated the fraud to be worth.

Seven years and more than $3 million? Hardened felons got less time and the amount was beyond jaw-dropping. The whole sentence was excessive. Niels reacted with visible anger and outrage. He had already hired the famed Harvard lawyer, Alan Dershowitz, to handle his appeal, and it now took on greater urgency.

I felt bad for my former friend and colleague, and beyond this, I couldn't help feeling anxious about what was in store for me. Both the prosecutors and my lawyers assured me not to worry. In light of what had just happened, however, I was not comforted.

On April 15, 2002, I entered the federal courthouse to learn my fate. Facing me, the judge declared I was a co-leader of the conspiracy. This meant trouble because it allowed Pauley to give me a stiffer penalty. And so it was: four months in federal prison followed by four months of home confinement and three years' probation. (Home confinement meant I could leave the apartment only for work, exercise, or a doctor's appointment.)

I was trying to wrap my head around what I had just heard, and I almost missed what came next. As a co-leader, the judge said, I was jointly responsible with Lauerson for the restitution of the $3.2 million. The court couldn't care less who paid it back. We were on the hook together until the debt was settled. Not especially fair, I reflected later, given that an anesthesiologist earns about one-tenth the salary of a surgeon.

Stunned, I stormed out of the courtroom without pausing to comment to the prosecutors or my lawyer. My mind was spinning, and I needed to collect my thoughts. The fresh air outside felt good but did nothing to change the reality that I was going to prison. I was in disbelief. I had done everything the feds asked of me, but the judge had the ultimate say, and he ignored recommendations of both the prosecutor and the probation department.

Years later, I learned that a particular incident from my past, which I was required to reveal during both trials, tipped the balance against me in Pauley's eyes. It involved how I got out of the Army during the Vietnam War. In 1969, when I left college to go into the music business, I knew I would lose my educational deferment and possibly get drafted. I strongly opposed the war and was determined not to take part in it. This left me with two choices: I could leave the country or try to get a medical excuse that would get me rejected.

A psychiatrist in Vermont known to be sympathetic to the cause accepted me as a patient. I went to him for a couple of office visits, took some psychological tests, and the doctor wrote a letter stating in detail the psychological reasons I was unfit to serve. It worked for me, but clearly not for the judge.

Now, pulled back into the present, I would need to report to Fort Dix Federal Correctional Institution in three months.

Over the following weeks, I prepared myself as well as I could. I read a book or two about federal prison, talked to a few guys who had been there, exercised a lot, and continued working with Charles. Our therapy sessions gave me the confidence I would be OK. Importantly, he encouraged me to use the experience as an opportunity for growth and personal development. Our last session was two days before I was to surrender myself voluntarily. We spent much of our time going over mental exercises Charles had taught me to quiet my mind. At the end, he had some words of advice:

"Neil, I want you to go away and figure out why you needed this experience. You created this opportunity."

This was difficult to hear, but I knew exactly what he meant. And he was right. Charles had taught me that we are co-creators of our own reality. I had put myself in the position I was in for a reason. Learning to not be a slave to the dollar was certainly a part of it. But going to prison was also a metaphor for something larger. The lesson would be something I couldn't get in any other way. My job was to find out what that lesson was.

"Oh, Neil, and one more thing...."

"What's that, Charles?"

"Have a fucking great time!!"

Charles was not being funny, he actually meant it, but not in a literal sense. His message was about living in the moment and getting the most out of all our experiences, both good and bad.

I hadn't seen or spoken to Michael since giving him anesthesia at Stu's office, and I didn't contact him after the sentencing. Frank called about a week later. He hadn't heard from me, and he was concerned. I gave him a brief rundown and asked him to tell Michael. He said he would and wished me luck.

As soon as I was sentenced, the State Medical Board came after me again. This time they wouldn't give up until they extracted their pound of flesh. I knew my specialist medical lawyer was working on something, and I wasn't surprised when he called me to his office. But it was the day before I had to report to prison, and I was in no shape to listen to what he had to say.

The deal he had negotiated with the State Medical Board called for punishment that had nothing to do with the crime. A license suspension for six months followed by five years in their drug program, the same program I had successfully completed years earlier.

I was incensed, and I let my lawyer know his so-called deal was total bullshit. The case was not about drugs, and I had been proved clean by random drug testing for more than ten years. I was outraged and didn't want to sign. My lawyer pushed harder. He must have told the Board it was a done deal already.

"Don't worry," he boasted to me. "I know the people up in Albany. Let's give them what they want now. We'll go up there and work it out after you're released. At least this way, you can leave with a clear head."

I reluctantly signed. When we went to Albany after I got out of prison, the Board wasn't moved by my lawyer's arguments, and I made my own pleas to no avail. At the end of the meeting, I told the Board and my lawyer that the agreement was unacceptable to me, and as a result, I never went back into the practice of medicine.

...

When it came time for me to surrender myself at the prison, I didn't want to involve family or friends. I asked two FBI agents who had worked on my case if they could help. They picked me up in their unmarked black car with U.S. government plates, and we headed to southern New Jersey. Approaching Fort Dix Correctional Institution on a hot, cloudless July day in 2002, I saw a large building looming over the treetops with guard towers and a fence of double-thick razor wire. We had arrived at the huge facility that housed both the military base and federal prison.

"Holy shit! This is a real prison."

I had prepared myself as well as I could, but how well can you really steel yourself to be incarcerated?

I had initially thought I was going to a "Club Fed," one of the few prison camps around the country that had tennis courts, cable TV, walking paths, and better food. Turned out those were a thing of the past. The judge had agreed to send me to a minimum-security prison camp and, although these weren't as cushy as the Club Feds, they were still the best place to be. They usually had low staff-to-inmate ratios, dormitories, few or no fences, and mostly nonviolent offenders. No one had informed me that I would be spending a week or two in the higher security prison before being sent to the adjacent minimum-security facility.

This place looked like the penitentiaries in old James Cagney and Edward G. Robinson movies. It was scary.

"Neil, we are not going to drive you up to the entrance of the prison," one of the agents said as we approached.

"Why not?"

"There are eyes in the windows. It will be better for you if they don't see you leaving a government car like ours."

Hmmm....

I exited the car wondering what prison would do to me.

Could I use the example of Nelson Mandela or would I end up an angry bitter man?

With that thought in mind, I walked toward the Fort Dix Correctional Facility.

A few minutes later, I stood in front of a blacked-out window with a camera lens aimed at my face. I had read that I was permitted to bring prescribed medication, and I carried a bag with a few drugs that I thought I might need, like antibiotics and allergy pills, in one hand. In the other, I held my eyeglasses.

"Name!" commanded a menacing voice from behind the window.

"Neil Ratner."

"What did you bring with you? A fucking pharmacy?"

I kept quiet.

"Look directly at the lens."

I heard the loud click of a camera followed by the sound of the faceless voice.

"Welcome to Fort Dix." This time the tone of sarcasm was unmistakable.

A corrections officer escorted me into a dingy, almost empty room. On one side were a few large cartons filled with laundered, but ratty T-shirts, old pants, and flimsy espadrilles. On the other side was a small empty carton.

"Strip naked," the officer directed, adding "Put your clothes in the empty carton."

"Bend over and spread 'em."

It was an unbelievably degrading experience.

I picked up a T-shirt, pants, and a pair of slippers. In another room, I received a towel, a sheet, a pillowcase, a bag containing basic toiletries, and two rolls of toilet paper. Prison time had begun.

After being processed in the administration building, a corrections officer led me to one of eight old Army barracks. They were long nondescript two and three-story brick buildings built during World War II. The officer took me to a dormitory-style room with eight bunk beds lined up four to a wall. Tall gray metal lockers stood on either side of the beds.

"This upper is yours," he said, pointing to a bed near the door.

"What about a locker?"

"That one," he said and left.   A young black guy with a head full of cornrows was sleeping next to my locker. It was 2:30 p.m. and he was the only one in the room. I woke him up. He was not a happy camper. He didn't say a word, but never took his eyes off me as he cleaned his things out of the locker that was now mine.

He removed items of clothing, a few rolls of toilet paper, and more than ten sardine-size cans of mackerel.

What an odd food choice and why so many?

It didn't take long to find out. Business exists anywhere there are enterprising individuals. The only thing unusual in prison was the unit of currency. Although cigarettes may have been used to trade for goods and services at one time, in the new millennium, the unit of currency was a can of "mack" as it was called. Cans were wrapped in red paper, contained two fish filets, and could be bought at the commissary for a dollar and five cents. It was treated as the equivalent of a buck.

If you wanted your laundry washed, dried, and folded, it cost three macks; it was ten macks to have your room cleaned. You could also eat the contents as a good source of protein, and many people did.

An inmate could buy up to twenty cans at a time, and stock no more than fifty cans in a locker. Stiff punishment, including time in solitary confinement, was in store for both the buyer and the entrepreneur if they got caught exchanging macks for goods. The guards busted inmates whenever they could, but they knew they were never going to stop the commerce. After all, prison was filled with criminals.

I sat on my bed for a few minutes, but I couldn't sit still. I was upset from all that had already happened that day, and I desperately needed some fresh air.

Behind the housing units was a large field with a baseball diamond and a running track. Groups of inmates hung out, seemingly segregated by race and color, and the clusters included some threatening and scary-looking characters. I didn't want to make eye contact with anyone.

I felt lost and disoriented. Fort Dix prison had 4,299 other inmates and me, and I stuck out like a sore thumb. Aside from the fact that the prison had a predominantly young nonwhite population, I was the only one dressed in a t-shirt, old chinos and slippers. The rest of the population was dressed in standard prison issued khakis which I would eventually get. But since I had arrived late on a Friday afternoon, when the storehouse was closed, I would have to get by with what I was given at admissions until Monday morning when the storehouse reopened.

I walked the compound for more than an hour trying to grasp the reality that I was really in prison. I had been an occasional smoker but, in that moment, I was craving a cigarette. There were plenty of people smoking, but none I felt comfortable approaching, especially to bum a smoke.

Finally, I saw a tall skinny white guy with unkempt thin gray hair smoking a cigarette off in a corner. He didn't look too threatening, and I decided to approach him.

John was about sixty years old. He was wearing a pair of poorly fitted, large black glasses. He handed me a cigarette, and we began to talk.

"What are you in for?" I asked.

"You shouldn't ask guys in here that question."

"Why?" I responded nervously.

"Most inmates think they don't belong here, and some get very touchy talking about the situation that put them here."

"I don't mind talking about it," he continued. "I was involved in health food stores in Florida and got sentenced to three years for selling bogus vitamins. I have less than a year to go. What about you?"

"I'm in for insurance fraud."

"How long?"

"Four months."

John gave me a strange look.

"That's a pretty short sentence."

"I cooperated with the government," I answered. "I shouldn't have gotten any time."

He looked me in the eye and schooled me:

"That's the second thing you don't want to be talking about in here. Being labeled a snitch could get you into a lot of trouble."

How stupid could I be? I had to be more careful.

We talked for a while longer. He wished me luck. I felt completely overwhelmed.

That first night etched itself into my brain. The air was thick and sticky, with only a couple of useless, large fans blowing around the July heat. The night was equally thick with humanity. More than one hundred and fifty men of assorted races, colors, and levels of rage were crowded together in a large recreation room, shouting, trash talking, and singing in a cacophony of languages, all against the background of the blaring TV. Meanwhile, the six microwave ovens against the back wall were continuously in use, reheating everything from rice and beans to spicy curry.

I sat in an easy chair in the lounge area and closed my eyes. The sounds and smells transported me to the open-air markets of Africa's slums. In my mind's eye, I could see the African women dressed in brightly colored wraps hawking their vegetables and fresh killed meat. A loud car commercial snapped me back to reality. Lights went out at 11:30 p.m., but the TV droned on until two.

The mattress on my bed was basically four sides with no middle and looked left over from World War II. I tossed and turned for what seemed like forever. The hour hand on the wall clock crawled toward 4 a.m. while I tried to come to grips with my situation. Obsessively, I rewound a certain conversation I had at Lauerson's office years before. Louise Weidel, the embryologist, had just spoken to me. She was worried.

"Neil, do you think we will all go to jail for this?"

"No, Louise, if there is a problem, it will be Lauerson's problem. Don't worry about it. We'll be cool."

Thinking back to that comment, I was ashamed of my arrogance.

It took a few weeks to get phone privileges. The first person I spoke with was Leann. Although I had only been gone a few weeks, I could hear the loneliness in her voice.

Most days during our twenty-six-year marriage, we had always tried to eat at least a meal together and have a little chat, and now I wasn't there.

She brought me up to date and told me about a few conversations she had had with my parents. By then they had accepted the fact that their son was in jail, but they were private people who didn't like to air their dirty laundry and since the case was public, and everyone was aware of my fate, it placed additional stress on them.

I felt very badly about putting Leann and my parents in the position they were in and spent many prison hours thinking about the consequences of my actions on others close to me.

Next, Leann told me about the surprise call she had received. From the soft-spoken voice, she knew right away it was Michael. He asked to speak to me, and Leann told him I was serving time. He said he knew, but he just wanted to be sure that I was OK.

Leann told him she hadn't spoken to me yet but that she was confident I would be all right. Michael agreed, and the call was over. Leann and I talked for a few more minutes. She told me not to worry, that she was strong and we would both get through this rough time.

I hung up and nodded to the next inmate, whose turn it was for his ten minutes on the telephone. Calls were made from designated phones located in a public hallway, and inmates lined up before the time permitted for phone use.

As I walked back to the lounge, I realized how different my life in prison was from the somewhat charmed life I had led. It was a sobering thought, but at least I gained a little solace from knowing that my friend Michael Jackson had cared enough to call to see how I was getting along.

33

Unexpected Benefits

Two weeks after I arrived at Fort Dix, I was transferred from the main part of the prison to the low-security camp across the street.

Before the summer of 2002, the word "camp" meant the place where I spent my summers when I was young, bunking in a cabin with friends, having fun, and being away from my parents. More recently, it meant going on safari and staying in a tent deep in the bush surrounded by wildlife. This camp was entirely different, and now the word would never hold the same meaning for me.

The lower-security prison camp was a big improvement from the 1930s-style penitentiary I had just come from. The double razor wire and the fences were gone, but I was still incarcerated.

Four hundred and fifty of us lived in one building. The only other camp facility was about a hundred yards away. I would get to know it well since it would become the site of my employment: the kitchen and dining room. Outside of the kitchen was a large open area with picnic tables and two covered areas with cement benches, which to my surprise were outdoor TV viewing areas.

One evening after dinner, I wandered over to a picnic table close to the housing unit, and I heard what seemed to be live music. I followed the sounds to a closed door with a sign on it, "Authorized Inmates Only." I hesitated, not wanting to get into trouble, but I decided to take my chances. I turned the knob and stepped into the room.

What I saw in front of me seemed like a mirage: A live Latin rock band was playing "Oye Como Va," a song by Tito Puente, most famously covered by Santana. The ensemble included two guitar players, a bass player, a keyboard player, a drummer, and a few guys playing a variety of Latin percussion instruments. There were as many onlookers as the room could hold.

I listened for a while. Most of these guys were good. I noticed a cowbell on the floor, and I couldn't resist picking it up and joining in. Although I hadn't played in a band in quite a few years, drumming and playing percussion was like riding a bicycle, once you learned the basics, it was something you never forgot. Nobody objected, and I continued for the rest of the rehearsal. I knew somehow, I had to play in that band.

There was one guy the other musicians called Ramon. He commanded a lot of respect and was obviously the bandleader. He was in his late thirties and was a real tough guy. I latter found out that Ramon was a bona fide musician prior to being incarcerated, and it showed.

I walked up to him as the room was emptying.

"I saw the way you played the cowbell. You played before?"

He wasn't interested in small talk.

"Si, puedo tocar," I said.

He looked at me with surprise.

"Come back next weekend."

He had a smile on his face.

The music room opened at 5 p.m. every Saturday night, and I made sure to get there very early the following week. Luckily there was no bongo player in the band. Not that I had any real expertise in playing bongos, but I could get by. After a song or two, Ramon, caught the vibe that I was a real drummer. He suggested putting the bongos on a stand so I could play them with sticks.

Carl, a white former construction worker, was the band's drummer. I knew I could play better than him, but this was not the circumstance to be pushy.

I was quickly accepted as a member of the group with the advantage that I spoke Spanish. When you are in a prison environment where more than 60 percent of the inmates are Latino, you command more respect when you speak and understand their language.

As Labor Day approached, Ramon told us we would be doing a show for the camp. The band had done shows before, so this was not uncommon.

A new set of Pearl drums arrived. Although I was enjoying the bongos, I longed to play on the kit. Of course, Carl was excited, too, and he claimed that with the new set, he could play the drums much better.

Ramon was a tyrant in the music room with no tolerance for mediocrity. He acted like we were a professional band playing every week for big money. At a rehearsal before the gig, Carl couldn't keep up on one of the tunes. He and Ramon got into it, and Ramon told him to let me sit in on that song. As long as it was Ramon who suggested it, I was pretty sure Carl wouldn't be pissed off at me, and he wasn't. Fortunately, Ramon was happy with my chops, and at last, I got my chance to play the drum set.

On Labor Day, steady rain ended the plan to hold our show outdoors. It was moved to the visiting room, a too-small space for the hundred or so inmates, visitors, and guards who packed in to hear us. Still the crowd was extremely enthusiastic.

I played the bongos at the beginning of the set.

"Now we are going old school with Neil on the drums," Ramon announced.

My style of playing was representative of '70s R&B and funk. Luckily Elliot, another non-Latino, and also the piano player, was also from that era.

Ramon featured me playing the kit for three songs. The few new prison friends I had made cheered loudly every time I did a drum break. It was easy to forget where I was. I was living in the moment and I was finally—and, ironically—where I had wanted to be for so many years: on stage playing drums.

...

Gary Lloyd had a country way about him with an easy-going manner and a slight southern drawl. Even though we were in a prison work camp, and everyone had to have a job, Gary never did. Each time he was assigned to work, he was able to finagle his way out of it. He owned a big farm in southern New Jersey and had been busted for running a methamphetamine lab.

I liked Gary and we talked often. When I told him about Charles and my interest in Native American spirituality, I was surprised to hear that he had let a group of Native Americans build a sweat lodge on his property. But what he said next floored me, "You know there is a sweat lodge right here at the camp, and there is a chief and a group of people that holds a ceremony and sweat lodge every week."

Even though Gary had never done sweat lodge, he had really wanted to approach the chief, but he was waiting for someone who would participate with him. He asked if I would be interested.

"Are you kidding me?" I told Gary excitedly. "I haven't done it yet either, but Charles and I spoke about it often, and I am very familiar with the ceremony and its meaning."

He said he would ask the chief. A few days later, Gary told me we were invited to come to their meeting Friday night after dinner.

Clyde Rogers, the chief and leader of the Native American group at Fort Dix, was about my age. He was 5'10", of average build, and had heavily tattooed arms. His salt-and-pepper hair was long and pulled back into a ponytail, and he wore a bandana tied around his forehead. His face had a weathered look, and his eyes seemed to convey hard-fought wisdom.

I introduced myself and told him of my experience with Charles and the Native American community.

"Brother, here you don't have to be Native American to participate in the group," he said. "All that's necessary is an honest desire to learn, and I can see by your experience that you have that. I welcome you both!"

"How is it possible to have a sweat lodge in prison?"

"Religious freedom is every prisoner's right," Clyde answered. "That means all religions."

He went on to tell us about a 1972 U.S. Supreme Court decision that found, "Reasonable opportunities must be afforded to all prisoners to exercise the religious freedom guaranteed by the First and Fourteenth Amendments without fear of penalty."

We were sitting in a fenced-off area in a corner of the prison yard specifically designated for sweat lodge. There was a small, prefabricated wooden shed, which contained blankets and firewood, a large fire pit, a smaller fire pit, and an area with log stumps for sitting and talking.

I arrived the next morning at 7 a.m. As a group of us constructed the sweat lodge, another inmate, the designated fire-keeper, stoked a large fire, at the bottom of which were molten rocks, or grandfathers, as they were called.

The sweat lodge structure, or inipi, had to be built and taken down for each ceremony. Constructed of blankets layered over a willow frame, once complete, the inipi was pitch black inside and almost airtight. Some of the blankets formed a door, which could only be opened from the outside.

I knew from my previous spiritual work that once you commit to going through any type of challenging emotional experience, suppressed feelings come to the surface, and I was anxious about this. But the sense of community and the spiritual nature of what we were doing helped to keep my uncomfortable feelings under control.

It was a hot August morning with the temperature in the mid-eighties. There were five of us. After stripping down to a pair of gym shorts and being purified with smoke (smudged), I entered the inipi already sweating.

The ceremony consisted of four parts called doors, each lasting approximately fifteen minutes. This meant four separate sessions with the sweat lodge closed to the outside. Drinking water was allowed only between doors when the inipi was opened.

Clyde called for the grandfathers. Seven molten rocks were taken from the large fire pit outside and placed in the small pit dug inside the inipi. I could feel the heat emanating from each one as it was added into the pit. Once the seven were in place, the opening was closed. The proximity of the heat was a new experience. It was like being attacked by little hot pins and needles, and it took a few minutes to get used to.

The first door began. Clyde beat a drum and chanted Native American prayers. We had been given a copy of the songs and prayers the day before, and we all joined in. As the ceremony went on, I understood why Clyde was the chief. He knew how to keep the group engaged, and he made sure everyone was an integral part of what was going on.

We went through different songs intermingled with periods of prayer and encouragement. Towards the end of the first door, Clyde began pouring water on to the rocks. I felt like the waves of heat and steam would scald me. At times I didn't think I could stand the intensity, but I was determined to persevere.

Just when I thought I couldn't take it anymore, Clyde yelled "Mitakuye Oyasin" (all my relations), a Lakota phrase used to symbolize the harmony of all life. It was also a signal for the fire-keeper to open the door to the outside. Although I was drenched in sweat, I felt strangely peaceful.

We had a brief respite to drink water, after which the fire-keeper brought in the next seven grandfathers and closed the inipi. As the second door began, I became seriously uncomfortable. It wasn't only the stifling heat. The sweat lodge is not just a place of purification for the body. More essentially, it is for purification of the soul. I knew I had to confront my demons and go through a painful personal encounter.

I wrestled with my thoughts in the baking heat, trying to overcome the idea that I was a failure in life. The extreme closeness of the heat was getting to me, and I remembered something Clyde had said, "If the heat gets too intense, get as close to the ground as possible."

I kept creeping lower and lower until I felt as if I was talking to the grass. Clyde began to speak, but I just wanted him to finish. He poured more water on the rocks and it was suffocating. Mercifully, after what seemed like hours, but was just about fifteen minutes, he yelled, "Mitakuye Oyasin" and the ceremony ended.

I had had it. I didn't think I could take anymore. Then a curious thing happened. We drank some water and did a pipe ceremony during our short break. In the Native American tradition, a combination of tobacco and herbs are smoked through a special pipe, and the smoke is meant to carry prayers to spirit. Strange as it may seem, the ritual gave me renewed energy and the strength and determination to continue.

By the time the third door began, my previous feelings of discomfort were gone. They were replaced by a profound sense of peacefulness and serenity. As hot as it was, and it was intensely hot, I was able to dissociate from my body throughout the third door. As it ended, and Clyde poured water over the rocks, I stayed in an upright sitting position. My body felt immune to the heat.

In between the third and fourth door, it was as if I was somewhere else. My body felt like spirit had wrapped me in a blanket of comfort. My mind was at peace.

The last ceremony was the shortest, but the most intense. Seven more grandfathers were put into the pit making a total of twenty-eight. But for me, this was no problem. I was spiritually in another dimension. As Roger poured water on the rocks, I welcomed the steam and the intense heat. When he shouted "Mitake Oyasin!" for the last time, I yelled "A ho!" a native expression I learned from Charles, which literally means, "I agree with you," but is often used as a substitute for "Amen."

Walking out of our special fenced-in area into the main part of the camp seemed like traveling back into another, now incomprehensible dimension. The reality of where I was smacked into me like a clear glass wall. Prison.

Maybe so, but as I suddenly comprehended, I was different. For me, prison life had come with a certain base level of nervousness and unease, feelings that I suddenly no longer had. In that moment, I felt instead a sense of peace and calm. I didn't know how long the feeling would last, but I knew I would be back the following week and every week thereafter until I walked free.

I participated in sweat lodge for the next ten weeks. Each ceremony was unique, but the best came last. Clyde addressed the group the night before my last sweat.

"Neil, our brother, will be with us for the final time tomorrow. We will do five doors and the last is dedicated to him."

I was surprised and honored, but I protested that this wasn't necessary. "We send all of our brothers out in the world this way," Clyde replied, looking me in the eyes. "No one has ever returned. It's strong medicine."

Returning his gaze, I knew he meant it.

Clyde was a man I came to admire greatly. He told me he was in for drugs and sentenced to fourteen years, but he never discussed the circumstances. As he explained it, he was not a good person in his younger days. He didn't follow the way of his people, and he did bad things. This was not the Clyde I had come to know;

humble, wise, caring, deeply spiritual, and committed to living his life in a positive way. Over the years, he had come to grips with himself and made profound changes. Before prison, he trusted no one. Now he trusted spirit. He had learned patience, tolerance, and the ability to be honest with himself. Prison didn't rehabilitate him. He used the experience to rehabilitate himself.

The fifth door began much the same way as the others––with the beating of the drum accompanied by chanting and singing. Clyde spoke of my participation in the circle and my strength in the lodge. I had a tremendous amount of emotion built up inside of me. Throughout my entire five-and-a-half-year ordeal, I hadn't shed a tear. Now I couldn't hold on any longer. The well of emotion I had been adding to for all those years erupted. The tears would not stop. When it was time for me to speak, I couldn't even express the words I wanted to say. It wasn't until we left the inipi that I composed myself and thanked the group for the strength and support they had given me. Letting go of all that sadness, shame, and sorrow lifted a great weight off my shoulders.

I wasn't a big shot New York doctor in jail or Michael Jackson's friend, or a rock-and-roll entrepreneur, I was just another inmate and, believe me, it was a humbling experience. How could I not have gratitude for the life I had, especially when I looked around and saw so many young black and Hispanic inmates who ended up in jail mainly because of the life they were born into?

I left prison a better person than when I arrived, more patient and tolerant, and much more appreciative of my freedom. I wasn't sure what life had in store for me, but I was sure that I was ready and eager to turn the page and start anew.

34

Road To Redemption

IT was ten o'clock on a beautiful mid-November morning, and I was relishing the fact that in a short time I would be free again. A group of us who were ready for discharge had been moved to a large holding room. Our papers were stamped, and a guard walked us to the open front gate.

Four months of prison was over. Although I was never threatened in any way, I still felt tremendously relieved to be out. I scanned the group of cars parked outside the entrance to Fort Dix, and immediately spotted the one belonging to my parents. Leann was back in the city getting the apartment ready for my arrival.

We stopped at the first gas station we saw, and I went into the bathroom and happily changed out of the khaki shirt and pants that had been my prison uniform. It felt amazing to be free and wearing normal street clothes again, but many challenges lay ahead.

Since I was not going to abide by the deal the medical board was insisting on, my life as an anesthesiologist was over. I had mixed feelings. On the one hand, I was deeply saddened that I would no longer be able to practice as a physician. I had very much enjoyed the challenge of taking a treatment room in a doctor's office and making it into a safe comfortable operating room. And there was nothing like the feeling of satisfaction I got when a patient opened their eyes at the end of the operation after a successful anesthetic experience. On the other, I was thankful that my life as an office anesthesiologist was over. Every day I had gone to work with the fear that I might hurt somebody. Fortunately, I never had, and now it wasn't something I had to think about anymore.

Under the terms of my home confinement, I would spend the following four months mostly in my apartment. I didn't have a job to go to, but I was determined to use my time well. The first thing I did was buy a set of electronic drums. Playing in jail had reignited my love of drumming, and I knew the discipline of practicing every day would put me in a good frame of mind.

I had a little money left from my years in practice, and it was going fast. Added to this, wondering how I could ever pay restitution had become a recurring nightmare, jolting me awake on many nights. Luckily, as it turned out, the feds understood my position. They let me know that as long as I paid something every month, they would be satisfied.

Now that medicine was no longer a part of my, life, I looked into working in the music business again. Gary Hasse and another producer I had worked with at the Dream Factory both needed help with management. This provided me with a small stream of income, but not nearly enough to support Leann and myself.

I was surprised and pleased when my father offered to help create an opportunity for me. An old friend of mine from high school that my dad knew and liked owned a construction company in Woodstock, New York, about ninety miles north of Manhattan.

He felt the two of us could get along in a business venture, and he would make that possible by financing the building of a house. I could draw a small salary during the construction and see if the business interested me.

As I spent more time in the Woodstock area, I began to think the town would make a perfect new home for Leann and me. Made famous by the 1969 music festival, Woodstock had attracted a unique blend of musicians, artists, writers, and free-spirited people. And funny enough, I had started my journey in the music business living with Edgar Winter's White Trash in Clinton Corners, just across the Hudson River from Woodstock. At first Leann was hesitant to leave the city, but as she got to know the area, she liked Woodstock as much as I did.

The construction business wasn't one that attracted me. What's more, the market was soft, and our efforts earned no profit. There was a huge upside to the experience however: It got Leann and me to Woodstock.

We rented an old house right outside of town with a big yard and a screened-in porch. After settling in, I got to work on a new project creating an internet-based, digital record label.

I also got in the habit of reading the *Woodstock Times,* our once-a-week local newspaper. About a year after we arrived, an article caught my eye. It featured Dan Leader, the Woodstock-based owner and founder of a small successful bakery chain called Bread Alone. In the piece, he described the satisfaction he had gained from teaching a bread-baking class to a group of HIV-positive moms in Johannesburg. Dan had traveled there as a consultant for a grocery chain and had visited Nkosi's Haven, a compound that housed single HIV-positive women and their children.

I understood Dan's feelings from the years I'd spent working in Kenya. Being involved in charity work had been profound for me, and I missed having a project to work on. One thing I had thought a lot about in prison was how important it was to give back. Even with my misadventures, I had been an incredibly fortunate person. The best way to express my gratitude, I knew, was to join in some type of volunteer charity work. I also remembered my conversation with Mandela:

"Doctor, I hope you will consider coming to South Africa to create one of your worthy projects for our people."

"President Mandela, you can be sure I will."

I had many contacts in South Africa, and as I read more of the article, I envisioned Dan and me working together on some sort of project there. Mutual friends put us in touch, and we met at Dan's bakery, a cozy spot in downtown Woodstock fragrant with the smell of fresh baked bread. Dan was about ten years younger than me, divorced twice, businesslike, and completely open to collaborating. Our initial idea was to make inexpensive healthy whole-grain bread, but we were unclear about where it would be made and how it would be distributed. We quickly realized we could do better: Why not build the bakery to make the bread?

"Give a man a loaf of bread and you feed him for a day. Teach a man to bake a loaf of bread, and you can feed a village for a lifetime."

Unfortunately, we had no idea how to begin. Then a friend told us about a contest the Dutch government was holding called the BID Network Challenge. Its slogan was "Make Poverty Your

Business," and our idea of creating small self-sustaining bakeries in under-resourced areas fit right in with what the sponsors were looking for. Over the next six months, we spent many hours working on the detailed application, which required a business plan and three-year projections. Much to our surprise, the judges chose our project as a finalist. Dan, Leann, and I traveled to Amsterdam to make our presentation. We were humbled and honored to win second prize, which included a check for seventy-five hundred euros to help make our plan a reality.

"The poorest of the poor" are those who have the least access to the basic needs of life: food, shelter, and security. Our mission, as International Community Bakeries, was to service their areas with community-based, community-run bakeries. In turn, these bakeries would generate employment, train disadvantaged youth, supply healthier bread in a cost-effective way, and provide a sustainable business model for these communities.

Dan had learned about Nkosi's Haven from a book he read called *We Are All The Same* by Jim Wooten. In it, Wooten tells the true story of Nkosi, a courageous black child who was living in a South African township with his single HIV-infected mother, and who was struggling to survive with AIDS. The book also relates the story of Gail Johnson, Nkosi's white foster mother, who became an activist and crossed class and race lines to care for him.

Nkosi and Gail fought for the rights of those living with HIV/AIDS, including their rights to a formal education. The South African government had been slow to respond to the crisis and for a while, minimized its effects. Simultaneously, the government banned all HIV-positive children from attending school. Gail and Nkosi fought an arduous battle through the courts to repeal this ruling. Ultimately, they won the right for Nkosi and others to attend school. The title of the book came from a speech Nkosi made at the 13th International AIDS Conference in Durban, South Africa:

"We are all the same. We are not different from one another. We all belong to one family. We love and we laugh, we hurt and we cry, we live and we die. Care for us and accept us. We are all human beings. We are normal. We have hands. We have feet. We can walk, we can talk—and we all have needs just like everyone else. Don't be afraid of us. We are all the same."

Nkosi died in 2001 at age twelve. Before his death, he and Gail created Nkosi's Haven, a home for HIV/AIDS-infected mothers and their children.

Dan and I made a short list for the location of our test bakery. Nkosi's Haven was a top contender, although we knew creating a bakery there would be a challenge. As we explored the possibility, we spoke with Gail many times about the stigma of HIV in South Africa and the challenges that we would face opening a site there. Our biggest problem was the fact that the public might not buy bread baked by HIV-positive women.

In one of our conversations, Gail mentioned how much Nkosi's Haven paid for bread on the open market. Dan and I realized that if the bakery merely supplied the needs of the moms and kids living there without ever selling to the public, the bakery would still be a great improvement and a financial success. At that moment, we knew we had found our first site.

We agreed the best way to start raising money would be to hold a fundraiser in New York City.

I wanted Dan Ntsala to be involved, and I thought that maybe he could raise additional money in South Africa. He said he would think about it. A few days later, he called. I could tell something was up.

"Doctor Lembay."

"Nice to hear from you, Dan. You sound fired up."

"I have some good news."

"Really?"

I got excited.

"I spoke to the old man."

This was Dan's code for Mandela. I had not asked him to speak to Mandela, although it had been in the back of my mind.

"What did he say?"

"He remembered you and wants to help. I am going to send you three of the official Mandela coffee table books. You can auction them off at your fundraiser. The old man will endorse them any way the buyer wants." Mandela's generosity left me speechless.

Dan sent me a sample copy and to my surprise there was already something written inside:

"To Leann and Neil Ratner,
     Best Wishes
     Mandela

Gail travelled to the States to speak at our fundraiser about the value of the new bakery for Nkosi's Haven. She stayed with us in Woodstock, and we got to know her well. Her fireball personality matched her signature flaming red hair. She told us about Nkosi and how sick he was when she agreed to take care of him. He was paper-thin and couldn't keep food down. But the biggest problem was the almost constant diarrhea. Somehow, with the aid of the newly available anti-retroviral drugs and her constant care and attention, she was able to nurse him back to a relatively reasonable state of health, but Nkosi was never really well.

Adopting him was not easy for her. Gail took a lot of backlash from both blacks and whites who questioned her intentions, some even accusing her of using Nkosi for her own gains. But through her work and dedication to the Haven, she demonstrated that her motives were sincere. She was now well known throughout South Africa and well respected for all she had done and continued to do.

The fundraiser was a success and brought in more than $35,000. Now we had to tackle logistics.

Space was a problem at the Haven. Where would we physically locate the bakery? As it turned out, Gail had plans for expansion in the works, which included moving to a bigger property just outside of Soweto. The new facility would have multiple buildings including housing for up to three hundred HIV-positive moms and their kids. The main building would include an administration area, clinic, and recreation room, as well as a commercial kitchen and dining room. Other buildings would provide the spaces for a computer room, a music room, and a child-care area for infants and babies.

Our idea for the bakery was to use a converted shipping container to create a self-contained "bakery in a box." Gail told us there was room for it right behind the kitchen, which worked out well because it gave us access to additional storage for baking supplies.

Dan Leader had been working with a large bakery supply firm in South Africa that was generous in getting us the equipment we needed at reduced rates and making the connections to enable us to obtain the container. In the meantime, Gail hired three of the moms to be our first bakers.

We ran into other challenges including getting the proper electric lines and having a foundation poured that immediately cracked. But nine months after we raised the money, we were ready to launch. We decided to open International Community Bakeries' first bakery in a box to coincide with the opening of the new facility, Nkosi's Village, on December 1, 2009, a day Gail had chosen because it was World AIDS Day.

The opening was a success, but it didn't take long before a major problem crept up. After a week or two of decent sales probably brought on by the press we got at the opening, our sales plummeted. Neither Dan nor I had an answer. We knew bread coming from an HIV facility could be a tough sell, but we foolishly thought that high nutrition, good taste and a very good price point would overcome any doubts people might have.

The answer to our problem came from a very unexpected source. I had recently been introduced to one of South Africa's leading humanitarians, a man named Bertie Lubner.

When we were first introduced, Bertie, realizing that I was Jewish, invited Leann and me to Friday night services at his temple in Johannesburg. As I have indicated, Temple was really not my thing, but I was encouraged by the friend who introduced us and the evening turned into the beginning of a wonderful friendship.

Bertie was passionate about charity. Twenty years earlier, he had started an organization called Africa Tikkun. The name was inspired by a Jewish principle called Tikkun Olam which literally translated means to repair the world. Now chaired by his son Marc, the organization's goal was to make a difference in the South African economy by developing and uplifting young people living in underprivileged communities. I told Bertie about International Community Bakeries, and he arranged for me to go to one of their centers outside of Johannesburg.

As I toured the kitchen of the Africa Tikkun facility, I saw multiple loafs of store-bought white bread and the bells in my head went off. I spoke to Bertie after the tour and asked him to arrange a meeting with his son Marc. My idea was to have that center buy bread from Gail's bakery which would be healthier and more cost effective than the store-bought brand they were presently using. Bertie liked the idea and was impressed by the goals we were trying to accomplish with our bakeries and he wanted to help in any way he could. Marc saw the wisdom of it immediately and within a few weeks we had our first steady client. The bread was well received and we were on our way to self-sustainability.

35

The Day The Music Died

LEANN and I were driving to a showcase in Albany to see a band I hoped to sign when a bulletin interrupted the radio, "Michael Jackson is dead...." It was June 25, 2009.

At first the news flash didn't register. My mind couldn't take in what I was hearing. A cacophony of questions ricocheted through my head:

Died?! What do you mean, he died? From what? How? Who was there? Could this be a hoax?

The news had come out of nowhere, and it left me literally stunned and almost unable to focus on the road.

I rushed through the showcase, and we headed home. Every station was carrying news about Michael's death. The reality of what had happened was beginning to sink in for me. He was really dead, found that morning at his home in cardiac arrest. I was overwhelmed with sadness and disturbed by the few details I heard. At the same time, a small part of me was not especially surprised.

As I approached the front door of my house, I could hear the phone ringing. It was Wayne, and he sounded as shocked as I felt.

"Ratner, where the fuck have you been? I have trying to reach you for the past two hours. Can you believe it?!"

"I know, Wayne. I can't believe it. I am beyond freaked out!"

"It was drugs wasn't it?"

"I don't know. I haven't heard enough yet, but it wouldn't surprise me."

Wayne and I had stayed in touch. We spoke about once a week, and our conversation often turned to Michael's downhill slide. We had suspected that he was high when we saw him on the news, announcing the This Is It Tour. When the pressure got too intense, Michael cancelled shows, and it was easy for us to see that he would never be able to complete the ever-increasing number of concerts the promoters were planning.

"Ratner, it's a damn shame! Such a talented man."

I could hear the shock and upset in Wayne's voice, but Wayne was stubborn. Even after all these years, he still held a grudge and wouldn't admit that he felt terrible about Michael's death.

"The only good thing is that we weren't there," he continued. "I knew, Rat, I knew it was the right time to get out."

In the months before he quit, Wayne had stressed to me many times that he had felt Michael had changed, and he didn't want to work for him anymore. Part of it was the way he fired Skip and the fact that the deals he and Michael's manger put together were going nowhere, but it was also Michael's behavior. Wayne knew Michael was different in ways he didn't like and couldn't change, and he didn't want to be around when the shit hit the fan.

"I guess so, Wayne, but maybe if we were there, this wouldn't have happened. Let's see what the real story is."

As soon as I hung up the phone, my landline rang again. I picked it up without thinking.

"Doctor Ratner, why did you kill Michael Jackson?"

The anonymous, accusatory male voice rattled me big time, and a jolt of fear shot through me. Leann saw the color drain from my face.

What's wrong?' she asked.

I told her what the caller said.

"They think YOU had something to do with this!" she replied, shocked.

I could hear the terror in her voice. That was the last time I picked up the phone without first looking at the caller ID.

When I heard about Conrad Murray's presence at Michel's bedside, I could imagine the scenario. For me, the situation was confirmed when the nurse, Cherilyn Lee, came forward and explained how Michael begged for Diprivan, a brand name for propofol.

Calls from CNN started a few days later. The first was from Anderson Cooper's producer. I politely told her, "I have nothing to say." That evening it was Sanjay Gupta, their medical correspondent. He said he had information about me accompanying Michael on tour in the '90s. His sources said I traveled with what he called a "mini clinic." He pushed harder.

"I am flying out of LA tomorrow, and I am coming up to Woodstock to interview you."

"Don't bother," I said and hung up.

I called my lawyer, and he and I agreed it was time to leave town for a while.

The next morning Gupta called again. I had already packed a suitcase because Leann and I had decided to go to our house in the Hamptons.

"You know, Dr. Ratner, you really should do the interview. You are going to have to talk sooner or later. Better to just do it now and get it out of the way."

"Listen, I told you before. I have nothing to say."

I was pissed off, and I wanted him to know it.

"Doctor Ratner, we are sending the live truck, and I will do the interview in front of your house whether you are there or not."

"Why do you want to do that?" I pleaded. "Don't send a truck to my house!"

"I can't stop it; that's what my boss wants." I slammed the phone down. I couldn't shake my sorrow for Michael, but increasingly it was being replaced by a sense of dread.

We needed to leave as quickly as possible. Leann was in the bedroom trying to pack. We had no idea how long we would have to be away. I ran upstairs and told her to hurry. Clothes were scattered everywhere.

"Don't worry about what to take, let's just go," I shouted.

Our dog, Finnegan, an 80-pound Saluki, heard the urgency in my voice and began to bark loudly. I hurried back downstairs, grabbed the keys, and went out to start the car. A black SUV came screeching around the corner and stopped directly in front of our house. Out jumped Gupta and a cameraman.

He must have been lying in wait. Who knows how long he had been in Woodstock? He began talking right away.

"We've come here because your name was obviously associated with Michael Jackson. And people said there was a question of whether or not you gave anesthesia to him while he was on tour. And we just wanted to come to the source, you, and hear and find out if that had happened."

I took a breath and thought fast. I knew I didn't want to react in anger and haste to Gupta's adversarial tone. Then the words found me:

"I'm very upset. I'm distraught," I told the correspondent. "Michael was a good person. I can't talk about it right now. It's really something I don't want to talk about right now. I've lost a friend, and I feel very badly about that."

I didn't say anything more. The story ran on Anderson Cooper's show on CNN, and it attracted even more attention from the press. I was devastated and in a state of despair, especially since we had to leave our home for five weeks until everything died down. In time, the story faded to opinion and commentary, and my mood lightened. As they say, "Today's news is tomorrow's fish wrapping."

We were still away when the family held Michael's memorial service. It was hard for me to process that he was *dead* and, as I had said to Wayne, I guess somewhere deep inside, I felt if I had been around maybe things would have been different. I hadn't tried to contact Michael after I got out of prison. I was busy dealing with all kinds of personal issues, and I wanted to wait a while before I reached out. Once he was charged with child molestation for the second time in 2003, I knew any association with me, a convicted felon, would be of no benefit to him.

It didn't matter that we hadn't seen or spoken to one another in seven years. We had the kind of bond that if we had seen each other again, it would have been as if no time had passed.

Leann and I both teared up as we watched the service on TV, but it was only at the end that I lost it. The family escorted the gold-plated solid bronze casket out of the Staples arena while an instrumental version of "Man in the Mirror" played. The beam of a single spotlight stayed lit on an empty microphone. I couldn't hold back any longer, and I cried loud and long.

Wayne and I were talking a few times a day to catch each other up on the latest developments. He had not been invited to the memorial service, and I was upset on his behalf. Michael would have wanted him there. Wayne didn't make a big deal of it, but I knew it hurt him.

After much delay, plans were announced that Michael would be laid to rest on Aug 11, more than a month after the memorial service.

"Hey, Rat," Wayne said the next time he called. "I wanted to call to tell you what just happened."

"What was that?"

"I spoke to Miss Jackson."

"Katherine?"

"Yeah, Rat. She wanted to invite me personally to the burial. She couldn't understand why I wasn't at the memorial service, so she took it upon herself to invite me."

"I am really glad, Wayne. I'm happy you'll have a chance to pay your respects."

36

Man In The Mirror

THEY say the older you get the faster time goes, maybe because each year represents less of your life. In the weeks and months following Michael's death, however, it seemed as if time stood still.

I read that Michael's brother Jermaine found it strange that Michael was considered a joke for years before his death and an iconic saint afterward – we love to hit them when they're down and praise them when they're dead. To me, Michael was neither a joke nor a saint. He was a complicated human being just like the rest of us.

Michael wanted to be like everyone else: go to the movies, shop, hang with friends. Not possible. He was MICHAEL JACKSON, KING OF POP, a persona he carefully created and nurtured without regard to the personal toll it took on him.

Michael had the bad habit of distancing himself from people who got too close, especially when they challenged him on anything personal. It was a little different with me. When I told him no, he knew he had to accept it. That didn't mean he wouldn't try to get what he wanted anyway, but that was Michael: "I want what I want, and I want it *now*!"

I've heard people talk about how someone should have intervened and made Michael get help, go to rehab, but I know from my own experience that no one can force you to change. I, like most other users, had to hit bottom before I was ready to look at life in a different way. Michael never got there.

The real problem with Michael and others in similar positions is that even if they want to change, most don't have the courage to face themselves. Michael needed to change and inside I'm sure he knew it. He just didn't have the capacity, and he wouldn't go far enough to let people in to help him.

Although Michael is long gone, I am still sad when I think about him. But I am comforted to know that his spirit will live on forever in the incredible dancing and music that he created for all of us.

Michael and I frequently talked about charity and giving back, and I deeply appreciated the example he provided and the encouragement he gave me. Of all the choices I have made, the ones that have given me the most satisfaction involve giving back, going to poverty-stricken areas, getting to know the people, and finding out what their true feelings and needs are.

Mandela's example of humility, and his generosity in helping us raise the money for our first bakery, inspired me to continue working as a social entrepreneur.

Michael was a friend who changed me in meaningful ways. Thanks man, I will be forever grateful! I am only sorry we couldn't walk this path together.

...

The mothers had started baking at dawn and continued as a few hundred guests gathered to mark the occasion of the dual opening of Nkosi's Village and our new bakery. The smell of fresh, wholesome bread permeated the air, adding to the crowd's eager excitement.

The loaves were warm and tasted delicious, and virtually everyone wanted to bring one home. Since the opening was a charity event, and the money raised would go back to the Village, Dan and I sold the bread that morning for as much as we could get.

I wished Mandela could have been there to see the result of his generosity. Dan told me the old man smiled broadly when he told him of our opening.

Michael's presence was with me throughout the day. As I sat and listened to the speeches, I heard his words echo:

"Hey, Rat, you love South Africa too, don't you?"

"Rat, we have to do something together. We must do it for the children. Like Albert Schweitzer, we'll build a children's hospital."

"We all have to give, and we all have to do what we can to help end the needless suffering in the world...."

At the end of the ceremony, Gail spoke, thanking us. I thought about the journey that had taken me to this point, and for a moment, Gail's words were eclipsed by an image of Michael singing:

I'm starting with the man in the mirror,   I'm asking him to change his ways.

"Hey, Rat.... You are the man in the mirror ...."

He he he ....

EPILOGUE

Woodstock, New York
February 2018

NEXT year will mark the 10th anniversary of Michael Jackson's untimely death. It's hard to believe that much time has passed. I don't see Michael's name in the news much anymore, but his memory will remain in my heart forever.

Leann and I continue to live in the wonderful town of Woodstock, New York. Since we have no children, we wanted to be part of a tight knit community composed of people that care about each other, and Woodstock has been that and more.

It was important for both of us to change and adapt to our new life. Leann didn't want to work as an exercise trainer anymore and shortly after we arrived, she began studying yoga. She took to it right away and over the years became adept at the practice. Through her participation in the yoga community, Leann has developed a large circle of friends about whom she cares deeply, and who admire and respect her for all that she has accomplished in her life.

In 2013 I was approached by a Town Board member to become a candidate for the Woodstock Ethics Board, a voluntary non-paid position. It was obvious that the board member knew nothing about my background and at first, I thought it best to refuse. But on further reflection, I felt that since I had a very personal experience with ethical issues, I was either the best or the worst person for the job, and I went through with the application and the interview.

During the interview, it again became quite clear to me that neither the Town Supervisor nor the Board members had done their due diligence. They still had not checked my background. So, I decided to stop the questioning and tell an abbreviated version of my life story.

The Board seemed impressed that I would be so honest, but I still wasn't sure what they would do. It didn't take long to find out. Less than 24 hours later I got a phone call informing me that I had been approved unanimously, and I have been a member ever since. I really enjoy my time on the board. The issues brought before us are quite thought provoking, and we play an important role in our town. It feels good to give back in this way and be a valued member of the community.

Niels Lauerson got out of prison in 2006. He pleaded poverty and did not pay any restitution. When Judge Pauley learned about Lauerson's hidden finances, he brought him back into court and threatened Lauerson with further jail time and a suspension of his probation if the 3.2 million dollar restitution was not paid in full by him within six months. Lauerson complied and incredibly, I was off the hook.

When I first moved to Woodstock, I tried a few different businesses including a t-shirt company and a digital record label before getting serious about writing this book. Although the record label is still in existence, it produces very little revenue. We support ourselves mainly with income from real estate we had owned and sold and occasional gifts from my family. It hasn't been easy reconstructing my life or writing this book. Not surprisingly, the two have gone hand in hand.

Writing my life story has been a catharsis and has helped show me the way to redemption and a new life.

When I began writing the book, I realized that I needed help,
and I asked my old friend Stewart Young to assist me with the project. Stewart had continued working in music management throughout the past 45 years and has many contacts. One of them, Peter Ruppert, a social media expert, made me aware of the value of my early music business experience to others, particularly those in my generation, and we resurrected my alter ego, the Rock Doc.

Posting my old Rock and Roll experiences, as well as little known details about artists and songs on social media, has given me a new purpose, and I am awed and humbled by the mostly positive worldwide response that I have received. Thank you Stewart, Peter, and all the followers of Neil Ratner Rock Doc on social media.

Finally, my desire to help others and continue doing charity work has only become stronger over the years. In 2011 we opened our second bakery in South Africa. This one is in the township of Khayelitsha, a slum of close to 400,000 people located in the Cape Flats, an area surrounding Cape Town.

When I was approached by the Irish Charity Soul of Haiti in 2012 to establish one of our bakeries in San Martin, Haiti, a very poor neighborhood of Port Au Prince, I wasn't sure it would be possible. St Martin is one of the most economically deprived areas in Port-au-Prince. It is inhabited by approximately 100,000 people in an area not much bigger than a few square kilometers. Plagued by gang violence and an unemployment rate approaching 90%, the neighborhood has limited electricity, no sanitation and little to no running water.

The challenges were many. We enlisted the help of the Enactus team from Syracuse University. Enactus is an organization with chapters in 1600 Universities in 36 countries. Each University forms a team dedicated to creating or improving existing triple bottom-line social welfare projects. Triple bottom-line means that the projects address social, environmental (or ecological) and financial goals. Our bakeries were a natural fit for the Enactus mission since they were self-sustaining businesses dedicated to improving the lives of those involved in the business as well as the surrounding underserved communities.

Providing a propane oven and a solar array connected to a small generator solved our electricity problem. A rooftop water tank provided us with enough storage in between water deliveries, and a new floor and roof gave us a bright work space.

I am very proud and happy to report that as of this writing, all three bakeries are operational, and we feel confident that there will be more in the future.

Life has taught me the importance of patience, tolerance, humility, gratitude, and giving back. I have also learned never to give up on your dreams. Throughout my life people told me YOU'LL NEVER: you'll never be in the music business, become a doctor, be friends with Michael Jackson and a thousand more things which if I had listened to, they would have been right. "Follow your bliss" as Joseph Campbell famously said, and if things are not working out don't be afraid to "Make That Change." We always have choices in life even if they don't seem obvious.

Bertie Lubner, my South African friend and mentor, once told me, "Neil, life is about giving back. Whatever riches you manage to accumulate both materially and spiritually mean nothing if you are not willing to share them with others." And as I move forward into the next stage of this great adventure, that's exactly what I intend to do.

Rock

ABOVE: Drumming in 1962

ABOVE: Mother and sister
RIGHT: Father

LEFT: Road manager Edgar Winters, White Trash

BELOW: Edgar Winter's White Trash road book

April 5, 1971

2 Shows

Fillmore EAST.
Good people +
Good PA.

Supposed to Play
with Tull but he didn't
show so crowd was
only ½ to ¾ what
it would have been

time onstage to offstage
including encore 1 hr.

2nd show

	Time	Crowd
Where would I Be	5:36	ok
Sunshine	7:15	ok
I've Got News.	6:50	good
SAve the Planet	7:30	ok
fore light	7.35	good
Tobacco Rd.	14:25	good
Get Ready	6:07	good

BELOW:
ELP concert Switzerland

ABOVE: Interview with Swiss television

BELOW: Circus Talents Ltd production for ELP

TOP LEFT: Puddie Watts

TOP RIGHT: Peter Watts

ABOVE: Rick Derringer

RIGHT: Edgar Winter

Doc

LEFT:
Medical student in Mexico

BELOW:
Treating young warriors from
Adam's village

BOTTOM:
Typical Samburu dwelling

RIGHT:
Adam with kids from
his village

ABOVE: Waiting in line
for treatment

RIGHT: Samburu bush
clinic with government
nurse

LEFT: Teaching at clinic supported by Ian and Oria Douglass Hamilton at Lake Naivasha Kenya

ABOVE LEFT: Visiting bombing victims in Nairobi
ABOVE RIGHT: Operating on bombing victims; BELOW: Working with Kenyan doctors

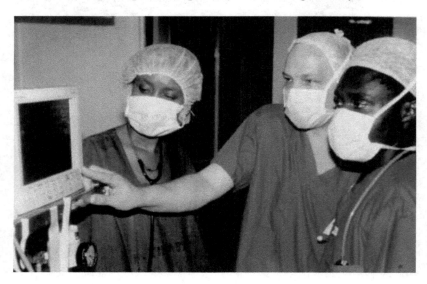

RIGHT: Drumming with a group of anesthesiologists called 'The Gas Band'

LEFT:
Niels Lauerson
and Denise Rich

BELOW:
Working in the kitchen
at Fort Dix

Michael Jackson

ABOVE LEFT: Michael and Neil
ABOVE RIGHT: MJ with security chief Wayne Nagin
BELOW: MJ at the Lost city

LEFT: In the boat with MJ

RIGHT: MJ

BELOW:
MJ at the lion park

LEFT: MJ and Lisa Marie enjoying the show at Sun City

BELOW: MJ and Lisa Marie

BELOW:
An afternoon with MJ

An incredible afternoon with Nelson Mandela

Introducing Madiba to MJ's kids

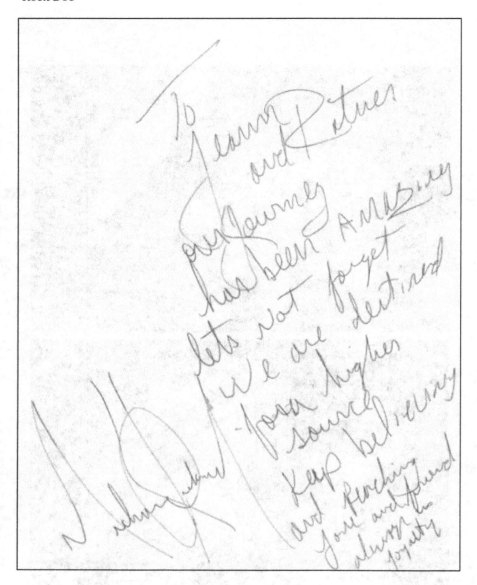

MJ note of appreciation

Rock Doc

LEFT: Wedding in 1976

RIGHT: Procession for Massai wedding

BELOW: Wedding Pary

RIGHT: Irene Mugambe and Leann

BELOW: Massai Wedding

BOTTOM: Leann celebrating

ABOVE:
Charles Lawrence and
Credo Mutha in celebration
of our 25th anniversary

MIDDLE LEFT: Dan Ntsala

BOTTOM LEFT:
One of our safari vehicles

ABOVE: Meeting Nelson Mandela
BELOW: International Community Bakeries at Nkosi's Village

ABOVE: Freshly baked
bread at Nkosi's Village

RIGHT: Nkosi's Village

CPSIA information can be obtained
at www.ICGtesting.com
Printed in the USA
LVHW020727030121
675538LV00016BA/2629